Violence Against Women

Karen F. Balkin, *Book Editor*

Daniel Leone, *President*
Bonnie Szumski, *Publisher*
Scott Barbour, *Managing Editor*
Helen Cothran, *Senior Editor*

CURRENT CONTROVERSIES

GREENHAVEN
PRESS®

THOMSON
™
GALE

San Diego • Detroit • New York • San Francisco • Cleveland
New Haven, Conn. • Waterville, Maine • London • Munich

LIBRARY OF CONGRESS CATALOGING-IN-PUBLICATION DATA
Violence against women / Karen F. Balkin, book editor.
p. cm. — (Current controversies)
Includes bibliographical references and index.
ISBN 0-7377-2042-5 (pbk. : alk. paper) —
ISBN 0-7377-2041-7 (lib. bdg. : alk. paper)
1. Women—Violence against. 2. Women—Violence against—United States.
I. Balkin, Karen F., 1949– . II. Series.
HV6250.4.W65V536 2004
362.88'082—dc21   2003048328

Printed in the United States of America

Contents

No: The Problem of Violence Against Women in the United States Has Been Exaggerated

Chapter 2: What Causes Violence Against Women?

safety. The Violence Against Women Act offers federal remedies to abused women who have not been adequately protected by state laws.

No: Current Legal and Social Remedies Are Ineffective

Chapter 4: What Is the Extent of Violence Against Women Worldwide?

Foreword

By definition, controversies are "discussions of questions in which opposing opinions clash" (Webster's Twentieth Century Dictionary Unabridged). Few would deny that controversies are a pervasive part of the human condition and exist on virtually every level of human enterprise. Controversies transpire between individuals and among groups, within nations and between nations. Controversies supply the grist necessary for progress by providing challenges and challengers to the status quo. They also create atmospheres where strife and warfare can flourish. A world without controversies would be a peaceful world; but it also would be, by and large, static and prosaic.

The Series' Purpose

The purpose of the Current Controversies series is to explore many of the social, political, and economic controversies dominating the national and international scenes today. Titles selected for inclusion in the series are highly focused and specific. For example, from the larger category of criminal justice, Current Controversies deals with specific topics such as police brutality, gun control, white collar crime, and others. The debates in Current Controversies also are presented in a useful, timeless fashion. Articles and book excerpts included in each title are selected if they contribute valuable, long-range ideas to the overall debate. And wherever possible, current information is enhanced with historical documents and other relevant materials. Thus, while individual titles are current in focus, every effort is made to ensure that they will not become quickly outdated. Books in the Current Controversies series will remain important resources for librarians, teachers, and students for many years.

In addition to keeping the titles focused and specific, great care is taken in the editorial format of each book in the series. Book introductions and chapter prefaces are offered to provide background material for readers. Chapters are organized around several key questions that are answered with diverse opinions representing all points on the political spectrum. Materials in each chapter include opinions in which authors clearly disagree as well as alternative opinions in which authors may agree on a broader issue but disagree on the possible solutions. In this way, the content of each volume in Current Controversies mirrors the mosaic of opinions encountered in society. Readers will quickly realize that there are many viable answers to these complex issues. By questioning each author's conclusions, students and casual readers can begin to develop the critical thinking skills so important to evaluating opinionated material.

Current Controversies is also ideal for controlled research. Each anthology in the series is composed of primary sources taken from a wide gamut of informational categories including periodicals, newspapers, books, United States and foreign government documents, and the publications of private and public organizations. Readers will find factual support for reports, debates, and research papers covering all areas of important issues. In addition, an annotated table of contents, an index, a book and periodical bibliography, and a list of organizations to contact are included in each book to expedite further research.

Perhaps more than ever before in history, people are confronted with diverse and contradictory information. During the Persian Gulf War, for example, the public was not only treated to minute-to-minute coverage of the war, it was also inundated with critiques of the coverage and countless analyses of the factors motivating U.S. involvement. Being able to sort through the plethora of opinions accompanying today's major issues, and to draw one's own conclusions, can be a complicated and frustrating struggle. It is the editors' hope that Current Controversies will help readers with this struggle.

"The admission of expert testimony regarding battered woman syndrome can be a crucial part of [battered women's] defense and thus an important element in combating violence against women."

Introduction

The night Marva Wallace shot her husband, he had beaten her, threatened her life, and forced her to perform a sex act while their two-year-old daughter watched. During their year-long marriage, Wallace's face was always bruised, her eye was perpetually black—"like it was part of my makeup," she said. Wallace was convicted of murdering her husband in 1985 and sentenced to twenty-seven years to life in a California state prison. However, she was freed in 2002 under the provisions of a newly enacted state law. In January 2002 inmates convicted before the battered woman syndrome was allowed as testimony were permitted one last legal avenue to seek a new trial, have the severity of their offense reduced, or even be released with time served. California Superior Court judge David Wesley ordered a new trial for Marva Wallace. During this trial testimony of her battering was presented, and she was allowed to plead guilty to a lesser charge, voluntary manslaughter. Wallace was sentenced to eight years of time already served with no parole required. After seventeen years in prison, Marva Wallace, a battered woman who killed her batterer, was free. Unlike Marva Wallace, most battered women are able to escape their abusers without resorting to violence—battered women rarely become murderers. However, if they do, the admission of expert testimony regarding battered woman syndrome can be a crucial part of their defense and thus an important element in combating violence against women. California courts began admitting expert testimony regarding battered woman syndrome (BWS) for women accused of killing their abusive partners in 1992 (seven years after Wallace was convicted). In 1996 a state Supreme Court ruling allowed acquittals of battered women who could prove they acted in self-defense. However, it was not until the California legislature enacted two laws in the years between 2000 and 2002 that women such as Marva Wallace were given a second chance. One law required the state parole board to review petitions for clemency and determine at the time of a woman's hearing if she was suffering from battered woman syndrome when she committed the crime. The other law, the one that freed Marva Wallace, allowed women to have testimony of their battering presented as evidence and BWS used in their defense at a new trial.

According to BWS attorney Mira Mihajlovich, testimony concerning BWS is used to support a battered woman's self-defense claim, not to explain away her actions or give her a special defense that would allow her to "destroy her tormentor at her own discretion." Jane Parrish, a consultant for the National Clearinghouse for the Defense of Battered Women, argues: "Defendants—including battered women defendants—should be able to introduce all relevant evidence at their trials, including evidence of and expert testimony about their experiences of abuse, that can help the jurors better understand their situations." Further, Parrish notes that this type of social context for behavior is not unique to the BWS defense. In the case of a barroom brawl, for example, a defendant may show evidence of the victim's prior threats against him to support the claim that his actions in self-defense were reasonable. Similarly, expert testimony on the nature and effects of battering can help convince a jury that a woman who killed her abusive partner held a reasonable belief that she was in imminent danger and acted in self-defense.

Further, women who have been physically, emotionally, or sexually battered for years may lose all self-confidence and self-respect and even come to doubt their own sanity. While most battered women are not insane, many may suffer from battered woman syndrome. The concept of the battered woman syndrome was originated by Lenore E. Walker and advanced in her books *The Battered Woman* and *The Battered Woman Syndrome*. "Battered woman's syndrome describes a pattern of psychological and behavioral symptoms found in women in battering relationships," she explains. According to Walker, there are four general characteristics of the syndrome: The battered woman believes the violence is her fault; the battered woman has an inability to place the responsibility for the violence elsewhere; the battered woman fears for her life and/or her children's lives; and the woman has an irrational belief that the abuser is omnipresent and omniscient. Walker claims that many BWS victims experience "learned helplessness," a condition brought about by the battered woman's futile attempts to protect herself from her abuser. In addition, after being subjected to several cycles of violence—where they are battered, try to leave their batterers, and are drawn back into the relationship when the abuser is contrite and loving—many BWS sufferers develop a form of posttraumatic stress disorder and may even experience flashbacks. They may come to believe that killing their abusers is their only way out. While neither the criminal justice system nor the general public agrees that murder is the answer to violence against women, an understanding of the years of abuse a woman has endured provides a proper perspective for evaluating the BWS defense.

While Walker introduced BWS to the public in the mid-1970s, it was not until the 1980s that legal and academic debate began concerning the syndrome. The U.S. legal system was slow to accept BWS as a factor in the self-defense pleas of battered women accused of murdering their batterers. Thus, it was the late 1980s before testimony about a battered woman's psychological state and the brutality and violence she suffered at the hands of her batterer could be used at her trial. Until that time, women accused of killing their husbands or domestic partners often received harsh sentences because juries were unaware of the circumstances surrounding the crime. Even after BWS was allowed as testimony, activists and legal experts were able to gain clemency for only a few women using BWS as part of their defense.

Then in 1990, outgoing Ohio governor Richard Celeste freed twenty-five women—state prison inmates—who had not had the opportunity to present testimony at their trials about the abuse they had suffered. As the BWS movement advanced, then-governor Donald Schaefer of Maryland commuted the sentences of eight women convicted of murdering their abusive partners in 1991; then-governor William Weld of Massachusetts freed seven of the eight abused petitioners who sought clemency from him in 1992; and then-governor Pete Wilson of California granted three of the thirty-five clemency petitions brought before him in the same year.

By 1995, twelve states had passed statutes allowing expert testimony on battering and its effects. However, while requests for clemency continued into the late 1990s, few of these petitions were granted. The momentum behind granting clemency based on the BWS defense began dissipating. While advocates tried to continue clemency petitioning, there was little interest and little funding available. Recent statistics support the "out of sight, out of mind" viewpoint: Florida has seen no domestic violence clemencies since 1999; no battered women have been freed in New York since 1996; John Engler, governor of Michigan in 2000, denied eight petitions that year.

BWS advocates are hopeful that Marva Wallace's release from a California prison may signal a positive change in public interest in and legal decisions on BWS. Critics of the BWS defense are less enthusiastic. In his book *More Than Victims*, Donald Alexander Downs contends that the logic of the battered woman syndrome denies women their reason and will and reinforces their victimization. He argues that battered women often show heroic survival techniques, retaining accurate, reasoned perceptions concerning the actions and intentions of their abusers. Portraying them as lacking reason and will undermines the validity of their rightful self-defense claims and causes them greater harm. Downs promotes a more moderate approach where specific situations relevant to the battered woman's life and accurate perceptions of danger are taken into account rather than relying on psychological incapacity, the cornerstone of the BWS defense.

Cathy Young, vice president of the Woman's Freedom Network, is also skeptical of the BWS defense, but for other reasons. She claims that BWS "sounds more like an ideological concoction to justify acts that would not fall under the category of self-defense." Young argues that the theory that repeated batterings cause a woman to become too passive to escape is unfounded. "The theory [is that] the victim becomes completely passive. It's an interesting sort of reasoning became it assumes the woman is so passive she can't leave a relationship, but she's not too passive to kill."

BWS is just one of the controversial issues surrounding the complex problem of abused women. Authors in *Current Controversies: Violence Against Women* explore other aspects of violence against women, including its causes, the effectiveness of current legal and social remedies for it, and its worldwide impact.

Chapter 1

Is Violence Against Women in the United States a Serious Problem?

Chapter Preface

Domestic violence is one of the most pervasive of all social ills. Women in big cities and sprawling suburban communities, women in small towns and rural areas, rich women and poor women are all vulnerable to violence. It is not surprising then that women in military families, either as enlisted personnel themselves or as the wives of soldiers, sailors, marines, or airmen, suffer as well from the effects of domestic violence. The most compelling statistic regarding domestic abuse in the military comes from Pentagon records. CBS news staffers analyzing Pentagon records for "The War at Home," a 1999 segment of the newsmagazine *60 Minutes*, found that the incidence of domestic violence in the military was five times higher than in the civilian population for the years 1992 to 1996.

However, the Department of Defense (DOD) argues that comparing domestic violence data between the military community and civilian society is inappropriate and misleading. According to the DOD, there are major differences in the way domestic violence studies are designed for each community. The military counts emotional abuse in its total; national studies frequently include other types of violence such as robberies. In addition, different demographics are studied; for example, the average age of the military population is lower than the population at large, and studies show that domestic violence occurs most frequently among people under thirty. Another problem is that researchers studying the military use a much narrower definition of domestic violence. When studying the military, only abuse within married couples is considered domestic violence; intimate partner abuse by single servicemembers and gay and lesbian servicemembers is not counted. All of these different research methods result in skewed data that cannot be used for an accurate comparison.

Officially, there is a zero tolerance policy toward violence against women associated with the military. In practice, however, the DOD admits that its approach to the elimination of domestic abuse has been less than successful. Lack of awareness and understanding of the signs and dynamics of family violence and the services available to address it are major problems in all branches of the service. Further, inconsistent support from commanders for the Family Advocacy Program—the program established for the prevention, investigation, and treatment of domestic violence and child abuse—often makes it difficult if not impossible to help abused women. Moreover, if the abused woman is in the military but her abusive husband is not, the military has no authority over him; military authorities can do little to help the abused servicewoman except offer counseling and encourage her to report the abuse to civilian police.

Abusive situations for military wives are further complicated by an amendment to the Gun Control Act of 1968, the Domestic Violence Offender Gun Ban, which prohibits members of the military who are domestic abusers from possessing firearms. The DOD points to its steadfastness on this issue as affirmation of its commitment to fighting violence against women. Unfortunately, this strict observance of the gun ban law often makes battered wives reluctant to report abuse. They are concerned that their allegations will mean that their husbands can no longer possess guns and will therefore be dishonorably discharged from the service. However, statistics show that fear of negative consequences is out of proportion to the true impact. Less than 5 percent of military abuse cases result in a court-martial, and 75 to 84 percent of alleged offenders are honorably discharged when they do decide to leave the military.

Domestic abuse is devastating whether it occurs in military families or in the civilian population. Authors in the following chapter explore the seriousness of violence against women.

Violence Against Women Is a Serious Problem

by Patricia Tjaden and Nancy Thoennes

About the authors: *Patricia Tjaden is a senior researcher at the Center for Policy Research; Nancy Thoennes is associate director at the center. The Center for Policy Research is a private, nonprofit research firm in Denver, Colorado.*

Research on violence against women has exploded in the past 20 years, particularly in the areas of intimate partner violence and sexual assault. Despite this outpouring of research, many gaps exist in our understanding of violence against women. For instance, reliable information on minority women's experiences with violence is still lacking. Few empirical data exist on the relationship between different forms of violence against women, such as victimization in childhood and subsequent victimization. Finally, empirical data on the consequences of violence against women, including their injury rates and use of medical services, are lacking.

To further understanding of violence against women, the National Institute of Justice (NIJ) and the Centers for Disease Control and Prevention jointly sponsored, through a grant to the Center for Policy Research, a national survey that was conducted from November 1995 to May 1996. The National Violence Against Women (NVAW) Survey sampled both women and men and thus provides comparable data on women's and men's experiences with violent victimization.

Key Issues

Respondents to the survey were asked about:
• Physical assault they experienced as children by adult caretakers.
• Physical assault they experienced as adults by any type of assailant.
• Forcible rape and stalking they experienced at any time in their life by any type of perpetrator.

Respondents who disclosed that they had been victimized were asked detailed questions about the characteristics and consequences of their victimization, in-

Patricia Tjaden and Nancy Thoennes, *Full Report of the Prevalence, Incidence, and Consequences of Violence Against Women: Executive Summary*. Washington, DC: National Institute of Justice, Office of Justice Programs, 2000.

cluding injuries they sustained and their use of medical services.

This NIJ Research Report presents findings from the NVAW Survey on the prevalence and incidence of rape, physical assault, and stalking; the rate of injury among rape and physical assault victims; and injured victims' use of medical services. The data show that violence is more widespread and injurious to women's and men's health than previously thought—an important finding for legislators, policymakers, intervention planners, and researchers as well as the public health and criminal justice communities.

Women Are Assaulted Early

Analysis of survey data on the prevalence, incidence, and consequences of violence against women produced the following results:

• Physical assault is widespread among adults in the United States: 51.9 percent of surveyed women and 66.4 percent of surveyed men said they were physically assaulted as a child by an adult caretaker and/or as an adult by any type of attacker. An estimated 1.9 million women and 3.2 million men are physically assaulted annually in the United States.

• Many American women are raped at an early age: Of the 17.6 percent of all women surveyed who said they had been the victim of a completed or attempted rape at some time in their life, 21.6 percent were younger than age 12 when they were first raped, and 32.4 percent were ages 12 to 17. Thus, more than half (54 percent) of the female rape victims identified by the survey were younger than age 18 when they experienced their first attempted or completed rape.

• Stalking is more prevalent than previously thought: 8.1 percent of surveyed women and 2.2 percent of surveyed men reported being stalked at some time in their life; 1.0 percent of women surveyed and 0.4 percent of men surveyed reported being stalked in the 12 months preceding the survey. Approximately 1 million women and 371,000 men are stalked annually in the United States.

• American Indian/Alaska Native women and men report more violent victimization than do women and men of other racial backgrounds: American Indian/Alaska Native women were significantly more likely than white women, African-American women, or mixed-race women to report they were raped. They also were significantly more likely than white women or African-American women to report they were stalked. American Indian/Alaska Native men were significantly more likely than Asian men to report they were physically assaulted.

> *"An estimated 1.9 million women . . . are physically assaulted annually in the United States."*

Women Are Assaulted Often

• Rape prevalence varies between Hispanic and non-Hispanic women: Hispanic women were significantly less likely than non-Hispanic women to report they were raped at some time in their life.

• There is a relationship between victimization as a minor and subsequent victimization: Women who reported they were raped before age 18 were twice as likely to report being raped as an adult. Women who reported they were physically assaulted as a child by an adult caretaker were twice as likely to report being physically assaulted as an adult. Women who reported they were stalked before age 18 were seven times more likely to report being stalked as an adult.

> *"Violence against women, particularly intimate partner violence, should be classified as a major public health and criminal justice concern in the United States."*

• Women experience more intimate partner violence than do men: 22.1 percent of surveyed women, compared with 7.4 percent of surveyed men, reported they were physically assaulted by a current or former spouse, cohabiting partner, boyfriend or girlfriend, or date in their lifetime; 1.3 percent of surveyed women and 0.9 percent of surveyed men reported experiencing such violence in the previous 12 months. Approximately 1.3 million women and 835,000 men are physically assaulted by an intimate partner annually in the United States.

An Intimate Partner Is Usually the Perp

• Violence against women is primarily intimate partner violence: 64.0 percent of the women who reported being raped, physically assaulted, and/or stalked since age 18 were victimized by a current or former husband, cohabiting partner, boyfriend, or date. In comparison, only 16.2 percent of the men who reported being raped and/or physically assaulted since age 18 were victimized by such a perpetrator.

• Women are significantly more likely than men to be injured during an assault: 31.5 percent of female rape victims, compared with 16.1 percent of male rape victims, reported being injured during their most recent rape; 39.0 percent of female physical assault victims, compared with 24.8 percent of male physical assault victims, reported being injured during their most recent physical assault.

• The risk of injury increases among female rape and physical assault victims when their assailant is a current or former intimate: Women who were raped or physically assaulted by a current or former spouse, cohabiting partner, boyfriend, or date were significantly more likely than women who were raped or physically assaulted by other types of perpetrators to report being injured during their most recent rape or physical assault.

• Approximately one-third of injured female rape and physical assault victims receive medical treatment: 35.6 percent of the women injured during their most recent rape and 30.2 percent of the women injured during their most recent physical assault received medical treatment.

Persons Victimized by an Intimate Partner[a] in Lifetime and Previous 12 Months by Type of Victimization

Type of Victimization	In Lifetime			
	Percentage		Number[b]	
	Women	Men	Women (100,697,000)	Men (92,748,000)
Rape	7.7	0.3	7,753,669	278,244
Physical assault	22.1	7.4	22,254,037	6,863,352
Rape and/or physical assault	24.8	7.6	24,972,856	7,048,848
Stalking	4.8	0.6	4,833,456	556,488
Total victimized	25.5	7.9	25,677,735	7,327,092
	In Previous 12 Months			
Rape	0.2	—	201,394	—
Physical assault	1.3	0.9	1,309,061	834,732
Rape and/or physical assault	1.5	0.9	1,510,455	834,732
Stalking	0.5	0.2	503,485	185,496
Total victimized	1.8	1.1	1,812,546	1,020,228

[a] Intimate partners include current and former spouses, opposite-sex and same-sex cohabiting partners, boyfriends/girlfriends, and dates.
[b] Based on estimates of women and men age 18 and older. U.S. Population: Wetrogan, Signe I., *Projections of the Population of States by Age, Sex, and Race: 1988 to 2010*. Current Population Reports, Washington, DC: U.S. Bureau of the Census, 1988: 25–1017.

Violence Against Women Is Pervasive

Information generated by the NVAW Survey validates opinions held by professionals in the field about the pervasiveness and injurious consequences of violence against women. This study's findings on the frequency with which women are victimized by intimate partners confirms previous reports that violence against women is primarily intimate partner violence. The study makes it clear that violence against women, particularly intimate partner violence, should be classified as a major public health and criminal justice concern in the United States. The large number of rape, physical assault, and stalking victimizations committed against women each year and the early age at which violence starts for many women strongly suggest that violence against women is endemic. Because most victimizations are perpetrated against women by current and former intimates and because women are more likely to be injured if their assailant is a current or former intimate, violence prevention strategies for women that focus on how they can protect themselves from intimate partners are needed. Injury and medical utilization data provide compelling evidence of the physical and social costs associated with violence against women. The findings suggest that future researchers should pay greater attention to demographic, social, and environmental factors that may account for variations in victimization rates among women of different racial and ethnic backgrounds and to the link between victimization they experience as a minor and subsequent victimization.

Rape Is a Serious Problem for Women

by Alyn Pearson

About the author: *Alyn Pearson is an occasional contributor to* Off Our Backs, *a feminist publication. She was a student intern when this viewpoint was written.*

Rape is the common cold of society. Although rape is much more serious than the common cold, the systems are the same. We have assimilated rape into our everyday culture much as we have the cold. Like the folklore surrounding the common cold, there is folklore about rape, like the notion that if a woman wears revealing clothing or goes to a bar alone, she is likely to "get raped." But in fact a woman is no more likely to be raped from these activities than from simply dating a man or being home alone.

There is a silence surrounding the recognition that we live in a cultural environment where rape is endemic, but it is true. The rape culture is much like the poor sanitation conditions which led to typhoid—it provides an environment in which acts of rape are fostered. Look through any supposed women's publication and notice the ads that display women at the mercy of a man or at the mercy of the male gaze. Notice the articles that emphasize dependence and passivity and avoid portraying independence and strength in women. Watch TV shows that display precocious models of sexually manipulated teen-aged women. Walk into any bar and watch the women primp and the men pounce, and watch, too, as the number of unreported rapes turns into the number of women socialized into accepting this sort of sexual behavior as standard—not even recognizing rape when it occurs. Rape is part of the natural flora of our society and our world.

I go to Bard College, a secluded little haven in New York State.

BRAVE, Bard's Response to Rape and Associated Violence Education, is the group on my campus that deals with rape, incest, sexual assault and harassment, domestic abuse, and gender-related violence issues that arise in our small community and, often, in the community-at-large. . . . Before attending college, I, like much of my generation, tended to not see rape as violence against women, but rather as a removed sort of problem that was often misused by women looking for sympathy. I was seduced by the post-modern rejection of feminism, believing instead in the inclusion of every opposite. I was socialized not to see the discrepancies, but to accept them. . . .

Training as a Peer Rape Counselor

Before joining BRAVE, I had this incredibly twisted and formed view of rape: specifically, that I was never a victim and I never could be. I was also convinced that women often lied about rape. Why did I think this way? Because social training, media propaganda, and backlash had me as a dedicated pupil. Fortunately, I was not too far gone in my hipster cynicism to grasp the facts of the matter. Rape, I learned, is not a removed, unrestricted, free flowing sort of problem that randomly strikes unfortunate women in dark parking lots or in frat houses.

This past January, I was trained to be a peer rape counselor. The training was my version of medical school—I can now identify the symptoms of rape everywhere, see the disease in everyone, and take the steps to cure it. . . .

A disease is merely a set of symptoms combined into a neat medically identified package and labeled for public. The germs are everywhere. The disease of rape is simply the set of symptoms of a socially oppressive system that allows men all the power and leaves women with all the shame. In fact, rape is quite pervasive and rigidly fixed into our social system. Everything from TV commercials for dish soap to the exchanges between men and women in supermarkets are symptoms of the rape culture. It is part of the natural flora, the way things are. Men are trained to rape and women to take it. Rape is taught and learned through these patterns and paradigms without the word rape ever being uttered. . . .

Young Women and the Rape Culture

Because of feminism's many successes, women have been seduced into submission once again. In the beginning of the 21st century, many more women than not are convinced that we have reached equality with men. This is a dangerous conviction, primarily because it is not true. The reason the rape culture is endemic to American women is because we have the illusion that we exist in a safe space, where rape only happens to women who jog late at night in Central Park. The term "date rape" is often mocked among my peers as a creation by sexually insecure women. And feminism is a dirty word, as those of us with vocal feminist views know all too well.

> *"I may be a smart, educated, self-confident woman . . . but any man who wants to can rape me because he is stronger."*

The advertisements and music videos depict women in skimpy clothing with beckoning looks on their faces. Women with small and impossible bodies are what we aspire to because that is what men are attracted to. And women are first and foremost supposed to be attractive to men. But women, particularly women in college, are also told that we are smart, liberated, equal to men, and have some inner goddess—strength. These contradictory messages can be confusing and keep us enthralled by the rape culture if we let the belief

> *"Rape is endemic because it pervades every aspect of our complex social structure."*

that we have social equality blind us to the subliminal messages embedded in the media.

To be a young woman today means to live with the rape culture in all its subtleties. It means to act in accordance with the roles that keep men forever in power. I may be a smart, educated, self-confident woman of the modern day, but any man who wants to can rape me because he is stronger. Not only physically stronger, but psychologically stronger because he was taught by the system to be aggressive and take what he feels he deserves. To be a young woman often means to buy *Glamour* and *Vogue* and take the advice that pleases men. It means to fluctuate body weight to please the day's fashion archetype. Being a young woman today means to be unhappy if men don't like the way you look. I have cried many a night because of my big shoulders and my skinny, white legs, and I still struggle to find my own definition of what is sexy. . . .

Rape Is Endemic

Rape is endemic because it pervades every aspect of our complex social structure. In order to vaccinate against it, we would have to change many parts of society that people are fully comfortable with and accepting of. Patriarchy is still very much at work, only more subtly. There is a defiance of admitting weakness because weakness is devalued and to be raped in these flicked up days, is to be weak. Postmodern theory waxes on about inclusion and identity politics; liberals pretend equality has been achieved. And because of the code of sex-positive cool, young women accept these stances at face value and ignore the ongoing perpetuation of rape culture.

Rape is not an epidemic that spiked mysteriously in the mid-seventies when feminists called attention to it. It is not a sudden outbreak that can be cured with a single vaccine. It is an endemic social disease that pervades every walk of life imaginable. This is the rape culture—millions of small-seeming social germs translate into sexual assault as they reach the bedroom.

In rape-crisis training, I learned what makes men rape. And it is not some inbred sexual urge that is just part of man's biology. It is power and privilege. I learned what keeps women silent. It is fear. . . . We can stop rape in this new century—if we are ready to identify the aspects of our cultural environment that foster rape and eliminate them.

Chapter 1

Rape Culture: Media and Message

Something was taken from me the other day as I, in a fit of self-destruction, picked up *Glamour* magazine and decided to read it for pleasure. What was taken from me was my ironclad sense of immunity, because the advertisements and the articles got to me and made me hate myself and want to buy a cure over the counter. I do not feel safe when I look into the pages of pop culture and I feel even less safe when I watch TV. . . . The media gives us gender roles and social norms to mimic and worship as creed. To disobey is to be outcast from the religion of normal, of popular.

Nearly every advertisement is sexist in some way. *Ms. Magazine* and *Bitch* have monthly critiques of ads that display the American way of misogyny through objectification of and disrespect to the female figure and to female existence. . . .

Unfortunately this style of ad is not rare. Candies [a fashion and accessories retailer] has a whole campaign of misogynist, subtly violent ads that sell various products. You can hop onto their website and see a wide variety of images of violence against women in the name of "sex sells." They call it racy and they call it daring. I call it the rape culture. I call their game. . . .

The world, or at least the majority of it, is convinced that this is sex. That we live in an era where violent sex is okay. . . .

Walk Out on Movie Rape Scenes

In the book *Cunt*, Inga Muscio encourages women to walk out of movies that have rape scenes. At first I wondered why. I thought that movie rape scenes must really show men how horrible rape is and encourage them not to do it. But then I thought about all the movies I have seen with rape scenes. . . . And I realized that these cinematic forays into the crime of rape make it sexy. They depict rape as rough, unwanted sex, that is nevertheless sexy. They show the frail, beautiful woman and the big, beautiful man engaged in sexual intercourse that just happens to be accompanied by mutters of no and some tears, or some serious drunken sleeping. Rape scenes in movies are geared to turn people on, not shock them. And as long as the public is being seduced by the myth that rape is about sex and not about power, and that rape is about lust and not oppressive violence, then the rape culture can continue to thrive and to destroy women.

Ads . . . and the rape scenes in movies portray violence as sexy and acceptable. They seduce viewers into being believers in rape culture and help create another generation of rapists who believe that rape is not violence, but merely sexual intercourse that sometimes goes "wrong."

The only "good" rape scene I have ever seen is in *Boys Don't Cry*, a movie about the true story of a transgender female to male who was discovered to be a woman born and was therefore raped brutally and violently. The movie showed that the men raping Brandon Teena were not doing it to get off sexually, but to violently enforce gender roles. They raped her because she had a vagina and she had threatened their concept of gender.

I can't really say I want to see more movies portray scenes like this either, because I threw up afterwards. I don't want to live in a place where we have to endure such realities. But I also don't want to live in a place that candy coats these realities into normative sexuality in order to support social roles and a culture that normalizes rape.

TV Reinforces Rape Culture

While ads and movies are normalizing rape, TV is busy making it just disappear entirely. When I was in high school there was an episode of the ever-popular [TV series] *Beverly Hills 90210* that depicted a woman being coerced into sex by a regular on the show. . . . The mass media managed to wrap centuries of oppression into one tiny hour and depict it totally according to rape culture's social roles. . . .

That episode along with many other prime time dramas sent the incorrect message that rape is an oops on the boy's part and can be easily wrapped up and erased between commercials for toothpaste. But rape, sexual harassment, sexual assault, and coercion are in real life incredibly difficult emotional ordeals for women.

In this TV show, which represents a microcosm of the youth mainstream and their social assumptions, the gender norms that create the rape culture were reinforced and the reality of rape was pushed far into the subconscious of youthful viewers.

The power of TV and other media to influence the values, personalities, and lifestyles of all of us cannot be overestimated. . . . In a culture obsessed with sound bites and quick gratification, young women read blurbs in exploitive magazines and get advice from advertisements. In a culture seduced by the almighty dollar, capitalism is allowed to replicate the rape culture by selling it maniacally as sex. . . . Today women learn to be women and men learn to be men immersed in rape culture; and the day ends and begins on the same note of silence from viewers of the mass media.

Rape Culture: A Personal Story

I was trained for 40 plus hours to be a peer rape counselor, and my friend and trainer Melanie remembers my face during the sessions as one of boredom. She thought I was zonked out of my mind from being assaulted with constant information and having to sit through it for 8 or more hours a day. I suppose I have my facial muscles as trained as my thoughts to avoid giving anything away, because I was not bored. While Melanie looked at me and thought I was bored, this is what I was thinking. . . .

There was a boy who came to visit my first college often, he was a friend of a boy that I really liked and had hooked up with a few times. Nick, the boy I liked, did not return the feelings and I was resentful. His friend liked everything with a vagina and I was vulnerable enough to think I was more. We drank beers and talked about Pearl Jam, a love we both shared. We drunkenly went to my room, kicked my roommate out and went for it. I had never, ever been in a situation so aggressive in my life. The other boys of that year were soft in their sexual advances. He was writhing on top of me touching body parts that I never wanted him to touch, I wanted to make out and rub backs or something. I whispered slow down or whoa or something to no response other than moans and it'll be fine. I thought perhaps that the other boys hadn't really liked me and that TJ did and that this was how it was supposed to be. Rough aggressive, with me powerless, with me on the bottom. A few red lights flashed at first but I was so scared to say no because why? Why? Because I want him to like me and I want Nick to be jealous and I want to be popular and sexy and not disappoint this boy on top of me by not allowing him to complete this charade. I want to be the cool chick who could fuck without feeling way more than I want to be the strong woman who took a stand and said get the hell out you are scaring me.

Rape Culture: Ignoring Fear and Instincts

I remember feeling very small. I remember his whole body pressing down on me and not being able to kiss him back because I could not breathe. I remember not saying no. I remember wanting to. And thankfully, I remember Sara knocking on the door repeatedly looking for me because she knew where I was and who I was with and wanted to rescue me from certain sexual shame. I answered her calls so she knew I was in there, even though TJ said shhhhhh. She heard me and did not relent so I found my way up and he left and I never saw him again, but I never told anyone how uncomfortable I had been in that small dark room and how scary it was not to be able to breathe and how much I hated myself for disappointing him and not following through like a little prude. All I ever told anyone was that we had "hooked up." In my head at the time that was truth, I saw nothing integrally wrong with how it went down and I ignored my fear and my instinct and my red lights. It became legend and I was a girl who hooked up and I had lots of lovers. . . .

> *"As long as the public is . . . seduced by the myth that rape is about sex and not about power . . . rape culture can continue to thrive and to destroy women."*

This situation is not an isolated incident in my early sexual past. I have slept with men I didn't love and didn't even know because I didn't think I had the social standing to say no. I have writhed beneath bodies with every muscle screaming no while my trained vocal chords made the appropriate sighs. And I hated myself every second during and too many more afterwards. . . .

It took my intense week of counselor training to infiltrate the secure stone wall of created consciousness that had prevented me from recognizing my own penetrability. As a woman born, I am vulnerable not only [to] the physical penetration of rape, but the mental penetration of the rape culture that socializes my womanhood. I didn't say no when I felt uncomfortable, I felt bad for disappointing him, I was rescued from SHAME not danger, and I convinced myself that the aggressive sexual attention is HOOKING up and not some flicked up manifestation of TJ's male privilege and power over my unsuspecting and passive female constitution.

I am lucky to have friends lurking around corners, but it is not always set up as such. Situations like this are normal, endemic to the dating scene. And nobody seems to recognize the violence proffered by magazine ads and television shows, by MTV videos or cigarette billboards. [Musician] Ani Difranco said "We learn America like a script," and I agree. Men and women are planted into roles and their character studies are media images.

Prison Rape Is a Serious Problem for Women

by Andrea C. Poe

About the author: *Andrea C. Poe is a freelance writer in the Washington, D.C., area.*

Robin Lucas was sentenced to 33 months in a minimum-security daily work camp program in a California women's prison in 1994 for illegally cashing traveler's checks. The following year, an altercation with another inmate landed her in corrective isolation. The "hole," as it's known, was located in an adjacent all-male facility. That's where Lucas' nightmare began.

Lying alone on her cot one night, she was awakened by a male inmate tugging at her. He claimed he'd paid to gain entrance, and demanded that she undress and have sex with him. When Lucas refused, he beat her until her head was gashed and bleeding. Seeing the blood, the assailant fled in fear.

The next morning, Lucas filed a complaint. Rather than investigate, the prison authorities subjected her to a lie detector test, questioned her repeatedly, and leaked her complaint to guards and inmates in the unit where she was being housed.

Retaliation soon followed. Inmates chanted her name and shouted threats from the surrounding cells. Her food was regularly sprayed with urine when it arrived.

One night, three inmates were given access to her cell by guards. Dragging Lucas from her cot, they clamped her down with handcuffs, beat, vaginally and anally raped her, and then urinated on her before leaving her semi-conscious on the floor. Afterward, she was denied medical treatment. Two weeks later, she was transported back to the women's facility.

It wasn't until 35 days after the attack that she finally received a medical exam.

While Lucas' story may be one of the most publicized, it isn't unique. Amnesty International (AI) charges that female inmates in the US are routinely raped and assaulted by guards.

A sample of recent court cases creates a grim outline of this growing problem. In Washington state, for example, a former prisoner was awarded $110,000 by the state for rape and impregnation by a guard. In West Virginia, a sheriff was sentenced to seven years in prison for forcing inmates to engage in sex acts with officers. And these cases aren't anomalies. Rather, they illustrate what goes on in women's prisons every day.

Fearing retaliation, most inmates remain silent about their abuse. According to Human Rights Watch, at least half of all female prisoners in the US experience sexual abuse: This constitutes a sexual abuse epidemic.

Women Prisoners Increase

The problem has worsened in recent years as the lock-up rate for women has surged. Since 1980, their numbers have exploded by 400 percent. The majority of the increase is due to the so-called War on Drugs, which requires mandatory sentences. The US female prison population has escalated from 2400 in 1986 to 23,700 as of 1996, according to the Sentencing Project, a group dedicated to finding imprisonment alternatives.

"At least half of all female prisoners in the US experience sexual abuse: This constitutes a sexual abuse epidemic."

Today, drugs account for about half of all women's state jail sentences. Only 25 percent are sentenced for violent crimes, 75 percent are between the ages of 25 and 34, and 50 percent were living in poverty at the time of their arrest. Black women are imprisoned at a rate eight times that of Whites; Hispanics, four times the White rate.

Unlike prisons in most other nations, it's primarily men rather than women who guard these mainly young prisoners. In the US, 70 percent of women's prison guards are men, while in Canada 91 percent are female. UN guidelines recommend that women should primarily staff women's prisons. In fact, Rule 53 of the UN's Standard Minimum Rules for the Treatment of Prisoners says that the role of males should be restricted in women's facilities. Yet, the US has opted to ignore this and continues staffing women's prisons with men.

America Is Lagging Behind

The rape of a prison inmate by staff is considered an act of torture according to the UN Convention and International Covenant on Civil and Political Rights, which the US ratified in 1993. The following year, the US also ratified the Convention against Torture and Other Cruel, Inhuman or Degrading Treatment or Punishment. Nevertheless, only 10 US states have laws prohibiting all members of staff from engaging in sexual abuse of prisoners. The rest, as well as the District of Columbia and the US Bureau of Prisons, have no such laws.

Further, 14 states had no laws against sexual misconduct by staff until 1998. As of 2001, Alabama, Minnesota, Oregon, Vermont, and Wisconsin still haven't passed legislation. And only two states—Kansas and Oklahoma—have statutes that meet the minimum standards set forth by AI to protect the human rights of prisoners.

In certain states, an inmate can actually be held criminally liable for engaging in sexual conduct. In Arizona, a prisoner can be charged even if she is raped. In California, oral sex is punishable, and, in Delaware and Nevada, a prisoner can be charged if she can't prove rape. In Missouri, Colorado, and Wyoming, staff can avoid being charged with misconduct simply by claiming the sex was consensual.

Making matters worse, the US is the only developed country that hasn't accepted the UN Convention to Eliminate All Forms of Discrimination against Women (CEDAW). Among other things, CEDAW makes it a crime for female prisoners to be sexually violated while incarcerated. Over 100 countries have ratified it, including developing nations like Cameroon, Sri Lanka, and Tajikistan. The US stands almost alone in its refusal to get behind CEDAW's important provisions.

A Small Victory

As for Robin Lucas, once transferred back to the women's facility she was able to contact family members, and they helped her secure an attorney. With two other women who had suffered similar experiences in the prison, she initiated a lawsuit in 1995. In a landmark decision, they won that legal battle and were awarded half a million dollars in damages.

This also led to some policy reforms. The women's prison in Northern California no longer houses women in the male facility, even temporarily. And the Federal Bureau of Prisons now puts guards through a training program designed to make them more aware of potential sexual abuse problems.

Yet, the victory wasn't complete. Although Lucas also filed criminal charges against her attackers and the guards who made the assault possible, they were dismissed by the state. Sadder still, she's still considered one of the lucky few to have won some measure of justice.

Violence Against Women of Color Is a Serious Problem

by Angela Davis

About the author: *Angela Davis is a longtime activist and author who teaches at the University of California at Santa Cruz.*

Editor's Note: The following viewpoint was excerpted from the author's keynote address at the Color of Violence Conference in Santa Cruz, California.

I feel extremely honored to have been invited to deliver this keynote address. This conference deserves to be called "historic" on many accounts. It is the first of its kind, and this is precisely the right intellectual season for such a gathering. The breadth and complexity of its concerns show the contradictions and possibilities of this historical moment. And just such a gathering can help us to imagine ways of attending to the ubiquitous violence in the lives of women of color that also radically subvert the institutions and discourses within which we are compelled by necessity to think and work.

I predict that this conference will be remembered as a milestone for feminist scholars and activists, marking a new moment in the history of anti-violence scholarship and organizing.

Many years ago when I was a student in San Diego, I was driving down the freeway with a friend when we encountered a black woman wandering along the shoulder. Her story was extremely disturbing. Despite her uncontrollable weeping, we were able to surmise that she had been raped and dumped along the side of the road. After a while, she was able to wave down a police car, thinking that they would help her. However, when the white policeman picked her up, he did not comfort her, but rather seized upon the opportunity to rape her once more.

I relate this story not for its sensational value, but for its metaphorical power.

Angela Davis, "The Color of Violence Against Women," *ColorLines*, vol. 3, Fall 2000, pp. 4–8.

Given the racist and patriarchal patterns of the state, it is difficult to envision the state as the holder of solutions to the problem of violence against women of color. However, as the anti-violence movement has been institutionalized and professionalized, the state plays an increasingly dominant role in how we conceptualize and create strategies to minimize violence against women.

One of the major tasks of this conference, and of the anti-violence movement as a whole, is to address this contradiction, especially as it presents itself to poor communities of color.

The Advent of "Domestic Violence"

Violence is one of those words that is a powerful ideological conductor, one whose meaning constantly mutates. Before we do anything else, we need to pay tribute to the activists and scholars whose ideological critiques made it possible to apply the category of "domestic violence" to those concealed layers of aggression systematically directed at women. These acts were for so long relegated to secrecy or, worse, considered normal.

Many of us now take for granted that misogynist violence is a legitimate political issue, but let us remember that a little more than two decades ago, most people considered "domestic violence" to be a private concern and thus not a proper subject of public discourse or political intervention. Only one generation separates us from that era of silence. The first speak-out against rape occurred in the early 1970s, and the first national organization against domestic violence was founded toward the end of that decade.

We have since come to recognize the epidemic proportions of violence within intimate relationships and the pervasiveness of date and acquaintance rape, as well as violence within and against same-sex intimacy. But we must also learn how to oppose the racist fixation on people of color as the primary perpetrators of violence, including domestic and sexual violence, and at the same time to fiercely challenge the real violence that men of color inflict on women. These are precisely the men who are already reviled as the major purveyors of violence in our society: the gang members, the drug-dealers, the drive-by shooters, the burglars, and assailants. In short, the criminal is figured as a black or Latino man who must be locked into prison.

"We must . . . oppose the racist fixation on people of color as the primary perpetrators of violence . . . and . . . challenge the real violence that men of color inflict on women."

One of the major questions facing this conference is how to develop an analysis that furthers neither the conservative project of sequestering millions of men of color in accordance with the contemporary dictates of globalized capital and its prison industrial complex, nor the equally conservative project of abandoning poor women of color to a continuum of violence that extends from the sweatshops through the prisons, to shelters, and into bedrooms at home.

How do we develop analyses and organizing strategies against violence against women that acknowledge the race of gender and the gender of race?

Women of Color on the Frontlines

Women of color have been active in the anti-violence movement since its beginnings. The first national organization addressing domestic violence was founded in 1978 when the United States Civil Rights Commission Consultation on Battered Women led to the founding of the National Coalition Against Domestic Violence. In 1980, the Washington, D.C. Rape Crisis Center sponsored the First National Conference on Third World Women and Violence. The following year a Women of Color Task Force was created within the National Coalition Against Domestic Violence. To make some historical connections, it is significant that the U.S. Third World Women's Caucus formed that same year within the National Women Studies Association, and the groundbreaking book *This Bridge Called My Back* was first published.

Many of these activists have helped to develop a more complex understanding about the overlapping, crosscutting, and often contradictory relationships among race, class, gender, and sexuality that militate against a simplistic theory of privatized violence in women's lives. Clearly, the powerful slogan first initiated by the feminist movement—"the personal is political"—is far more complicated than it initially appeared to be.

> *"Can a state that is thoroughly infused with racism, male dominance, class-bias, and homophobia . . . act to minimize violence in the lives of women?"*

Violence Is Not Private

The early feminist argument that violence against women is not inherently a private matter, but has been privatized by the sexist structures of the state, the economy, and the family has had a powerful impact on public consciousness.

Yet, the effort to incorporate an analysis that does not reify gender has not been so successful. The argument that sexual and domestic violence is the structural foundation of male dominance sometimes leads to a hierarchical notion that genital mutilation in Africa and sati, or wife-burning, in India are the most dreadful and extreme forms of the same violence against women which can be discovered in less appalling manifestations in Western cultures.

Other analyses emphasize a greater incidence of misogynist violence in poor communities and communities of color, without necessarily acknowledging the greater extent of police surveillance in these communities—directly and through social service agencies. In other words, precisely because the primary strategies for addressing violence against women rely on the state and on constructing gendered assaults on women as "crimes," the criminalization process further bolsters the racism of the courts and prisons. Those institutions, in turn, further contribute to violence against women.

Government Reliance Is a Problem

On the one hand, we should applaud the courageous efforts of the many activists who are responsible for a new popular consciousness of violence against women, for a range of legal remedies, and for a network of shelters, crisis centers, and other sites where survivors are able to find support. But on the other hand, uncritical reliance on the government has resulted in serious problems. I suggest that we focus our thinking on this contradiction: Can a state that is thoroughly infused with racism, male dominance, class-bias, and homophobia and that constructs itself in and through violence act to minimize violence in the lives of women? Should we rely on the state as the answer to the problem of violence against women?

> *"The ... strategy ... of criminalizing violence against women will not put an end to violence against women—just as imprisonment has not put an end to 'crime' in general."*

The soon-to-be-released video by Nicole Cusino (assisted by Ruth Gilmore) on California prison expansion and its economic impact on rural and urban communities includes a poignant scene in which Vanessa Gomez describes how the deployment of police and court anti-violence strategies put her husband away under the Three Strikes law. She describes a verbal altercation between herself and her husband, who was angry with her for not cutting up liver for their dog's meal, since, she said, it was her turn to cut the liver.

According to her account, she insisted that she would prepare the dog's food, but he said no, he was already doing it. She says that she grabbed him and, in trying to take the knife away from him, seriously cut her fingers. In the hospital, the incident was reported to the police. Despite the fact that Ms. Gomez contested the prosecutor's version of the events, her husband was convicted of assault. Because of two previous convictions as a juvenile, he received a sentence under California's Three Strikes law of 25 years to life, which he is currently serving.

I relate this incident because it so plainly shows the facility with which the state can assimilate our opposition to gender domination into projects of racial—which also means gender—domination.

Militarized Violence

Gina Dent has observed that one of the most important accomplishments of this conference is to foreground Native American women within the category "women of color." As Kimberle Crenshaw's germinal study on violence against women suggests, the situation of Native American women shows that we must also include within our analytical framework the persisting colonial domination of indigenous nations and national formations within and outside the presumed territorial boundaries of the U.S. The U.S. colonial state's racist, sexist, and homophobic brutality in dealing with Native Americans once again shows the futility of relying upon the juridical or legislative processes of the state to resolve these problems.

How then can one expect the state to solve the problem of violence against women, when it constantly recapitulates its own history of colonialism, racism, and war? How can we ask the state to intervene when, in fact, its armed forces have always practiced rape and battery against "enemy" women? In fact, sexual and intimate violence against women has been a central military tactic of war and domination.

Women Are in Agencies of Violence

Yet the approach of the neoliberal state is to incorporate women into these agencies of violence—to integrate the armed forces and the police.

How do we deal with the police killing Amadou Diallo, whose wallet was putatively misapprehended as a gun—or Tanya Haggerty in Chicago, whose cell phone was a potential weapon that allowed police to justify her killing? By hiring more women as police officers? Does the argument that women are victimized by violence render them inefficient agents of violence? Does giving women greater access to official violence help to minimize informal violence? Even if this were the case, would we want to embrace this as a solution? Are women essentially immune from the forms of adaptation to violence that are so foundational to police and military culture?

> *"We need to develop an approach that relies on political mobilization rather than legal remedies or social service delivery."*

Carol Burke, a civilian teaching in the U.S. Naval Academy, argues that "sadomasochistic cadence calls have increased since women entered the brigade of midshipmen in 1976." She quotes military songs that are so cruelly pornographic that I would feel uncomfortable quoting them in public, but let me give one comparatively less offensive example:

> *The ugliest girl I ever did see*
> *Was beatin' her face against a tree*
> *I picked her up; I punched her twice.*
> *She said, "Oh Middy, you're much too nice.*

If we concede that something about the training structures and the operations they are expected to carry out makes the men (and perhaps also women) in these institutions more likely to engage in violence within their intimate relationships, why then is it so difficult to develop an analysis of violence against women that takes the violence of the state into account?

The major strategy relied on by the women's anti-violence movement of criminalizing violence against women will not put an end to violence against women—just as imprisonment has not put an end to "crime" in general.

I should say that this is one of the most vexing issues confronting feminists today. On the one hand, it is necessary to create legal remedies for women who are survivors of violence. But on the other hand, when the remedies rely on punishment within institutions that further promote violence—against women and men—how do we work with this contradiction?

How do we avoid the assumption that previously "private" modes of violence can only be rendered public within the context of the state's apparatus of violence?

The Crime Bill

It is significant that the 1994 Violence Against Women Act was passed by Congress as Title IV of the Violent Crime Control and Law Enforcement Act of 1994—the Crime Bill. This bill attempted to address violence against women within domestic contexts, but at the same time it facilitated the incarceration of more women—through Three Strikes and other provisions. The growth of police forces provided for by the Crime Bill will certainly increase the numbers of people subject to the brutality of police violence.

Prisons are violent institutions. Like the military, they render women vulnerable in an even more systematic way to the forms of violence they may have experienced in their homes and in their communities. Women's prison experiences point to a continuum of violence at the intersection of racism, patriarchy, and state power.

Sexual Abuse Is Rampant

A Human Rights Watch report entitled *All Too Familiar: Sexual Abuse of Women in U.S. Prisons* says: "Our findings indicate that being a woman prisoner in U.S. state prisons can be a terrifying experience. If you are sexually abused, you cannot escape from your abuser. Grievance or investigatory procedures, where they exist, are often ineffectual, and correctional employees continue to engage in abuse because they believe they will rarely be held accountable, administratively or criminally. Few people outside the prison walls know what is going on or care if they do know. Fewer still do anything to address the problem."

Recently, 31 women filed a class action[1] law suit against the Michigan Department of Corrections, charging that the department failed to prevent sexual

---

1. In addition to the inmates' law suit, the U.S. Department of Justice filed its own action against the Michigan Department of Corrections under the Civil Rights of Institutionalized Persons Act, alleging pervasive sexual misconduct against women prisoners. A settlement was reached in both cases, excluding male officers from female inmates' housing units where women were more vulnerable to sexual abuse by guards.

violence and abuse by guards and civilian staff. These women have been subjected to serious retaliations, including being raped again!

At Valley State Prison in California, the chief medical officer told Ted Koppel on national television that he and his staff routinely subjected women to pelvic examinations, even if they just had colds. He explained that these women have been imprisoned for a long time and have no male contact, and so they actually enjoy these pelvic examinations. Koppel sent the tape of this interview to the prison and he was eventually dismissed. According to the Department of Corrections, he will never be allowed to have contact with patients again. But this is just the tip of the iceberg. The fact that he felt able to say this on national television gives you a sense of the horrendous conditions in women's prisons.

Political Mobilization Is Necessary

There are no easy solutions to all the issues I have raised and that so many of you are working on. But what is clear is that we need to come together to work toward a far more nuanced framework and strategy than the anti-violence movement has ever yet been able to elaborate.

We want to continue to contest the neglect of domestic violence against women, the tendency to dismiss it as a private matter. We need to develop an approach that relies on political mobilization rather than legal remedies or social service delivery. We need to fight for temporary and long-term solutions to violence and simultaneously think about and link global capitalism, global colonialism, racism, and patriarchy—all the forces that shape violence against women of color. Can we, for example, link a strong demand for remedies for women of color who are targets of rape and domestic violence with a strategy that calls for the abolition of the prison system?

I conclude by asking you to support the new organization [INCITE! Women of Color Against Violence] initiated by Andrea Smith, the organizer of this conference. Such an organization contesting violence against women of color is especially needed to connect, advance, and organize our analytic and organizing efforts. Hopefully this organization will act as a catalyst to keep us thinking and moving together in the future.

Violence in Lesbian Relationships Is a Serious Problem

by Jacqueline Williams and Kathleen O'Connell

About the authors: *Jacqueline Williams is a member of the Coalition Against Same-Sex Partner Abuse (CASSPA) and facilitates groups on lesbian relationships. Kathleen O'Connell is a social worker who provides individual and group counseling to women who are at risk of or who have experienced violence in their lives. She is also a member of CASSPA.*

Much is known and understood about violence in heterosexual relationships. The campaign against 'wife assault' and domestic violence has enlightened many about violence in intimate male-female relationships. Unfortunately, the same cannot be said about violence in same-sex relationships. Education is needed so that violence in lesbian relationships will be seen as an issue in need of attention and intervention. Addressing violence in same-sex relationships means challenging our theories about gender-based violence as well as our stereotypes about women and about lesbians/bisexual women.

In 1997 and 1998, two ten week support groups for women who had been abused were sponsored by Parkdale Community Health Centre. From the beginning, there were a number of challenges. Providing a safe location was important and there were pros and cons for having a group in an identifiable gay/lesbian location and for a location that provides mainstream services.

We found that a comprehensive intake process was critical in order to screen out women who were in fact abusive to their partners. Some women defend themselves from an abusive partner and other women believe they may have joined in and were abusive as well to their partners. This continues to be a complex issue and raises questions around who should be included and excluded from a group.

The support groups provided lesbians/bisexual women with a space to talk

Jacqueline Williams and Kathleen O'Connell, "What's Love Got to Do With It! Examining Abuse in Lesbian Relationships," www.womanabuseprevention.com, November 25, 2001. Copyright © 2001 by Education Wife Assault. Also available at *Education Wife Assault Newsletter*, vol. 9, issue 2, Spring 1999. Reproduced by permission.

about their losses, their fears and ways to rebuild their lives. Feelings such as anger, embarrassment, sadness and shame were focused on. Anger at oneself, at an abusive partner and at the community for not addressing the issue more openly were discussed in the group. Rebuilding trust with self and others was an important theme. We discussed patterns of abusive behaviour and developed a list of "warning signs" which could indicate that a partner might become abusive. The tremendous support and validation women offered each other in the groups reduced feelings of isolation, self blame and guilt and helped women move forward in their lives.

Barriers for Women in Seeking Support

Resources are scarce for women in same-sex relationships who have experienced abuse or who have been abusive. Homophobia is usually present in agencies and institutions. Lesbians/bisexual women who attempt to get help from institutions are often met with homophobia, disbelief and blame. We have heard some reports of lesbians/bisexual women having positive experiences with systems, for example, the police and legal system, but many have described attitudes that are oppressive: misogynist, homophobic, racist, etc. This results in lesbians feeling reluctant to seek out these avenues of support. Lesbians/bisexual women told us that they often felt triply victimized: initially by their partners, by services/institutions that are supposed to be there to help and by the lack of positive response in their communities. Furthermore, if a lesbian does decide to seek support, it may create a double crisis. First, she has to "come out" to a stranger at a time when she is very distressed, and then she has to disclose the violence in her relationship.

When other oppressions such as racism, classism, anti-Semitism, ageism and ableism exist, the abused lesbian may feel further deterred from disclosing abuse. This can be experienced as a triple whammy; for example, a Black lesbian already deals with sexism, racism and homophobia, and now she is faced with disclosing that she is being abused. Lesbian/bisexual communities are small, and even smaller for Black lesbians, lesbians of colour and Aboriginal women. As a result, women from these communities can feel even more concerned about privacy and confidentiality. Sometimes a woman and her abusive partner may approach the same services requesting help, which can raise difficult issues for agencies providing support.

> *"Education is needed so that violence in lesbian relationships will be seen as an issue in need of attention and intervention."*

If a lesbian/bisexual woman decides to go to a shelter or the police, for example, she may find that she feels inhibited from disclosing her sexuality and thus may not receive the thorough and adequate attention she may desperately need. Shelters are supposed to be safe spaces for women, but when a woman uses a shelter to escape from the violence of another woman, the methods shelters use to keep out abusive male partners do not work in deterring female abusers from gaining access to shelters. Some lesbians/bisexual women have spoken about their experiences in shelters—that they did not feel safe and accepted because of the homophobia that exists in shelters.

Same-Sex Partner Abuse Is Invisible

Other challenges faced by lesbians/bisexual women seeking support are the attitudes and perceptions of others in the lesbian/gay/bisexual/transgendered communities. There is an assumption that women interact in a caring and supportive manner and therefore cannot be abusive. This stereotype and the invisibility of same-sex partner abuse make it even more difficult for lesbians/bisexual women themselves to recognize they are being abused, and create barriers when women reach out for help, because the attitude that women would not be abusive exists in the larger community as well.

Most theories about the causes of violence are gender-based and assume that the violence is being perpetrated by men—men raised in a patriarchal and sexist society. How then are these theories to be transferred or utilized in the incidence of violence between female and intimate partners? Without accepting some stereotypes about the nature and dynamics of lesbian relationships (namely that lesbian relationships have a "butch/male" partner and a "femme/female partner"), this theory is not very helpful. Even when lesbians do adopt explicit roles, these roles do not predict who has the power in a relationship and who in the relationship might be abusive.

Lesbian Violence Is a Surprise to Many

A number of women expressed their surprise and shock that their female partner was violent. Women spoke about their beliefs that women would not be violent and because of this, when violence did happen, it was doubly hard to name and address.

Safety, confidentiality and upholding a woman's right to privacy is always a concern for lesbians/bisexual women who are seeking support. When a woman finally decides to come forward and name the violence which has been perpetrated against her, it can be a frightening and overwhelming experience. It is extremely important that disclosure is made in an environment that is safe and lesbian-positive.

Anti-homophobia and anti-heterosexism training and education about violence in same-sex relationships are crucial in this work. Some shelters and other agencies have begun this work. We need to be allies in addressing the issue of violence in same-sex relationships, so that the statement that all women deserve to live free of violence has meaning for us all.

The Problem of Violence Against Women in the United States Is Exaggerated

by Richard L. Davis

About the author: *Richard L. Davis is a contributor to the website Domestic Violence Against Men in Colorado (www.dvmen.org) and the author of* Domestic Violence: Facts and Fallacies.

No, this is not an Andy Rooney *Sixty Minutes* piece. However, "have you ever wondered" why we are constantly bombarded with dramatically different numbers of women who are being beaten and battered by an intimate partner? Is it 188,000, 876,340, 1.3 million, 1.8 million, 4.8 million, 18 million, 27 million, or 60 million? I'm sure that I am not the only person who has wondered just what the heck is going on here? And, I didn't make these numbers up. These are real numbers presented to us by real people who expect us to believe them.

The 188,000 and 1.8 million numbers are from the *1975 National Family Violence Survey*, authored by Murray Straus and Richard Gelles and sponsored by the National Institute of Mental Health. They estimate that 84 percent of American families are not violent and that 16 percent do engage in some form of physical assault against each other. The 188,000 is the number of women who are injured severely enough to seek medical attention and the 1.8 million are women who suffer through severe violence such as kicking, punching, or using some type of a weapon.

The 876,340 number is by Callie Marie Rennison and Sarah Welchans from the Bureau of Justice Statistics Special Report, Intimate Partner Violence of May 2000. They get their numbers from a study of the National Crime Victimization Survey of 1998. The survey estimates that about 1 million violent crimes were committed against people by their current or former spouse, boyfriend, or girlfriend. About 85 percent of the victims were women and 15 percent men. It is worth noting here that often we read that male against female intimate partner violence is reported to be as high as 95 percent. That is a number offered by the [Denver-based] National Coalition Against Domestic Violence (NCADV) and almost always used by women's rights groups. They claim that number comes from the U.S. Department of Justice, however, the Rennison and Welchans report is from the Department of Justice and they make no such claim.

Both the 1.3 million and the 4.8 million both come from Patricia Tjaden and Nancy Thoennes in the findings from the National Violence Against Women Survey and their numbers vary depending on which of their two reports you read. The Full Report of the Prevalence, Incidence, and Consequences of Violence Against Women, November 2000 reports the 1.3 million number. The 4.8 million is from the Extent, Nature, and Consequences of Intimate Partner Violence, July 2000.

Data Collection Lacks Validity

The 18 million number is attributed to the National Coalition Against Domestic Violence who estimate that annually more than one third of all married women are being battered. The 27 million is an estimate that more than half of all married women will experience violence during their marriage. These "numbers" are often repeated by domestic violence advocates and printed by the media, although it seems as if they may have been pulled out of thin air. Rita Smith of NCADV when asked where these numbers came from stated that they were estimates based on what NCADV "hears" from battered women's shelters and others. I think we would all agree that this type of data collection lacks the validity of an empirical scientific study. However, they may at least be possible, as compared to the mythical number of 60 million.

A Miami talk show host, Pat Stevens, conjured up the 60 million number. Stevens appeared on CNN's *Crossfire* show and made the claim that all of the numbers concerning battered women are incorrect and in fact, Stevens claimed, when the real numbers are adjusted for under reporting, the true number for battered women is 60 million. No single person on the show disputed Mr. Stevens. No one bothered to inform Mr. Stevens that his "guesstimate" is more than all of the women in the United States who are married or living with a man in some form of spousal relationship. I do admit that in all the years I have been involved with the issue of domestic violence, I never once heard anyone, not the

> *"The attempt by . . . the women's rights movement to inflate the number of victims . . . has resulted in driving many men and women away from the issue."*

most radical of women's rights advocates, anywhere, at any time repeat this inane claim. Never the less, it went undisputed on a respectable, nationally televised show.

The real fact is, that numbers such as those presented by Stevens and those that appear to be pulled out of the air by the NCADV, in the long run hurt and not help the cause of battered women. How or why can we expect men to become involved with domestic violence when they are constantly being painted with a broad brush as demonic males who beat and bash women with impunity? And even more troublesome is the fact that most of those other numbers cited above, despite their radical differences, are numbers that can be substantiated. How can this be? . . .

Definitions of Battering Differ

The larger numbers of 60 million, 18 million, or in fact any numbers that seem unbelievable, are most often just that, unbelievable. Some of the numbers reported are simply pulled out of a hat for effect. Smaller numbers such as 188,000, 1.3 million, 1.8 million, 4.8 million or other numbers that do seem possible are often based on fact and are real numbers. However, what accounts for the numerical difference in numbers presented by researchers and the women's rights movement is that they do not necessarily report the number of women who are being systematically battered by a man. Agreement concerning just who is a "battered woman" continues to plague researchers and impede proper intervention. Researchers, professionals, and the women's rights movement have been disputing this definition for years. The actual number of women who are "battered" still remain in the eye of the beholder. How can we agree on numbers if we cannot agree on definition?

> *"Many . . . have come to distrust . . . the women's rights movement because . . . they continue to present flawed and dramatically differing numbers of abusers and victims."*

Most researchers and professionals agree that a "battered woman" suffers from what is often labeled "patriarchial terrorism." Most researchers and professionals agree that a "battered woman" is a woman whose life is thoroughly, extensively, and completely controlled by a man and her behavior purposely altered to suit a man's desires while they live in a familial styled relationship. The batterer systematically uses physical violence, economic subordination, threats, isolation, and a variety of other behavioral controlling tactics to ensure she does what he wants her to do. The problem with the numbers documented above, and often reported elsewhere, is that the vast majority of data that purport to demonstrate the number of "battered women" do not document the above type of victim or abuser.

The vast majority of studies used to measure the number of "battered women" employ some form of the Conflict Tactics Scale (CTS) developed by University of New Hampshire in 1971. CTS is the most common measure of non-sexual family violence. It measures three styles of interpersonal conflict in familial styled relationships. It measures, most often through telephone interviews, the use of rational verbal agreement and disagreement, the use of verbal and non-verbal aggressive behavior, and the use of physical force or violent behavior. It is not designed to measure in any rational context the reason or motivation for the behavior of either abuser or victim.

CTS Measures Nonsexual Family Violence

Almost all of the modified versions of the CTS ask questions such as:
• Did you have something thrown towards you that could hurt if it hit you?
• Were you grabbed, pushed, or shoved?
• Were you slapped, hit, bitten, or kicked?
• Were you hit with an object, choked, or beaten up?
• Were you threatened with a knife, gun, or other weapon?
• Was a knife, gun, or other weapon used against you?

The question begged here is, how many of us have not been guilty of, or a victim of, some form of the behavior described by the CTS scale? How does a single yes answer to any one of the above questions document that a victim of an isolated event is a "battered woman" or that the actor is a "batterer?" And just as important is the fact that the motivational dynamic is rarely asked and, hence, rarely answered. No one, not the most ardent feminist or male chauvinist, can argue with any degree of reason or certainty that some of these self-reported behaviors could not have been motivated by an isolated argument, anger, jealousy or revenge for some perceived prior behavior and/or fueled by an excessive use of alcohol or drugs.

Simple and cursory research concerning the "battered woman model" documents the phenomenon is very real. I believe that most police officers in this nation honestly agree that both the batterer and victim, noted above, exist in their community. None of what I write is an attempt to dispute that fact. My concern is just the opposite. What I proffer is the attempt by many in the women's rights movement to inflate the number of victims and to paint all men as batterers and all women equally at risk of being battered has resulted in driving many men and woman away from the issue. The victims of battering, the majority who are at the lower end of the socioeconomic, educational ladder, become marginalized because of the claim that all women are equally at risk for battering. All studies document quite clearly that women who suffer social, economic, and educational deprivation and lack family support are at a greater risk of severe battering. These victims are the ones who most need our help and their batterers need sure, swift, and just sanctions.

Women's Rights Activists Call All Men Batterers

The constant attempt by the women's rights movement to paint all men as batterers has caused many men to minimize, deny or ignore this type of behavior even when they suspect a friend might be a batterer. Many men fear being caught in the women's rights legal dragnet for batterers. After all, many in the women's rights movement continue to profess that these witnesses are men and;

hence, they must be guilty of something. The continued drumbeat by many in the women's rights movement and some researchers that all men are demonic batterers and all women angelic victims has resulted in the majority of men and women in America, who are not batterers or victims, to ignore the plight of many battered women that lack resources or family support.

Many women, and African-American women in particular, during the 1800's came to distrust white suffragettes led by Susan B. Anthony and Elizabeth Cady Stanton because of their repeated attack on marriage and in particular when both turned their support away from the rights of African-American women in the South to vote. Today, many men and women, who are neither batterer or victim, have come to distrust many in the women's rights movement because of their repeated attack on all men and because they continue to present flawed and dramatically differing numbers of abusers and victims simply to support their position. And once again many very real victims are marginalized in society because of their social, economic, and educational status.

Feminists Exaggerate the Prevalence of Rape

by Wendy McElroy

About the author: *Wendy McElroy is the editor of the website ifeminists.com and a research fellow at the Independent Institute, a libertarian think tank. She is also the editor of* Freedom, Feminism, and the State, *a historical overview of individualist feminism in America.*

The mother of all feminist myths on campuses today is that one in four female students has been the victim of rape or attempted rape. So states the conservative Independent Women's Forum [IWF] in a recent advertisement in student newspapers across the country. The ad referred to feminism as a "cult" and warned that anyone who believed two or more of the ten listed myths might need "de-programming." The backlash was swift. Women's rights groups at [University of California, Los Angeles] UCLA held a rally specifically to protest the ad.

The source of the myth is a study published in 1987, which was commissioned by *Ms. Magazine* and conducted by Mary Koss—a researcher chosen by [renowed feminist] Gloria Steinem. Since then the "one-quarter" stat has become commonplace in newspapers and commentary. Yet Koss herself admitted that, of the 27.5% reported "victims," fully 73% were not "aware" of having been raped. Over 40% continued to date their "rapists." Koss seemed to prefer her interpretation of the data over the words and actions of her research subjects. Feminists agreed: the subjects had been raped because their experiences met the definition of rape, which was "sex without consent."

The validity of Koss' study is crucial. PC feminists rabidly defend the one-quarter stat because laws, campus policies and massive funding have been based upon it. They would rather create an atmosphere of sexual and anti-male paranoia, than endanger their financial support or political agenda. As Kate Kennedy, IWF campus projects manager, stated, "What we see time and again is the lack of truth on college campuses and faulty statistics that we feel creates a certain form of national hysteria on campuses."

Rape Redefined

Key to this hysteria is the redefinition of "rape" that has been going on for decades. The word "rape" comes from the Latin *rapere*, which means "to take by force." Although the feminist re-wording of "to take without consent" may seem innocuous, the new definition expands the boundaries of rape beyond all reason. The "presence of force" standard has clear evidence such as bruises, a struggle, cries of protest, a police report. The "absence of consent" standard is so vague that radical feminists such as Catharine MacKinnon have stated, "Politically, I call it rape whenever a woman has sex and *feels* violated." Liz Kelly, in her book *Surviving Sexual Violence*, captures how rape is defined on many campuses. She writes, "Sexual violence includes any physical, visual, verbal or sexual act that is *experienced* by the woman or girl, at the time *or later*, as a threat, invasion or assault, that has the effect of hurting her or degrading her and/or takes away her ability to control intimate contact." [Emphasis added in both.]

This guideline is rampantly subjective and heavily loaded against men. By its standards, a woman who experienced no threat during sex may accuse the man of rape if she feels "threatened" later upon remembering or regretting the act. Moreover, anything she "experiences" as violence is considered to be *de facto* violent. A few years ago, a survey by two sociologists at Carleton University, financed by a $236,000 government grant, found that 81 percent of female students at Canadian universities and colleges had suffered sexual abuse. The study caused a maelstrom of controversy. Then it was revealed that the researchers had included insults hurled during lover's quarrels within their definition of "sexual abuse."

> *"My concern is about the trivialization of rape that occurs when 'abusive' comments are classified as assault."*

Lack of Consent

This re-definition of sexual violence underlies many anti-male policies on campus—like the extreme Sexual Misconduct Policy at Columbia University. Columbia's policy defines sexual misconduct as "nonconsensual, intentional physical contact with a person's genitals, buttocks, and/or breasts. Lack of consent may be inferred from the use of force, coercion, physical intimidation, or advantage gained by the victim's mental and/or physical impairment or incapacity, of which the perpetrator was, or should have been, aware." The wording "should have been aware" is dangerously subjective.

Even worse, in the hysteria surrounding sexual violence, Columbia has implemented the policy in a manner that utterly suspends due process for the accused who is almost always male. For example, the process does not allow a "defendant" to face his accuser or cross-examine witnesses. Indeed, it is not clear whether he can even hear the testimony of witnesses: the Policy states, "the student does not necessarily have the right to be present to hear other witnesses."

The defendant is not allowed to have an attorney present. With a maximum of ten days notice and with little information as to the specific charges—which can be brought five years after the fact—the defendant is expected to prepare a defense. His career might hinge upon the result. If found guilty, he can be denied the degree for which he has worked for years and a file tagged "sexual offender" may follow him forever.

Rape Must Not Be Trivialized

Redefinition also fuels attempts to change how the legal system treats rape. A section of the 1994 Violence Against Women Act (VAWA) was recently struck down by the Supreme Court. The section allowed an alleged rape victim to sue her attacker for damages in federal civil court for violating her civil rights. The first case filed concerned a campus rape. In 1995, Christy Brzonkala sued two male students for civil damages in federal court for a rape that allegedly occurred at Virginia Polytechnic Institute. The men had been cleared by both a university judicial committee and a criminal grand jury. But the VAWA would have allowed them to be tried for rape in a civil court, which would have been more favorable to a vague definiton of rape that did not require stringent evidence. In a criminal court, rape must be sustained beyond a "reasonable doubt," often defined as 99 percent certainty. Civil court requires only a preponderance of the evidence, often defined as 51 percent certainty. And the rules of evidence are far more relaxed.

As a woman who has been raped, I will never diminish the importance of preventing sexual violence. Quite the contrary. My concern is about the trivialization of rape that occurs when "abusive" comments are classified as assault. I worry about the danger to male students when their freedom of speech—albeit, poorly exercised—is treated as a physical attack. Or when an alleged attack does not require evidence to be sustained. The hysteria will only be ended when parents are as concerned about the well-being of their sons as they are about their daughters.

Advocacy Groups Exaggerate the Prevalence of Female Rape in Prisons

by Dyanne Petersen

About the author: *Dyanne Petersen was an inmate at the Federal Prison Camp in Dublin, California, when she wrote this account for* Liberty *magazine, a libertarian publication.*

On March 30, 1999, a special investigator for violence against women, Radhika Coomaraswamy of Sri Lanka, issued her report in Geneva to the United Nations Human Rights Commission. One of her conclusions was that sexual misconduct by prison guards is common in women's prisons in the U.S., based on her June 1998 visits to state and Federal prisons in six states and Washington, D.C. As reported in the *New York Times*, "In some prisons, she said that she was told that 'at least two-thirds of the female inmates have been sexually or physically abused.'"

A few weeks earlier, Amnesty International [AI] issued a report, *Not Part of My Sentence: Violations of the Human Rights of Women in Custody*, which concluded that "sexual abuse is a fact of life for incarcerated women in the United States." Among other outrages, the study reported that rapes, sexual slavery and other sexual abuse had occurred at the Federal Correctional Institution (FCI) and Federal Prison Camp (FPC) in Dublin, California.

This was of more than academic interest to me. You see, I am an inmate at the FPC in Dublin, and I've had a chance to witness firsthand the activity alleged in these reports.

Federal Corrections Officer Jon C. Hyson was indicted February 17, 1999, by a federal grand jury in San Francisco on charges of engaging in sexual acts with female inmates at FCI and FPC Dublin where he had worked. The indictment included 17 counts of sexual acts and contact and five alleging that Hyson lied about the incidents to authorities. If convicted on all counts, Hyson could be

Dyanne Petersen, "Sex Behind Bars," *Liberty*, January 2000, p. 29. Copyright © 2000 by Liberty Publishing. Reproduced by permission.

sentenced to more than 20 years in prison and fined more than a million dollars.[1] The prosecution followed a ten-month investigation by the FBI and the Department of Justice Inspector General.

Less than a year before the Hyson Sex Scandal hit the news, the Bureau of Prisons agreed to pay a half-million dollars to three female inmates who claimed that in 1995 they were sexually assaulted, beaten and sold by guards as sex slaves to male prisoners. Their lawsuit accused eight federal prison officials of actively participating in or knowing about the sex slavery ring, while refusing the plaintiffs' repeated pleas for help.

Not surprisingly, the story got a lot of media attention. TV crews swarmed our facilities almost as much as when Unabomber Ted Kaczynski briefly stayed across the street at the Federal Detention Center. My family and friends saw the reports from as far away as Chicago and New York. Needless to say, they were concerned for my safety. Some were terrified for me.

But the media lost interest in the Hyson story. The prison grapevine gave staff and inmates news that Hyson's attorney was negotiating a plea agreement to lesser charges of sexual misconduct. Gossip about the inmates who had cooperated in the Hyson investigation continued but, for the most part, I thought the controversy had blown over. Then, in mid-April, a friend sent me the Spring 1999 issue of Amnesty International's newsletter, *Amnesty Action*, which presented its sensational study of sex abuse in prison, including its account of abuse at FCI/FPC Dublin, my home away from home.

AI's Distorted Report

My friend was understandably frightened for me. I wrote to him explaining that I wasn't in any particular danger. AI's account, I assured him, was grotesquely inaccurate. Contrary to the impression given in *Amnesty Action*, sexual abuse is *not* a fact of life for women incarcerated in either the FCI or FPC.

Jon Hyson was the Officer-in-Charge (OIC) when I was assigned to his housing unit upon my arrival at FCI Dublin in March 1994. During my first 4:00 stand-up count with OIC Hyson, I was shocked to see how my fellow inmates treated him. Wolf whistles followed him down the

> *"Any relatively young or good-looking male staffer found an abundance of sexually willing and eager women to tempt and proposition them."*

hall. Women stood in their doorways licking their lips, offering open mouths and tongues or making lewd comments and gestures.

1. On February 17, 1999, Jon Hyson was indicted on sixteen counts of sexual contact with prisoners, one count of attempted sexual contact, and five counts of lying to federal officers. On August 11, 1999, he pleaded guilty to four counts of engaging in illicit sexual acts and one count of making a false statement. He admitted to having sex with female prisoners when he was employed at the Federal Correctional Institution in Dublin, California. Hyson was sentenced in December 1999 to five months in prison, five months in a halfway house, and six months of home detention. The sentences were served consecutively.

Women flirted shamelessly with him. It was often impossible to reach him at his officer's station to ask a question or get one's mail because so many women were jockeying for his attention. And this was repeated on each of his work shifts. I witnessed scores of provocative women offer themselves to him during my full year at the FCI and for almost four years at the FPC.

The women's lack of respect for the officer and for themselves was disturbing and embarrassing. And the disrespect was not directed exclusively to Officer Hyson. Any relatively young or good-looking male staffer found an abundance of sexually willing and eager women to tempt and proposition them. Men who were less attractive or desirable were also propositioned, but the sexual favors they were offered often required payment in contraband cosmetics or other goodies.

Sex Was Consensual

In this sexually charged atmosphere it is inconceivable to me that Officer Hyson would seek out "victims" for non-consensual sex. What I do find conceivable is that inmates who had consented to sexual activity, but were later dissatisfied with the level of emotional commitment or special favors they received, registered complaints. Inmates who were suspicious or jealous of relationships between other inmates and staff, or who were envious of the special gifts and favors that come with such relationships, would also be probable sources of complaints.

> *"Inmates who had consented to sexual activity, but were later dissatisfied with the level of emotional commitment or special favors they received, registered complaints."*

What happened is this: The prison administration attempted to enforce its own policies to prevent inappropriate physical contact between inmates and staff. The "investigation" of Officer Hyson included using inmates to entrap him, to lure him into acts of sexual misconduct that he neither initiated nor coerced. The incentives for inmates to cooperate with such investigations range from simple vindictiveness against staff/officers, to promises—real or imagined—of administration-directed favors. Cooperating "victims" have the added incentive of pursuing civil litigation for monetary awards if the criminal charges against the "offender" are proven. There are plenty of crusading and feminist lawyers to offer *pro bono* assistance to the "victims," and even more ambitious attorneys who are willing to pursue large cash settlements on a contingency basis.

Sex Vacations at Club FDC

Several months after my transfer to the FPC, across the street from the FCI, a friend and two other campers were ordered into the Special Housing Unit (SHU/disciplinary segregation) for a marijuana possession investigation. Campers were normally taken to the SHU at the FCI, but because of overcrowding at that time, the women were put in temporary segregated custody at the Federal Detention Center (FDC), which houses male inmates. During the first half of 1995, FCI inmates, including the three female inmates who won the half-million dollar settlement from the Bureau of Prisons, were also sent to the FDC for disciplinary housing when the FCI SHU was full or under renovation. My friend and her companions returned to camp from their extended FDC segregation with happy

> *"I am safer from random acts of violence or rape than free women in Washington, D.C., Belfast or Kinshasa."*

stories of repeated sexual activity with the male inmates, facilitated by one or more FDC officers. Although these women couldn't verify the arrangements made between the cooperating parties, we assumed that the inmates paid officers for opportunities to be with the women of their choice. My friend and her companions were willing, eager, consenting participants in the sexual activity.

Once their stories spread through the FPC, an epidemic of bad behavior broke out among campers hoping for disciplinary action and housing with the male inmates at the FDC. The same thing happened among the FCI women who sought sex vacations at the FDC. It's not a pleasant story. But it's also not a story of coercion abuse or violence.

Women Are Hungry for Affection

The impression that all women in prison are weak, helpless, potential victims is Victorian, insulting nonsense. Women, like men, are sexual beings and most women inmates, separated from their husbands, lovers or children, are hungry for physical and emotional affection. Others use sex as a tool or weapon with officers and staff to secure lighter work details, special privileges, money or contraband. And some women become the sexual predators other women fear.

Prison policy prohibits consensual acts of sex for the same reasons that universities, the military and many corporations prohibit superior-subordinate sexual relationships: discipline and objectivity are compromised and opportunities for abuse and coercion increase in these relationships. I believe this policy is a good one.

But I would never advocate civil or criminal penalties for *consensual* relations. Abusive, rogue officers here are dismissed and frequently criminal charges are filed and convictions obtained. But abuses are also perpetrated by inmates who, out of anger, frustration, boredom, the desire for monetary awards or early release, are quite willing to destroy an officer's or staff member's reputation, career and family.

Many Women Do Not Belong in Prison

I witness truly tragic human rights violations every day and most are the result of legislation and the court of public opinion, a misguided, paternalistic team that will remove men and women from their families, friends, careers and communities for peaceful, non-aggressive, non-coercive, non-fraudulent and genuinely consensual activities, and warehouse them for years and decades with murderers, arsonists, terrorists, rapists and thieves. What outrages me, what I can't say loud enough or often enough, is that half the women don't belong here because they've done nothing wrong, they have no victims; the other half don't belong here because it's too good for them.

The model of egalitarianism that is prison, houses and feeds and punishes the marijuana grower and the serial killer together and in the same way—and at a cost to taxpayers of over $20,000 per year per inmate. This is an atrocity that far exceeds the questionable claims of possible sexual abuse from a nano-fraction percent of the thousands of women who have been in custody at FCI/FPC Dublin in the past five years.

Prison Is Safer than the Streets

Life in prison is far from my idea of a good time, but I've traveled enough in my pre-prison life to know and appreciate that women in FCI/FPC Dublin live, by any objective standard, better than three-quarters of the world's population. I am safer from random acts of violence or rape than free women in Washington, D.C., Belfast or Kinshasa. And I'm old enough to remember fugitive Black Panther Eldridge Cleaver's comment to the press when he returned from exile to face prison time in the U.S.: "I'd rather be incarcerated in America than free in Algeria."

There are real problems in our nation's prisons and I applaud AI's efforts to bring attention to and correct them. But more energy should be spent on reforming the draconian drug laws, mandatory minimums and sentencing guidelines that are filling up America's prisons, and on rallying support for the hundreds of thousands of victims of the War on Drugs, not just as "prisoners of war," but as "political prisoners" who are imprisoned for holding dear and expressing in practice the radical ideas of self-ownership and individualism.

Rape is *not* part of our sentence at FCI/FPC Dublin. It's not encouraged, condoned, sanctioned, nor is it a systemic problem: it is an anomaly, an ugly and infrequent exception to a vigorously enforced rule.

I don't fear sexual abuse here as much as I fear being released into an America with fewer and fewer personal freedoms and with increasing violations of the rights which used to enjoy constitutional guarantees and protections that made us the envy of the world.

Letter Sent to AI

I sent Amnesty International a letter detailing all this, suggesting that its report was inaccurate in many details. AI replied with a simple note that acknowledged receipt of my letter, and that was it.

About a week after I sent my letter to AI, Fox News ran a two-night *Segment*

Two report on prison sex scandals, the first part devoted exclusively to FCI/FPC Dublin. One of the officials interviewed in the Fox News report was Ralph Paige, from the U.S. Justice Department Office of Inspector General, the agency that assisted in Jon Hyson's investigation and which has the responsibility of accepting and investigating new complaints of sexual harassment and abuse from federal inmates. He reported receiving, on average, one complaint per month from the Dublin facilities since his office's phone number had been made available for free calls from inmates.

What Paige failed to make clear, or what was edited out of his interview, was the fact that on any given day, there are 1400–1500 female inmates in the two facilities of FCI/FPC Dublin and that some percentage of those complaints are without merit and undeserving of active investigation.

I would bet a carton of cigarettes (at tax-free prison prices, thank you) that free-world, private or public sector ombudsmen would welcome that rate of complaint, given today's litigious society and the legions of gender feminists coming out of Women's Studies programs and into the job market. I sent Mr. Paige my Amnesty letter with a note suggesting that he remember my perspective every time he and his colleagues receive complaints from Dublin.

I'm still waiting for his response.

Female Violence Against Men Is a Serious Problem

by Richard J. Gelles

About the author: *Richard J. Gelles holds the Joanne and Raymond Welsh Chair of Child Welfare and Family Violence at the University of Pennsylvania School of Social Work.*

I met Alan and Faith nearly twenty-five years ago. I was in the process of interviewing men and women on what was then both a taboo topic and an issue that had been treated as an unmentionable personal trouble—violence in the family. I was one of the first researchers in the United States to attempt to study the extent, patterns, and causes of what I then called "conjugal violence," and what today advocates label "domestic violence." There was precious little research or information to guide my study—the entire scientific literature was two journal articles. With the exception of the tabloids, the media and daytime talk shows had not yet discovered the dark side of family relations.

Both Alan and Faith discussed their experiences with violence in their respective intimate relations and marriages. The violence was sometimes severe, including a stabbing and broken bones. And yet, Alan and Faith ended up as mere footnotes in my initial book, *The Violent Home.* I admit now and knew then that I had overlooked the stories of Alan and Faith. The reason that their stories were relegated to mere notes was that they did not fit the perceptual framework of my research. Although I called my study an examination of family or conjugal violence, my main focus, the issue I hoped to raise consciousness about, was violence toward women. Alan, as it turned out, had never hit his wife. The broken bones and abrasions that occurred in his home were inflicted by his wife. But Faith was herself a victim of violence; her husband, ex-husband, and boyfriends had struck her and abused her numerous times. These events were dutifully counted and reported in my book and subsequent articles. Faith's situation was the focus of my article "Abused Wives: Why Do They Stay?" However, Faith's acts of violence, which included stabbing her husband while he read the morning paper, were reported only as a small quote in my book, with little analysis or discussion. In my first study of family violence, I had overlooked violence toward men. I would not, and could not, ever do that again.

Family Violence

My recognition of the issue of violence toward men came about in a strange way. In 1976, two years after my initial study of family violence, the American Sociological Association included a session on "Family Violence" as part of the association's annual meeting program. This was the first time this scholarly association had devoted precious meeting time and space to this topic. However, unlike most sessions, which are open to anyone registered for the meeting, this session required a reservation. I wrote the day I received my preliminary program to request admission to the session, and was subsequently informed that the session was "filled."

I do not believe I stopped to consider how or why a session could be completely filled as soon as it was announced. I was desperate, however, to link up with others in my field who were interested in the rarely studied topic of family violence. So, uninvited, I went to the session anyway and sat in the back of the room, hoping to hear what was going on, without being labeled a "gate crasher."

The session was held in a small ballroom, and there were about twenty people in attendance, all sitting in a circle. The room was far from overflowing. The session was chaired by two sociologists from Scotland who were about to publish their own book on family violence, titled *Violence Against Wives: A Case Against Patriarchy*. Much of the session focused on the application of feminist theory, or patriarchy theory, to explaining the extent and patterns of violence toward wives, both in contemporary society and over time and across cultures. Much of the discussion was informative and useful.

> *"Contrary to the claim that women hit only in self-defense, we found that women were as likely to initiate the violence as were men."*

No Male Victims

But eventually someone raised the question of whether men were also victims of domestic violence. The session leaders and many others in the group stated, categorically, there were no male victims of domestic violence. At this point, I raised my hand, risking discovery of being a gate crasher, and explained that I had indeed interviewed men and women who reported significant and sometimes severe violence toward husbands. I was not quite shouted down, but it was explained to me that I must certainly be wrong, and even if women did hit men, it was always in self-defense, and that women never used violence to coerce and control their partners, as did men.

Alan and Faith were suddenly no longer footnotes, but I did not fully appreciate the significance of this until two years later.

The research I conducted for *The Violent Home* was a small study, based on eighty interviews conducted in New Hampshire. That research pointed to the possibility that family violence was indeed widespread and the probability that social factors, such as income and family power, were causal factors. But the study was too small and too exploratory to be more than suggestive. To build a more solid knowledge base and an understanding of family violence, my colleagues Murray Straus and Suzanne Steinmetz and I conducted the First National Family Violence Survey in 1976.

High Rates of Violence Are Revealed

The survey interviewed a nationally representative sample of 2,143 individual family members. The results were reported in a number of scholarly articles and, finally, in the book *Behind Closed Doors: Violence in the American Family*. What surprised my colleagues and me the most were the high rates of violence toward children, between siblings, toward parents, and between partners that were reported by those we interviewed. Up until this point, annual estimates of child abuse and wife abuse were placed in the hundreds of thousands and no higher than one million. But our study, based on self-reports, placed the rates in the one to two million range.

The most controversial finding, as it turned out, was that the rate of female-to-male intimate violence was the same as the rate of male-to-female violence. Not only that, but the rate of abusive female-to-male violence was the same as the rate of abusive male-to-female violence. When my colleague Murray Straus presented these findings in 1977 at a conference on the subject of battered women, he was nearly hooted and booed from the stage. When my colleague Suzanne Steinmetz published a scholarly article, "The Battered Husband Syndrome," in 1978, the editor of the professional journal published, in the same issue, a critique of Suzanne's article.

Personal Attacks

The response to our finding that the rate of female-to-male family violence was equal to the rate of male-to-female violence not only produced heated scholarly criticism, but intense and long-lasting personal attacks. All three of us received death threats. Bomb threats were phoned in to conference centers and buildings where we were scheduled to speak.

Suzanne received the brunt of the attacks—individuals wrote and called her university urging that she be denied tenure; calls were made and letters were written to government agencies urging that her grant funding be rescinded. All three of us became "nonpersons" among domestic violence advocates. Invitations to conferences dwindled and dried up. Advocacy literature and feminist writing would cite our research, but not attribute it to us. Librarians publicly stated they would not order or shelve our books.

The more sophisticated critiques were not personal, but methodological. Those critiques focused on how we measured violence. We had developed an instrument, "The Conflict Tactics Scales." The measure met all the scientific standards for reliability and validity, so the criticisms focused on content. First, the measure assessed acts of violence and not outcomes—so it did not capture the consequence or injuries caused by violence. Second, the measure focused on acts and not context or process, so it did not assess who struck whom and whether the violence was in self-defense. These two criticisms, that the measure did not assess context or consequence, became a mantra-like critique that continued for the next two decades.

Criticism Continues

While the drumbeat of criticism continued, Murray Straus and I conducted the Second National Family Violence Survey in 1986. We attempted to address the two methodological criticisms of the Conflict Tactics Scales. In 1986 we interviewed a nationally representative sample of 6,002 individual family members over the telephone. This time we asked about the outcomes of violence and the process and context—who started the conflict and how.

"The real horror is the continued status of battered men as the 'missing persons' of the domestic violence problem."

The findings again included surprises. First, contrary to advocacy claims that there was an epidemic of child abuse and wife abuse, we found that the reported rates of violence toward children and violence toward women had declined. This made sense to us, as much effort and money had been expended between 1976 and 1986 to prevent and treat both child abuse and wife abuse. But female-to-male violence showed no decline and was actually higher and about as severe as male-to-female violence.

The examination of context and consequences also produced surprises. First, as advocates expected and as data from crime surveys bore out, women were much more likely to be injured by acts of domestic violence than were men. Second, contrary to the claim that women only hit in self-defense, we found that women were as likely to initiate the violence as were men. In order to correct for a possible bias in reporting, we re-examined our data looking only at the self-reports of women. The survey had asked subjects to talk about the last time there was partner violence: "In that particular instance, who started the physical contact, you or your spouse/partner?" The women reported similar rates of female-to-male violence compared to male-to-female, and women also reported they were as likely to initiate the violence as men.

When we reported the results of the Second National Family Violence Survey the personal attacks continued and the professional critiques simply ignored methodological revisions to the measurement instrument. This round of personal attacks was much more insidious—in particular, it was alleged that Murray had abused his wife. This is a rather typical critique in the field of family violence—men whose research results are contrary to political correctness are labeled "perps."

Up until now I have focused only on our own research. However, it is important to point out that our findings have been corroborated numerous times, by many different researchers, using many different methodological approaches. My colleague Murray Straus has found that every study among more than thirty describing some type of sample that is not self-selective (an example of self-selected samples are samples of women in battered woman shelters or women responding to advertisements recruiting research subjects; non-select selective samples are community samples, samples of college students, or representative samples) has found a rate of assault by women on male partners that is about the same as the rate by men on female partners. The only exceptions to this were the Justice Department's Uniform Crime Statistics, the National Crime Victims Survey, and the Department of Justice National Survey of Violence against Women. The Uniform Crime Statistics report the rate of fatal partner violence. While the rate and number for male and female victims was about the same twenty-five years ago, today [in 1999] female victims of partner homicide outnumber (and the rate is higher than) male victims. The National Crime Victims Survey and National Survey of Violence against Women both assess partner violence in the context of a crime survey. It is reasonable to suppose both men and women under-report female-to-male partner violence in a crime survey, since they do not conceptualize such behavior as a crime—whereas male-to-female violence is perceived as a crime.

Women Are More Likely to Be Injured

It is worth repeating, however, that almost all studies of domestic or partner violence agree that women are the most likely to be injured as a result of partner violence.

Two new studies add to our understanding of partner violence and the extent of violence toward men. First, psychologist David Fontes conducted a study of domestic violence perpetrated against heterosexual men in relationships compared to domestic violence against heterosexual women. The "Partner Conflict Survey" sample consisted of employees from the California Department of Social Services. Altogether, 136 surveys were returned out of 200 surveys distributed to employees in four locations (Sacramento, Roseville, Oakland, and Los Angeles). Not only did men experience the same rate of domestic violence as did women, but men reported the same rate of injury as did women.

More recently, a survey conducted by University of Wisconsin-Madison psychologist Terrie Moffit in New Zealand also found roughly the same rate of violence toward men as toward women in intimate relationships.

Chapter 1

Men Are Invisible Victims

Most journalistic accounts and many scholarly examinations of domestic violence toward women include descriptions of the horrors of intimate violence. Reports of remarkable cruelty and sadism accompany reports on domestic violence. Fatal injuries, disabling injuries, and systematic physical and emotional brutality are noted in detail. I have heard many of these accounts myself and reported them in my own books, articles, and interviews.

The "horror" of intimate violence toward men is somewhat different. There are, of course, hundreds of men killed each year by their partners. At a minimum, one-fourth of the men killed have not used violence toward their homicidal partners. Men have been shot, stabbed, beaten with objects, and been subjected to verbal assaults and humiliations. Nonetheless, I do not believe these are the "horrors" of violence toward men. The real horror is the continued status of battered men as the "missing persons" of the domestic violence problem. Male victims do not count and are not counted. The Federal Violence Against Women Act identified domestic violence as a gender crime. None of the nearly billion dollars of funding from this act is directed toward male victims. Some "Requests for Proposals" from the U.S. Justice Department specifically state that research on male victims or programs for male victims will not even be reviewed, let alone funded. Federal funds typically pass to a state coalition or to a branch of a state agency designated to deal with violence against women.

> *"It remains clear . . . that the problem is violence between intimates not violence against women."*

Battered Men May Lose Their Children

Battered men face a tragic apathy. Their one option is to call the police and hope that a jurisdiction will abide by a mandatory or presumptive arrest statute. But when the police do carry out an arrest on a male beating, they tend to engage in the practice of "dual arrest" and arrest both parties.

Battered men who flee their attackers find that the act of fleeing results in the men losing physical and even legal custody of their children. Those men who stay are thought to be "wimps" at best, and "perps" at worst, since if they stay, it is believed they are the true abusers in the home.

Thirty years ago battered women had no place to go and no place to turn for help and assistance. Today, there are places to go—more than 1,800 shelters—and many agencies to which to turn. For men, there still is no place to go and no one to turn to. On occasion a shelter for battered men is created, but it rarely lasts—first because it lacks on-going funding, and second because the shelter probably does not meet the needs of male victims. Men, for example, who retain their children in order to try to protect them from abusive mothers, often find themselves arrested for "child kidnapping."

Men Must Be Protected

The frustration men experience often bursts forth in rather remarkable obstreperous behavior at conferences, meetings, and forums on domestic violence. Such outbursts are almost immediately turned against the men by explaining that this behavior proves the men are not victims but are "perps."

Given the body of research on domestic violence that finds continued unexpectedly high rates of violence toward men in intimate relations, it is necessary to reframe domestic violence as something other than a "gender crime" or an example of "patriarchal coercive control." Protecting only the female victim and punishing only the male offender will not resolve the tragedy and costs of domestic violence. While this is certainly not a politically correct position, and is a position that will almost certainly ignite more personal attacks against me and my colleagues, it remains clear to me that the problem is violence between intimates not violence against women. Policy and practice must address the needs of male victims if we are to reduce the extent and toll of violence in the home.

Chapter 2

What Causes Violence Against Women?

Chapter Preface

While there is no single answer to the question of what causes violence against women, experts throughout the world agree that family violence is primarily a learned behavior. Children who grow up witnessing abuse, even if they are not the direct targets of the abuse, will internalize abusive behavior. They will learn that violence solves problems, and that men must be controlling, possessive, and abusive. Research over the past twenty years has shown that the most consistent risk factor for men being abusive to their own female partners is growing up in a home where they witnessed their father (or father-figure) abusing their mother (or mother-figure). When female children witness violence by their fathers against their mothers, they come to believe that it is normal for a woman to suffer abuse in a marriage. As Alan Rosenbaum, professor of psychology at Northern Illinois University and a faculty member of the university's Center for the Study of Family Violence and Sexual Assault explains, "Children of marital abusive couples mature into the next generation of abusive husbands and abused wives." Thus, domestic violence—learned as a child and practiced as an adult—is passed on from generation to generation.

Exposure to domestic violence can lead to numerous other difficulties for youngsters. Many of the developmental and behavioral problems a boy experiences as a result of the abuse he witnessed will ultimately contribute to his own risk of becoming an abuser. Experts agree that school-age boys from abusive homes often exhibit low self-esteem, have few friends, and have little confidence in the future. They feel guilty and ashamed about the abuse going on in their homes but feel powerless to do anything about it; this feeling of powerlessness then leads to anger. They act out in aggressive, antisocial ways that mark them as "troublemakers" from an early age. By the time young males who have witnessed domestic violence reach adolescence, they have higher rates of difficulties with all interpersonal relationships, especially with family members. Their lack of confidence in the future makes them fatalistic, and, as a result, they typically engage in an increased rate of risk-taking behavior such as substance abuse, truancy, and delinquency. In addition, they often engage in early sexual activity and are abusive in their dating relationships.

School-age girls from homes where their mothers are abused often have problems of a different nature that will lead to eventual victimization. According to psychologists, their lack of self-esteem is expressed in passive, often anxious behavior. They mistrust men from an early age, although it may seem that they try to gain their attention and affection. However, like boys who witness abuse, they may also feel guilty and humiliated by the violence in their homes and powerless to do anything to stop it. Their interpersonal relationships are difficult, and they also may engage in risk-taking behaviors like substance abuse and truancy. As they mature into adolescence, girls may try to avoid dating completely or fall into relationships that are physically or sexually abusive.

Researchers agree that not every boy or girl who grows up with domestic abuse exhibits these problems or goes on to become an abuser or a victim of abuse. However, the risk of becoming involved in family violence is so much greater among child witnesses of domestic violence that their experiences must be part of any exploration of the causes of violence against women. Authors in the following chapter debate several other causes as they try to understand this devastating problem.

Pornography Causes Violence Against Women

by Kristin Olson

About the author: *Kristin Olson was a third-year law student at the University of Oregon School of Law and associate editor of the* Oregon Law Review *when she wrote this viewpoint. She is now law clerk to the Hon. Robert Wolheim, judge at the Oregon Court of Appeals.*

Editor's Note: Originally written as a comment (a synopsis of a case including a detailed commentary) for the Oregon Law Review, *this viewpoint proposes model statutes that would offer civil and criminal remedies for those harmed by pornography. These suggested laws would hold the pornographer as well as the perpetrator of the violent acts liable for prosecution. The statutes were never submitted to the Oregon legislature.*

Violent depictions of women in submissive positions . . . exist throughout pornography and are replicated in sex crimes. In numerous instances, women and children have been forced to participate in acts that recreate pornographic images, which are primarily consumed by men. Consider the following examples: First, a woman named Jayne Stamen married a man who tortured her by acting out the violent pornographic images he consumed regularly. . . . Second, another woman married to a consumer of pornography recalled how her husband had rape and bondage magazines lying throughout the house and said, "'He used to tie me up and he tried those things on me.'" Third, "Steven Pennell, the infamous 'Corridor Killer,' kept a favorite triple-XXX [sic] video cued to a lurid sexual torture scene. He would replay it and replicate the scene on his victims until he had tortured them to death." Oregon victims of crimes such as these would have no recourse against the pornographers who produced and distributed the material which so clearly motivated the perpetrators. Currently, Oregon state law does not recognize injuries inflicted by pornography and does not provide redress to victims of pornography-motivated crimes. . . .

Kristin Olson, "Comprehensive Justice for Victims of Pornography—Driven Sex Crimes: Holding Pornographers Liable While Avoiding Constitutional Violation," *Oregon Law Review*, vol. 30, Fall 2001, p. 1. Copyright © 2001 by the *Oregon Law Review*. Reproduced by permission.

This Comment concludes that if pornographic material is replicated in a sex crime, pornographers should be found civilly or criminally liable and that this can be done without violation of either the Oregon Constitution or the United States Constitution.

Defining Pornography

The definition of pornography this Comment will follow is similar to that advanced by feminist Marianne Wesson, Professor of Law at the University of Colorado, with two modifications. Wesson defines pornography as material in any medium which depicts violence directed at, or pain inflicted on an unconsenting person or child and is aimed at real or apparent sexual gratification or arousal "in a context suggesting endorsement or approval of such behavior, and that is likely to promote or encourage similar behavior in those exposed to the depiction." The difficulty with Wesson's definition is that it excludes depictions of "consensual" acts, or of women gaining sexual pleasure from being tortured. . . .

Besides including sexually violent acts committed upon an apparently willing participant, this Comment will focus only on harm inflicted due to obscene material. Although the Oregon Constitution protects obscenity, the United States Constitution does not. . . . This Comment will explain why the definition of pornography it follows does not violate either the Oregon Constitution or the United States Constitution, despite the fact that the Oregon Constitution protects obscenity.

Miller v. California defined obscenity using five elements: (1) the reader is the average person; (2) the work must be taken as a whole; (3) it must appeal to the purient interest; (4) it must depict or describe sexually offensive conduct specifically forbidden by law to depict; and, finally (5) it must be without redeeming value. *Miller* further held that obscenity is not constitutionally protected under the United States Constitution and, therefore, that it is a form of speech subject to regulation.

> *"Pornography is dangerous because ninety-seven percent of pornographic rape stories 'end with the woman changing her mind . . . and being represented as enjoying rape.'"*

While it is necessary to limit the definition of pornography to obscene material, putting the definition of pornography in context by requiring the pornographer to endorse or approve of the material is also necessary because it ensures that the statute is not overly broad. It excludes suits against murder-mystery writers, rape education books, and televison documentaries which include reenactments. Therefore, the definition of pornography this Comment follows includes obscene material in any medium which depicts or describes violence directed at, or pain inflicted on, a person, and when such material is intended to cause real or apparent sexual gratification or arousal in a context where a reasonable person would conclude that the author is endorsing or approving such material.

Holding Pornographers Accountable

Even pornography as it is defined in this Comment is vehemently protected by many free speech advocates. Efforts to combat the violent pornography that contributes to crimes against women and children have been going on for years. They are consistently met with opposition and are hotly debated. Usually the arguments come down to a libertarian-style theory of free speech versus the radical feminist view that violent pornography causes specific harms to women. Resistance to anti-pornography efforts stems from liberal feminists (liberal in the sense that they adhere to modern liberal political thought), other libertarian-minded free speech theorists, and efforts by the pornography industry to protect itself.

Opponents of pornographer liability worry that holding the pornographer responsible may protect the perpetrator and provide him with a "psychological escape" from accountability for his actions. The most notorious example of this is Ted Bundy, the serial murderer who blamed his assaults, rapes, and murders on his consumption of pornography. However, even Bundy acknowledged that he was personally responsible for his crimes and made it clear that he was, in no way, blaming pornography for his actions. Pornographer liability would not shield the perpetrator. Serial murderers like Ted Bundy will not avoid criminal liability if the victims themselves, or their representatives, have the ability [to] sue the pornographers that influenced the perpetrator's action. . . . Further, research has revealed that pornographer liability would actually succeed in making pornographic images seem illicit and abnormal. Diana Scully studied men who committed sex crimes and were influenced by pornography, reporting that the reason criminals commit these acts is that the pornography is assuasive, telling them what they are doing is normal and acceptable and that their victims will enjoy the assault. The notion that once pornography is made actionable it becomes less normal to fantasize about and act upon makes sense, as that is what tort law is all about: using civil litigation to socially regulate people and things that are harmful to society. When pornography is no longer widespread in society because distributors and manufacturers cannot afford to put it in the marketplace, it becomes less available to the perpetrator, and it tells the perpetrator that the images he is viewing are illicit and wrong.

Another argument against the regulation of pornographic material . . . and a favorite of the liberal feminists, is that it is a manifestation of sexual Victorianism, or prudishness, and that pornography provides women an opportunity for sexual expression. However, the type of pornography this Comment discusses is in no way sexually liberating, as it causes harm to women. Pornography as it is defined in this Comment has nothing to do with benevolent eroticism. The material discussed in this Comment is sexual material that demonstrably causes injury. If the price society has to pay to suppress injury means that people are not able to express their eroticism, that is a price society should be willing to pay.

The most popular argument against the regulation of pornography is that it restricts free speech rights. Civil liberties in the tradition of liberalism are rights guaranteed to individuals, limited only to the extent that they interfere with the liberties of others. Traditional liberals, especially libertarians, tend to argue against efforts to regulate or restrict speech as if the Amendments in the Constitution (our civil liberties articulated) are absolute. Clearly, however, civil liberties are limited to the extent that they interfere with other's rights. The United States Supreme Court, for instance, has declared obscenity and child pornography unprotected forms of speech. Further, the Oregon Supreme Court ruled that although the state may not ban harmless speech per se, it can ban or punish speech when it causes harm.

"For some men it is just pornography—and nothing else—which creates the predisposition to commit sexual abuse."

This Comment will focus primarily on the free speech argument and show that both a criminal and a civil law can provide recourse to victims injured by violent pornography while withstanding constitutional scrutiny under Oregon's free speech clause, Article I, section 8, and under the First Amendment of the United States Constitution. Unfortunately, neither Oregon tort law nor criminal law has precedents or statutes providing recourse for pornography victims such as Jayne Stamen. To most efficiently withstand scrutiny under both Article I, section 8 and the First Amendment, this Comment will not focus on victims of pornography per se, such as women as a class of people who are generally injured and degraded by pornography (as discussed by feminist theorists Catharine MacKinnon and Andrea Dworkin), but rather victims of pornography who can demonstrate that a particular piece of material so closely resembled their sexual violation that it was a substantial factor in the commission of the offense. This Comment assumes that no expression is per se harmful, as that is the precept upon which Oregon constitutional analysis is founded. But, when harm does occur and a crime is committed, both criminal and civil strategies should be employed to hold pornographers accountable for pornography-driven crimes. . . .

Pornography Normalizes Violent Sexual Fantasies

Rice v Paladin Enterprises is illustrative of proving causation where the material that motivated the crime is followed so exactly that it is considered incitement and more than mere advocacy. In *Rice*, Paladin Enterprises published *Hit Man*, a how-to-commit-murder manual for independent contractors. *Hit Man* encouraged people to be independent contractors and showed them how to commit murder for hire. The book had an effect upon the behavior of a hit man hired by an estranged husband to murder his wife and handicapped son. The murderer followed the content of *Hit Man* so closely that the court held that the First Amendment did not preclude a cause of action against the manual's publisher. Under *Rice*, mere instruction and abstract advocacy is protected. Speech, therefore, is presumptively not protected. In the same way, pornography can tell a sex crime perpetrator that his violent sexual fantasies and desires are normal and show him how to act out his fantasies and desires on both willing and unwilling women.

To prove general causation, a plaintiff's attorney could introduce evidence showing that pornography substantially contributed to the plaintiff's injury by normalizing violent sex—much in the same way *Hit Man* normalized murder for hire. For example, sex offenders have discussed the way pornography normalized their activities and helped them overcome any reservations they might have had about committing sex crimes. Ray Wyre's work with offenders has documented that child abusers initially use child pornography "to legitimize their behaviour to themselves. . . . It is precisely because they know that what they are doing, or wanting to do, is wrong that they 'need' to use child pornography to rationalize it. It enables them to construct a different version of reality. . . ." Wyre explains that pornography is dangerous because ninety-seven percent of pornographic rape stories "end with the woman changing her mind . . . and being represented as enjoying rape. Sex offenders use this kind of pornography to justify and legitimate what they do. It provides them with an excuse and a reason for what they do."

Some experts believe pornography conditions one to adopt perpetrator-like behavior because of its normalization tendencies and because the orgasm positively reinforces the viewer's sexually violent experience. Wyre, who has worked with sex offenders since the mid-1970s, believes "for some men it is just pornography—and nothing else—which creates the predisposition to commit sexual abuse. I have little doubt that there are men who in reading pornography, and particularly child pornography, will acquire ideas that they will put into practice. Their ideas are initiated by pornography." Wyre sees a direct causal connection between pornography and some sex offenders and views the orgasm as part of the reinforcing behaviour. "Pornography makes the behaviour more acceptable and right because it reinforces the nice experience of sexual arousal and orgasm to something that is wrong. Pornography predisposes some men to act out their behaviour."

Viewers of Pornography Associate Sexuality with Violence

The orgasm as a positive reinforcer, as a contribution to the association of pleasure with pornographic violence, is known as "'masturbatory conditioning.'" Even for men who do not find rape sexually exciting, "masturbation subsequent to the movie reinforces the association.". . .

The most reliable evidence examining the effects of pornography is found in the work of [Edward I.] Donnerstein, [Daniel] Linz, and [Steven] Penrod. Donnerstein's work is compelling because he testified before the 1986 Attorney General's Commission on Pornography and his work was cited by the Commission when it argued for increased prosecution of pornographers. . . . This Comment does not attempt to comprehensively explain the intricacies involved in pornography studies, however, a summary of Donnerstein, Linz and Penrod's work is found in this quotation:

> Violent pornography influences attitudes and behaviors. . . . Viewers come to cognitively associate sexuality with violence, to endorse the idea that women want to be raped, and to trivialize the injuries suffered by a rape victim. As a result of the attitudinal changes, men may be more willing to abuse women physically (indeed, the laboratory aggression measures suggest such an outcome).

Critics note that one of the difficulties with studies on pornography is that laboratory conditions do not adequately replicate reality. However, this is because it is not practical to allow someone exposed to violent pornography to carry out violent behavior on a subject. Criticism aside, studies and expert opinions regarding the causal connection between pornography and violence are helpful for attorneys. Combined with a crime scene that strikingly resembles pornography found in the possession of the perpetrator, it will be easier for attorneys to argue that pornography is an invitation to commit a sex offense, rather than mere facilitation. . . .

Just as one who aids and abets a criminal in the commission of a crime or who encourages or incites a criminal to commit such a crime should be held criminally liable, so should a pornographer be held liable for his role in creating an environment where women are depicted enjoying rape, tied spread-eagled to the roof of a Jeep, and where, as a result, women are raped and then killed (as in "snuff films"). . . .

Pornography Increases Acceptance of Violence Against Women

The proposed legislation . . . target[s] pornography which includes sexual violence inflicted upon a person who appears to be a consenting participant. Radical feminist Andrea Dworkin notes that one of the most dangerous forms of pornography depicts brutalized women appearing to enjoy, or consent to, the torture. "The most enduring sexual truth in pornography . . . is that sexual violence is desired by the normal female, needed by her, suggested or demanded by her." It is quite possible that the reason some "men do not believe that rape or battery are violations of female will . . . [is] because . . . [they] have consumed pornography. . . ." Social science and psychological evidence has found that aggressive behaviors and other adverse consequences result "from exposure to coercive and/or violent sexually explicit material—especially portrayals in which women are shown tolerating, if not enjoying, abusive treatment as in the rape-myth scenario." Further, "studies have shown that viewing portrayals of sexual violence as having positive consequences increases male subjects' acceptance of violence against women.". . .

Understanding why the sexualization of male dominance is so dangerous to women requires recognizing that sexism exists. And sexism does exist. There is a wage gap, a mere 7.8% of United States women avoid being sexually harassed or assaulted in their lifetimes and a male-defined beauty myth has caused eating disorders that strike up to one-tenth of all young American women. Recognizing these facts makes it easier to understand why the objectification of women is so pervasive and why the sexualization of male dominance makes the objectification and dehumanization of women in pornographic material seem normal and acceptable, maintaining a sexist society.

While male dominance is especially dangerous due to the reality of sexism, (and this Comment certainly views pornography from a feminist perspective) it is also important to note that the laws advocated in this Comment are gender-neutral. Domination should be condemned in all its forms, and sadomasochistic depictions of women in the dominating position which motivate sex crimes should be actionable as well. Thus, sadomasochistic depictions of violence and torture (whether inflicted by males or females) that are instrumental in the commission of sex crimes should be included within the definition of pornography.

> *"The sexualization of male dominance makes the objectification and dehumanization of women in pornographic material seem normal and acceptable."*

Targeting pornography that includes violence inflicted upon a consenting participant does not infringe on protected speech. Regardless of whether the pornography involves two consenting participants, the statutes are limited to the extent that the defendant must know or have reason to know that the material would cause a perpetrator to commit a sex offense, and a reasonable person viewing the material must conclude that the author is endorsing or approving of the material (the violence).

Pornography vs. Free Speech

Therefore, holding pornographers liable for their role in sex crimes perpetrated primarily against women and children is consistent with efforts of the Oregon Constitution to prevent infringement upon free speech. Feminist arguments against pornography like those presented here (e.g., the argument that pornography contributes to sex crimes against women and children and therefore should be regulated accordingly) are sometimes viewed as contrary to efforts to protect the freedom of speech and many anti-censorship task-forces have dedicated themselves to opposing feminists who support the regulation of pornography. However, as libertarian and protective of free speech as the Oregon Constitution is, this Comment proves that feminist efforts to regulate pornography can exist while free speech remains unharmed. . . .

While recognizing that women and children are the prime targets of subordination in pornography, this Comment advocates laws and legal arguments that focus on all Oregon victims of crimes who currently have no recourse against the pornographers who produced and distributed the material which so clearly motivated their perpetrators.

Pornography Does Not Cause Violence Against Women

by the American Civil Liberties Union

About the author: *The American Civil Liberties Union (ACLU) is a national organization that works to safeguard Americans' civil rights.*

Sexually explicit material, in literature, art, film, photography and music, has always been controversial in the United States, from James Joyce's *Ulysses*—which was banned in the 1930s—to rap music performed by 2 Live Crew, a target of prosecution in the 1990s. Traditionally, political conservatives and religious fundamentalists have been the primary advocates of tight legal restrictions on sexual expression, based on their view that such expression undermines public morality. In the late 1970s, however, those traditional voices were joined by a small but extremely vocal segment of the feminist movement. These women, who do not by any means speak for all feminists, charge that "pornography" is a major cause of discrimination and violence against women and should, therefore, be suppressed.

Although unsupported by any reliable evidence, this theory has been especially influential on college and law school campuses, leading to several incidents in which speech and works of art—including works by women artists—have been labeled "pornographic" and censored. Even classics like Francisco de Goya's painting, *The Nude Maja*, have been targeted.

The American Civil Liberties Union (ACLU) has fought censorship from the time of its founding in 1920. In our early days, we defended sex educator/activists Margaret Sanger and Mary Ware Dennett against criminal obscenity charges. Today, we continue to defend the free speech rights of all expression, including sexual expression. We believe that the suppression of "pornography" is not only damaging to the First Amendment, but also impedes the struggle for women's rights.

Here are some answers to questions often asked by the public about the ACLU's opposition to the suppression of pornography.

Is Pornography Protected by the First Amendment?

Yes. The First Amendment absolutely forbids the suppression of ideas or images based on their content alone. Moreover, a basic tenet of U.S. Supreme Court jurisprudence is that laws must be "viewpoint" neutral. And even though the Court has carved out a narrow exception to the First Amendment for a category of sexually explicit material deemed "legally obscene," the term "pornography" has no legal significance at all.

The dictionary defines pornography simply as writing or visual images that are "intended to arouse sexual desire." Pro-censorship feminists have greatly expanded the common meaning of pornography, redefining it as "the sexually explicit subordination of women through pictures and/or words." They then define "subordination" as the depiction of women "in postures or positions of sexual submission, servility, or display." These extraordinarily subjective interpretations would apply to everything from religious imagery to news accounts of mass rape in Bosnia. Because the Supreme Court has consistently ruled that the government may not make content-based rules limiting free speech, material that depicts "the subordination of women" enjoys the same First Amendment protection afforded material that depicts women in other ways. Were that not so, the government could suppress any ideas it didn't like, rendering the First Amendment meaningless.

> *"The suppression of 'pornography' is not only damaging to the First Amendment, but also impedes the struggle for women's rights."*

Is Pornography a Form of Discrimination Against Women?

Sexually explicit words and images aimed at arousing sexual desire—pornography—constitute a form of expression. Pro-censorship feminists seek legal recognition of their counter-claim that such images are a form of sex discrimination because they reinforce stereotypes of women as inferior. The architects of the latter concept are law professor Catharine MacKinnon and writer Andrea Dworkin, who drafted a model law that would permit any woman claiming to have been harmed by pornography to bring a civil lawsuit for monetary damages, and to halt the production, distribution and sale of pornographic works.

The model law has been considered in numerous locales around the country, but when it was adopted by the Indianapolis City Council in 1984 it collapsed under a legal challenge brought by a coalition of booksellers and publishers and supported by the ACLU as a friend-of-the-court. Leaving no doubt that the law targeted expression, federal Judge Sara Barker wrote: "To deny free speech in order to engineer social change in the name of accomplishing a greater good for one sector of our society erodes the freedoms of all and . . . threatens tyranny and injustice for those subjected to the rule of such laws."

The ACLU's fears about the censorious effects of the MacKinnon/ Dworkin law have been borne out in Canada, where the Canadian Supreme Court incorporated that law's definition of pornography into a 1992 obscenity ruling. Since then, more than half of all feminist bookstores in Canada have had materials confiscated or the sales of some materials suspended by the government. The most susceptible to repression have been stores that specialize in lesbian and gay writings.

> *"'Demonstrated empirical links between pornography and sex crimes in general are weak or absent.'"*

Wouldn't Ridding Society of Pornography Reduce Sexism and Violence Against Women?

Although pro-censorship feminists base their efforts on the assumption that pornography causes violence against women, such a causal relationship has never been established. The National Research Council's Panel on Understanding and Preventing Violence concluded, in a 1993 survey of laboratory studies, that "demonstrated empirical links between pornography and sex crimes in general are weak or absent."

Correlational studies are similarly inconclusive, revealing no consistent correlations between the availability of pornography in various communities or countries and sexual offense rates. If anything, studies suggest that a greater availability of pornography seems to correlate with higher indices of sexual equality. Women in Sweden, with its highly permissive attitudes toward sexual expression, are much safer and have more civil rights than women in Singapore, where restrictions on pornography are very tight.

Doesn't Pornography Exploit the Women Who Participate in Its Production?

The ACLU supports the aggressive enforcement of already existing civil and criminal laws to protect women from sexual violence and coercion in the process of making sexually oriented material. At the same time, we oppose the notion, advanced by anti-pornography feminists, that women can never make free, voluntary choices to participate in the production of pornography, and that they are always coerced, whether they realize it or not. This infantilization of women denies them the freedom of choice to engage in otherwise legal activities.

There are cases of women who say they were coerced into working in the pornography industry, the most well known being "Linda Lovelace," who starred in the movie *Deep Throat*. But the majority of women who pose for sexually explicit material or act in pornographic films do so voluntarily. Indeed, these women resent attempts to outlaw their chosen occupation. As one actress exclaimed, "For them to tell me I can't make films about naked men and women making love is a grotesque violation of my civil rights."

Why Does the ACLU Say That Anti-Pornography Laws Harm Women's Struggle for Full Legal Equality?

A core idea of the anti-pornography movement is the proposition that sex per se degrades women (although not men). Even consensual, nonviolent sex, according to MacKinnon and Dworkin, is an evil from which women—like children—must be protected. Such thinking is a throwback to the archaic stereotypes of the 19th century that formed the basis for enacting laws to "protect" women from vulgar language (and from practicing law or sitting on juries lest they be subjected to such language). Paternalistic legislation such as that advocated by MacKinnon and Dworkin has always functioned to prevent women from achieving full legal equality.

Furthermore, history teaches that censorship is a dangerous weapon in the hands of government. Inevitably, it is used against those who want to change society, be they feminists, civil rights demonstrators or gay liberationists. Obscenity laws, especially, have been used to suppress information and art dealing with female sexuality and reproduction. Thus, the growing influence of anti-pornography feminism threatens to undermine long-established principles of free speech.

Finally, the focus on sexual imagery and symbols diverts attention from the real causes of discrimination and violence against women, as well as from problems such as unequal pay, lack of affordable childcare and sexual harassment in the workplace.

Men Are Biologically Inclined to Rape

by Randy Thornhill and Craig T. Palmer

About the authors: *Randy Thornhill is a University of New Mexico Regents professor of biology. Craig T. Palmer is an anthropologist at the University of Colorado at Colorado Springs. They are coauthors of* A Natural History of Rape: Biological Bases of Sexual Coercion.

For the last quarter of a century, attempts to prevent rape have been guided by the social-science explanation of rape.

This explanation holds that the motivation to rape has little, if anything, to do with sexual desire. Instead, it holds that rape is an attempt by men to dominate and control women. It also contends that rape only occurs when males are taught by their culture, directly or indirectly, to rape. In our new book, *A Natural History of Rape* (MIT Press), we challenge this established social-science explanation of rape.

We argue that although a given rapist may have numerous motivations for committing a rape, social scientists have failed to prove that sex is not one of these.

Rape Occurs in All Cultures

Although we agree that culture plays a major role in the cause of rape, we challenge the notion that rape only occurs when males are taught by their cultures to rape. Rape not only appears to occur in all known cultures, but in a wide variety of other species where there is certainly no cultural encouragement of such behavior.

We also argue that the best way to obtain a better understanding of the role of culture in the cause of human rape is to approach the subject from the only generally accepted scientific explanation of the behavior of living things: Darwinian evolution by natural selection.

Why have we chosen to make such an argument, knowing full well the criti cisms that challenging such a widely held position would cause to be rained down upon us?

The answer is that inaccurate knowledge about the causes of behavior hinder attempts to change behavior, and we want very badly to eradicate rape from human existence. Given the great amount of media attention our book, *A Natural History of Rape*, has already received, we thought the best way to summarize the book would be to contrast what you may have heard in the media with what the book actually says.

You have probably heard that our book says that rape is good because it is a part of the natural, biological world. If so, you might be surprised to find the following statement at the book's outset: "There is no connection here between what is biological or naturally selected and what is morally right or wrong. To assume a connection is to commit what is called the naturalistic fallacy."

Natural Does Not Mean Morally Right

This fallacy erroneously sees the facts of how nature is organized as moral truths. This fallacy still remains too common today, despite having been discarded in intellectual circles. Modern thinkers emphasize that nature is as nature is, period; right and wrong in the moral sense derive from humans pursuing their interests, not from the facts of nature.

You may have also heard that the book excuses rapists for their hideous acts. You will recognize this as another version of the naturalistic fallacy. What we really say is: "Contrary to the common view that an evolutionary explanation for human behavior removes individuals' responsibility for their actions, . . . knowledge of the self as having evolved by Darwinian selection provides an individual with tremendous potential for free will.

> *"Rape not only appears to occur in all known cultures, but in a wide variety of . . . species where there is . . . no cultural encouragement of such behavior."*

Moreover, refusal to refrain from damaging behavior in the face of scientific understanding could be seen as a ground for holding irresponsible individuals more culpable, not less so."

This is why, far from claiming that rapists should not be punished, the reader of our book will find that "we have stressed the value of punishment for changing human behavior."

Evolution allows the understanding of why certain experiences are punishments and others rewards. We don't suggest particular types of punishment for rape. We leave up to people the hard decision of how much cost to impose for this crime.

Knowledge from evolutionary biology, then, cannot tell us that rape is morally good or bad. People decide that distinction and have deemed it horrific. Our book is about how evolutionary knowledge may be useful for achieving the desirable social goal of reducing rape.

Another frequent depiction of our book claims that we say rape is inevitable because it is determined by genes. We are actually in full agreement with the eminent evolutionary biologist John Maynard Smith's observation that genetic determinism is "an incorrect idea."

We further point out that "most evolutionary works on humans (including ours) include an extended discussion of the inseparable and equally important influences of genes and environment. . . ."

Environmental Factors Are Important

This is why we can state, "The evolutionary approach holds that no behavior is inevitable," and that rape can best be prevented by addressing the "environmental factors" that lead to rape.

These environmental factors may include certain learning experiences during boys' upbringing, such as the conditions of poverty, limited enduring relationships and father absence.

The evolutionary approach focuses attention on specific experiences that would have been correlated with limited social and economic resources when boys achieved adulthood in human evolutionary history.

These limitations would have, in the deep-time history of the human past, reduced or eliminated access to consensual female sex partners, because recent research has shown that our female evolutionary ancestors preferred mates with status and resources.

This preference is indicated by the vast evidence from evolutionary psychology that women today have a psychological adaptation that functions to guide their romantic interests toward such men. Rape bypasses this preference and thereby circumvents a fundamental aspect of female reproductive strategy.

The reader may also be surprised to find that, contrary to media reports, we do not argue that rapists are driven by an urge to reproduce.

As is explained in detail in Chapter 1, this assertion confuses the motivations that form the immediate (what evolutionists call proximate) causes of a behavior with the evolutionary (what evolutionists call ultimate) effects of a behavior during countless past generations of evolutionary history.

Rapists may be motivated by many different immediate desires, but a desire for reproduction is probably one of them in only the rarest of instances. Sexual stimulation is a proximate cause of raping and is the common denominator across rapes of all kinds.

Sexual Motivation Depends on Selection Pressures

Men's sexual motivation is an ultimate product of selection pressures in human evolutionary history. In addition to the false claim that we excuse rapists, you have probably heard that we blame victims. This is also not true.

Instead, we emphasize that "educational programs aimed at reducing the vulnerability of women to sexual coercion are dependent on the acquisition of information concerning risk factors."

We also make a claim (which has been seen by some people as both an insane idea and a mortal sin, but by most others as too obvious to be worth debate) that a person's appearance and behavior might have some influence on these risk factors.

> *"Sexual stimulation is a proximate cause of raping and is the common denominator across rapes of all kinds."*

We stress in the book, however, that it is completely "unjustified" to argue that "a victim's dress and behavior should affect the degree of punishment a rapist receives."

Despite full awareness of the misguided criticisms that would rain down upon us, we chose to address this issue because, "The failure to distinguish between statements about causes and statements about responsibility has the consequence of suppressing knowledge about how to avoid dangerous situations."

It has also been claimed that our book is not a study, but only a theory, with only evidence from insects to support it.

The reader who has heard such a depiction may think they have bought the wrong book when they encounter the plethora of studies that make up the nearly 600 references in the bibliography.

Those particularly interested in insects will also be disappointed to find how relatively few of them concern that subject. We do discuss research on insects called scorpion flies that has identified a clamp on the top of the male's abdomen as an adaptation specifically for rape.

This illustrates what an adaptation for rape is, but it does not follow that because scorpion fly males, and males of other non-human species, have adaptation for rape, that, therefore, men do, too. This is an erroneous extrapolation that modern biologists don't engage in.

Further Research Is Needed

One hypothesis about how evolution and human rape are related is that men have rape-specific adaptation, but located in the brain.

We outline in the book how further research could test for the existence of six potential rape psychological adaptations.

Readers who have also heard that we assume every aspect of human behavior, including rape, is an adaptation directly favored by Darwinian selection will be surprised also to find an extended discussion in the book of the alternative hypothesis that rape itself is not an adaptation, but instead a by-product of other adaptations, such as men's psychological adaptation that motivates their pursuit of partner variety without commitment.

Our proposal that all men are potential rapists has been interpreted by the media as meaning that all men will rape. Actually, we emphasize that "many men don't rape and are not sexually aroused by laboratory depictions of rape.

This suggests that there are cues in the developmental environments of many men that prohibit raping behavior."

That all men are potential rapists is only bad news from science if people continue to ignore the utility of evolutionary biology for understanding rape's immediate causes, as it is only the full knowledge of these causes that could allow their elimination.

Although the media's distortion of our book has been extreme, it is understandable given the extreme emotions the horrible act of rape produces in all people.

This is why we don't begrudge our critics.

We only hope that as the initial emotions that have so colored their responses subside, they will take the effort to try and read our book as it is, not as they have feared it was.

After all, we all share the same goal of trying to end the immense pain caused by rape.

Claims That Men Are Biologically Inclined to Rape Are Faulty

by Laura Flanders

About the author: *Laura Flanders is a columnist for* In These Times, *a national biweekly magazine of news and opinion.*

All men are natural-born rapists. This is not the sort of allegation that usually gets serious treatment in the mainstream media. But Randy Thornhill and Craig T. Palmer have been journalistically feted from coast to coast for making just that charge. The attention has been enough to more than double the print-run of their book, *A Natural History of Rape*, three months before it will be released by MIT. Not bad for a couple of uncharismatic guys with a meandering theory based on bug research. The key to their success: They use their theory to criticize not rapists, but feminists.

Professors of evolutionary biology at the University of New Mexico and evolutionary anthropology at the University of Colorado, respectively, Thornhill and Palmer argue that rape has given rapists a reproductive edge in the contest for genetic selection. Rape may be hard-wired into the species. At the very least, it is a product of the male breeding drive.

While the writers say rape is wrong and that they are out to stop it, they contend we need to face facts. For a quarter of a century, they say, people informed by Susan Brownmiller's *Against Our Will* have viewed rape as "unnatural behavior having nothing to do with sex." That hasn't worked. But where feminists have failed, Darwin can come to the rescue.

Rape Impulse Is a Birthright

Heaven forbid. The techniques these guys propose to stop rape sound like suggestive counseling. Just in case a young man's thoughts have not naturally drifted to sexual violence, Thornhill and Palmer advise lecturing boys on the "impulses" that are their birthright. And they caution young women that because evolution has favored men who are quickly aroused, "the way they dress can put them at risk."

But in the excerpt that appears in the January-February edition of *The Sciences*, Thornhill and Palmer provide no data to back up the claim that the skimpily dressed are raped more often than the frumpy. Instead, much is made of a grabbing appendage on scorpionflies (insects Thornhill has studied in depth) that seems to suggest that the natural world designs

> *"I'm glad we're asking why men rape, but 'because it's natural' is no sort of answer."*

for better raping. The authors point to data that they say show that most rape is not "gratuitously" violent, that most raped women are of child-bearing age, and that the most "distressed" rape victims are fertile and married. But the studies they cite are 20 years old—done before a movement helped survivors to talk openly. Clearly their sources (absent in the abstract) deserve a closer look.

Author Is Accused of Sloppy Science

"It's advocacy and the science is sloppy," says Jerry Coyne, an evolutionary biologist at the University of Chicago. This is not the first time Thornhill has been accused of sloppy science. A few years back, *Time* dedicated its cover to a Thornhill "report" linking symmetrical features to genetic health and better sex. That too, was based on dubious data. But Coyne says half the reporters he has spoken to seem to have only the slightest idea of Thornhill and Palmer's thesis. "They've mostly read other media accounts," he says.

Indeed, the media have swept the two from the dry world of science journalism to the country's most popular talk shows. *Dateline* and *Today* interviewers have swallowed their science whole. The way Melinda Penkava introduced Thornhill on NPR's *Talk of the Nation* was typical: "Now evolutionary science enters the picture." "Scientist" Thornhill was put up against "feminist" Brownmiller.

And that's the point. There is no original research in *Why Men Rape*, and their theory ignores a multitude of contradictions. Stumped by homosexual rape, the rape of the old and the young, and by the impotence of many rapists, Thornhill and Palmer simply ignore assaults that make no reproductive sense. But even they know better. In an essay he co-authored in 1983, Thornhill was honest enough to point to a contemporary estimate that only "about 50 percent of rapes include ejaculation." He ignores that here.

The Book Attacks Social Science

What Thornhill and Palmer are really about is advancing the cause of biology against sociology. "This is the *Bell Curve* of anti-feminism," says Jackson Katz, creator of a new film from the Media Education Foundation, *Tough Guise: Vio-*

lence, Media and the Crisis of Masculinity. "It discourages tackling the economic, social and political factors that support male violence."

As Coyne—a biologist himself—puts it, "They're on a mission to swallow up social studies." That's why the first chapter of their book is dedicated not to rape, but to an attack on social scientists, who, they say, mistakenly overemphasize social learning. "In reality, every aspect of every living thing is by definition biological," they write.

Well, sure. We live and breathe with quirky equipment developed over generations. But thinking and choosing and wanting and hating are hard things to explain in a laboratory.

Thornhill and Palmer aren't the first to consider that maybe all men are potential rapists. Rape survivors often grapple with that thought. It occurred to Karen Pomer, who was raped in 1995 by a man who went on to rape an 83-year-old woman. But years of work on sexual violence led her to a different conclusion: "I don't think people do this if something didn't happen to them," she says. "I'm glad we're asking why men rape, but 'because it's natural' is no sort of answer."

Promoting Marriage to Reduce Poverty Will Increase Violence Against Women

by the Family Violence Prevention Fund

About the author: *The Family Violence Prevention Fund is an international organization that works to prevent violence within the home and in the community through public education and advocacy.*

Battered women's advocates are speaking out against Bush Administration proposals that could potentially endanger victims of domestic violence who receive public assistance.

At a time of broad and deep budget cuts, President George W. Bush proposes earmarking several million dollars in federal welfare funds for states and local communities to develop programs that encourage poor couples to marry and stay married. Some Administration officials have said that they do not want to force women into abusive relationships or make it more difficult for them to leave abusive relationships, but battered women's advocates think that is exactly what may happen.

Congress is putting reauthorization of the 1996 welfare reform law on a fast track, aiming to complete work by Memorial Day.[1] Although some experts doubt that Congress will meet that ambitious timeline, marriage promotion programs are becoming the focus of an intense debate.

In this highly charged atmosphere, the ultra-conservative Heritage Foundation last week released a new backgrounder, *Marriage: The Safest Place for Women and Children.* It uses select data from the U.S. Department of Justice's National Crime Victimization Survey (NCVS) and concludes, "the institution that most

---

1. In May 2000 Congress reauthorized the welfare program, including $300 million for marriage promotion.

strongly protects mothers and children from domestic abuse and violent crime is marriage."

"This report is misleading and dangerous," said Family Violence Prevention Fund President Esta Soler. "Responsible lawmakers will reject its conclusions."

While the Heritage Foundation paper claims to be a fresh analysis, it reaches conclusions about marriage's capacity for reducing domestic violence that are not fully supported by the NCVS. One reason is that the NCVS presents the annual rates of domestic violence for women in four categories: married, divorced, separated and never married. But *Marriage* uses NCVS statistics to divide women into only two categories: "never married" and "ever married," with the latter combining married, divorced and separated women. Based on this division, the report finds that the "never married" women have higher annual rates of domestic violence than the "ever married" women.

However, the U.S. Department of Justice's Bureau of Justice Statistics 2001 report *Intimate Partner Violence and Age of Victim, 1993–99* looks at the same data and reaches different conclusions. *Intimate Partner Violence* finds that, while the annual rate of domestic violence for never married women was higher than that of married women, it was lower than that of divorced or separated women. In fact, separated women experienced "significantly higher" annual rates of domestic violence than women in the other categories. *Intimate Partner Violence* does find that married women "reported experiencing intimate partner violence at rates lower than women in other marital categories," but cautions against interpreting any link between marriage and domestic violence.

"Caution is warranted in interpreting intimate partner violence and marital status in the NCVS because marital status may be related to a respondent's willingness or ability to disclose violence by an intimate partner," says *Intimate Partner Violence* in a section titled, "Special Considerations When Examining Marital Status and Intimate Partner Violence." The section continues, "a married woman may not view, may not wish to view, or may be unable to report the behavior of her partner as violent or criminal. That same woman, if separated or divorced, may view or may be able to report the same behavior as violent."

Marriage Promotion Has Conservative Support

The Heritage Foundation backgrounder supports conservative proposals for welfare policies that encourage marriage and discourage divorce, co-habitation and out-of-wedlock children.

Republican leaders in Congress are also expressing support for these proposals. In a guest editorial in [the] *New York Times*, Speaker of the House Dennis Hastert (R-IL) supports a plan that allocates $500 million to pay for "premarital marriage education divorce-reduction" programs. "In its current form, the welfare system discriminates against marriage," Hastert said in the editorial. "The federal government can further encourage marriage by financing . . . programs so that couples have support in building healthy marriages."

Battered women's advocates have joined with women's rights, anti-poverty and other advocates in supporting programs that support and strengthen all families, regardless of their make-up. But advocates strongly oppose using federal money to promote marriage and provide financial incentives for welfare recipients to marry or stay married.

> *"Welfare policies that encourage marriage through financial incentives are coercive and dangerous."*

"Welfare policies that encourage marriage through financial incentives are coercive and dangerous," said Soler. "They can even be deadly for battered women who may be forced to remain in abusive situations because they simply cannot afford to leave. Victims of domestic violence who rely on public assistance should not have to choose between their own safety and the crucial financial benefits they need to support themselves and their families."

Programs designed to promote marriage among welfare recipients are not new. The Welfare Reform Act of 1996 created Temporary Assistance for Needy Families (TANF) block grants that gave states federal money to fund programs designed to reduce welfare recipients' dependence on public assistance, including programs designed to promote marriage and discourage divorce. But since 1996, there has been no significant reduction in the number of single parent households in the United States.

[In June 2001], the U.S. House of Representatives Committee on Ways and Means, Subcommittee on Human Resources held hearings that focused on how states can use welfare funds to promote marriage. Some state legislatures have enacted or are considering legislation to fund policies that encourage or reward marriage. In West Virginia, for example, welfare parents who are married receive a $100 "marriage bonus" each month. Other states have enacted covenant marriage legislation—laws that strengthen the marriage contract and make it more difficult for couples to get divorced.

Bush, Hastert and their allies argue that programs that support "healthy marriages" and provide welfare recipients with financial incentives to get married and stay married will help reduce poverty, limit dependence on public assistance and foster self-sufficiency. The Heritage Foundation backgrounder also argues that British children in "intact families" are less likely to suffer from serious child abuse than British children in other types of families.

"Encouraging marriage will not keep women off welfare and it will not protect women and children on public assistance from abuse," Soler added. "There is no real evidence that promoting marriage can improve the well-being of women and their children. Government's role is not to force marriage. Lawmakers must recognize that battered women in poverty need programs that will help them to gain economic independence, not coerce them into remaining in life threatening situations."

Promoting Marriage to Reduce Poverty Will Decrease Violence Against Women

by Patrick F. Fagan and Kirk A. Johnson

About the authors: *Patrick F. Fagan is a William H.G. FitzGerald research fellow in family and cultural issues and Kirk A. Johnson is a senior policy analyst in the Center for Data Analysis at the Heritage Foundation.*

The institution that most strongly protects mothers and children from domestic abuse and violent crime is marriage. Analysis of the 1999 findings of the National Crime Victimization Survey (NCVS), which the U.S. Department of Justice (DOJ) has conducted since 1973, demonstrates that mothers who are or ever have been married are far less likely to suffer from violent crime than are mothers who never marry.

Specifically, data from the NCVS survey show that:

• *Marriage dramatically reduces the risk that mothers will suffer from domestic abuse.* In fact, the incidence of spousal, boyfriend, or domestic partner abuse is twice as high among mothers who have never been married as it is among mothers who have ever married (including those separated or divorced).

• *Marriage dramatically reduces the prospects that mothers will suffer from violent crime in general or at the hands of intimate acquaintances or strangers.* Mothers who have never married—including those who are single and living either alone or with a boyfriend and those who are cohabiting with their child's father—are nearly three times more likely to be victims of violent crime than are mothers who have ever married.

Other social science surveys demonstrate that marriage is the safest place for children as well. For example:

• *Children of divorced or never-married mothers are six to 30 times more likely to suffer from serious child abuse* than are children raised by both biological parents in marriage.

Without question, marriage is the safest place for a mother and her children to live, both at home and in the larger community. Nevertheless, current government policy is either indifferent to or actively hostile to the institution of marriage. The welfare system, for example, can penalize low-income parents who decide to marry. Such hostility toward marriage is poor public policy; government instead should foster healthy and enduring marriages, which would have many benefits for mothers and children, including reducing domestic violence.

Violence Against Mothers

The DOJ's National Crime Victimization Survey collects data on victimization through an ongoing survey of a nationally representative sample of Americans. The survey defines violent crime as rape, sexual assault, robbery, aggravated assault, and simple assault. Domestic or intimate abuse is defined as violent crimes performed by a spouse, former spouse, boyfriend, or former boyfriend.

The NCVS data reveal interesting patterns among mothers (ages 20–50) with children under the age of 12. Specifically:

• Never-married mothers experience more domestic abuse. Among those who have ever married (those married, divorced, or separated), the annual rate of domestic violence is 14.7 per 1,000 mothers. Among mothers who have never married, the annual domestic violence rate is 32.9 per 1,000.

Thus, never-married mothers suffer domestic violence at more than twice the rate of mothers who have been or currently are married. (See Chart 1).

• Never-married mothers suffer more violent crime. The NCVS provides data on total violent crime against mothers with children under the age of 12. Total violent crime covers rape, sexual assault, robbery, aggravated assault, and simple assault committed against the mother by any party. Total violent crime covers violence against mothers by former and current spouses and boyfriends as well as by relatives, acquaintances, and strangers.

As Chart 2 shows, ever-married mothers with children suffer from overall violent crime at an annual rate of 52.9 crimes per 1,000 mothers. Never-married mothers with children, by contrast, suffer 147.8 violent crimes per 1,000 mothers.

Thus, never-married mothers experience violent crime at almost three times the rate of ever-married mothers. The institution of marriage, in general, shelters mothers from the specter of violence.

Violence Against Children

Rates of victimization of children vary significantly by family structure, and the evidence shows that the married intact family is by far the safest place for children. Although the United States has yet to develop the capacity to measure child abuse by family structure, British data on child abuse are available. These

Chart 1: Annual Rates of Domestic Violence Against Mothers with Children*

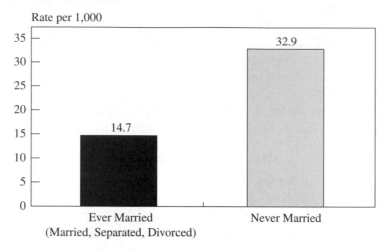

Rate per 1,000

Ever Married (Married, Separated, Divorced): 14.7
Never Married: 32.9

Note: * These data are limited to mothers over age 20 with children under age 12. Mothers with older children cannot be identified separately in the survey. Domestic or intimate violence is defined as violent crimes performed by a spouse, former spouse, boyfriend, or former boyfriend.

Source: U.S. Department of Justice, National Crime Victimization Survey, 1999.

Chart 2: Annual Rates of Total Victimization for Mothers with Children*

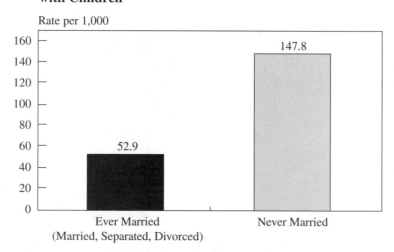

Rate per 1,000

Ever Married (Married, Separated, Divorced): 52.9
Never Married: 147.8

Note: * These data are limited to mothers over age 20 with children under age 12. Mothers with older children cannot be identified separately within the survey. The survey defines violent crime as rape, sexual assault, robbery, aggravated assault, and simple assault.

Source: U.S. Department of Justice, National Crime Victimization Survey, 1999.

data show that rates of serious abuse of children are lowest in the intact married family but six times higher in the step family, 14 times higher in the always–single-mother family, 20 times higher in cohabiting–biological parent families, and 33 times higher when the mother is cohabiting with a boyfriend who is not the father of her children.

When an abused child dies, the relationship between family structure and abuse gets stronger: It is lowest in intact always-married families, three times higher in the step family, nine times higher in the always–single-mother family, 18 times higher in the cohabiting–biological parents family, and 73 times higher in families where the mother cohabits with a boyfriend.

Policymakers Should Promote Marriage

In legislation and social policy, the government should not penalize parents for marrying. Given the rising evidence that non-married mothers and their children are at greater risk of violent crime and abuse, government policy should not encourage—either directly or in unintended ways—single mother-hood and cohabitation.

Yet that is what is being done in many of America's means-tested welfare programs. Because mothers and children are safest from harm within a married family, policymakers should begin the work of implementing policies to reduce the bias against marriage in welfare programs and to strengthen marriage as the primary institution for raising children.

> *"The institution of marriage, in general, shelters mothers from the specter of violence."*

Members of Congress should support President [George W.] Bush's proposal to spend $300 million per year on efforts to rebuild marriage among the poor.[1] It is the first serious proposal in this regard ever to come before Congress. His suggestions, if adopted into law, would begin the necessary work to recon-struct the institution of marriage, which failed welfare policies of the past have undermined. Now that the first stage of welfare reform—rebuilding an ethic of work—is well underway, Congress should support the President as he focuses on the second important stage: rebuilding a culture of marriage in American society.

The Marriage Penalty Should Be Eliminated

Members of Congress should begin to reduce and eventually eliminate the penalty against marriage in most means-tested welfare programs. For example, they could issue a joint resolution indicating their intent to achieve this goal. Then they could request that the Department of Health and Human Services submit a list of options that would be good candidates for this reform.

1. In May 2002 Congress reauthorized the welfare program, including $300 million for marriage promotion.

In establishing programs to help those who need assistance, the question before Congress should not simply be whether or not to fund a program, but how much its policies would improve the well-being of adults and children. Social science data clearly show that mothers and children are safest and thrive best in a married family. It is time for the government to adopt policies that reflect this knowledge and rebuild, rather than undermine, the institution of marriage.

Poverty Increases Women's Vulnerability to Abuse

by Susanne Beechey and Jacqueline Payne

About the authors: *Susanne Beechey and Jacqueline Payne are with the National Organization for Women Legal Defense and Education Fund. NOW Legal Defense pursues equality for women and girls in the workplace, the schools, the family, and the courts through litigation, education, and public information programs.*

Each year, approximately 1.5 million women are physically or sexually assaulted by an intimate partner in the United States. It is estimated that nearly 800,000 women a year seek some type of medical care as a result of injuries sustained by a sexual or physical assault. Each year approximately 500,000 women are stalked by an intimate partner.

Domestic violence survivors face a pattern of psychological assault and physical and sexual coercion by their intimate partners. Abusers often retain control over survivors by ensuring a survivor's economic dependency or instability. While survivors face a number of barriers to escaping abuse, poverty is among the most formidable. This is true for survivors for whom leaving the abuser means giving up economic security, as well as for those already trapped in poverty.

Poverty Traps Women

Domestic and sexual violence causes many women to enter poverty and traps many more in it. Studies consistently demonstrate the high rates of domestic violence among women turning to welfare.

- As many as 60% of women receiving welfare have been subjected to domestic violence as adults (compared to 22% of women in the general population), and as many as 30% reported abuse within the last year.
- A study of women in a welfare-to-work program in Allegheny County Pennsylvania found 38% of those enrolled reported that their current or

most recent partner hit, kicked or threw something at them; 27% were cut, bruised, choked or seriously physically abused by an intimate partner; 18% were forced or coerced into sex.

- Among a representative sample of the Massachusetts welfare caseload, using the state's definition of abuse 65% would be considered domestic violence victims of a current or former boyfriend or husband; and 20% had experienced abuse within the past 12 months.

> *"While survivors [of domestic violence] face a number of barriers to escaping abuse, poverty is among the most formidable."*

- In Utah, research found that 81% of long-term welfare recipients had lived with an abusive partner, and 79% had either called the police or sought a protective order. The individuals who had experienced domestic violence reported more barriers to employment (including higher rates of depression, post-traumatic stress disorder, and substance abuse) than individuals who had not experienced domestic violence.
- Domestic violence is a primary cause of homelessness among women—a circumstance that poses significant barriers to these women's workforce participation.
- Many welfare recipients who are current or past survivors of domestic violence were also victims of sexual or physical abuse as children.

Welfare Makes Escape Possible

Many domestic violence survivors depend on welfare to provide the economic support necessary to escape the violence.

- In a survey of CalWORKs recipients, 37% said that domestic violence was their entire reason for applying for aid, and another 18% said that violence contributed to their need for aid.
- A longitudinal study of low income women who were in a serious relationship with a man found that of women who had received more than one type of public assistance in their lives, 73% experienced moderate or severe violence, compared to 62% who had received one type of public assistance and 53% of those low-income women who had never received public assistance.
- Shelter programs have reported that a majority of shelter residents use welfare in their efforts to end the violence in their lives.
- In an Ohio survey of persons seeking services in domestic violence shelters, 51% said that income and basic needs were "very important" to them when deciding whether to stay or leave their current partners.

Abusers Interfere with Education and Work

Abusers often try to interfere with any efforts their partners make to gain economic independence, including efforts to find work, retain employment or continue studying. This is done in a variety of ways: by inflicting injuries and keeping women up all night with arguments before important events such as interviews or tests; preventing her from sleeping; turning off alarm clocks; destroying homework assignments; saying negative things about her ability to succeed; destroying clothing; inflicting visible facial injuries before job interviews or threatening to kidnap the children from school care centers.

In addition to the direct effect physical violence can have on a woman trying to hold down a job, conduct such as stalking, harassment, and an abuser's refusal to cooperate with child-care arrangements are all aspects of family violence that can be barriers to survivors' employment.

- Women interviewed in battered women's shelters consistently reveal that their abusers did not support and often prevented their employment.
- Abused women are 10 times more likely to have a current or former partner who would not like them going to school or work, compared to women who do not have an abusive partner.
- In a January 1997 month long survey of all persons who sought shelter or supportive services at 20 shelters across Ohio, approximately 75% of respondents stated that there were times that their current partner made it difficult for them to get or keep a job, and 20% said their partner was the cause of injuries that affected their ability to work.
- Another study found increased physical and psychological abuse is closely linked with increased work and school interference.

Abuse Makes It Difficult to Comply with Requirements

- A survey of Passaic County education and training program participants showed that 14.6% were currently survivors of physical domestic violence and 57.3% had been subjected to physical domestic violence in the past. 47% stated that boyfriends do not encourage them to participate in education and training and 39.7% of currently abused women reported that their partners actively try to prevent them from obtaining education and training.
- An assessment of public assistance applicants in four Colorado welfare offices in 1997 found that 44% of domestic violence survivors reported their abusive ex-partners had prevented them from working.

"Many domestic violence survivors depend on welfare to provide the economic support necessary to escape the violence."

- In one urban county in Michigan, 23% of welfare recipients reported that they needed to miss work or school because of something a husband or partner had done to them; and 48% of those who experienced severe violence in the past 12 months reported some form of direct work interference.
- A Utah survey of women receiving long-term welfare benefits found that 42%

reported having been harassed at work by abusive partners and 36% reported having to stay at home from work due to domestic violence at some point in their adult lives. 29% said that their partner objecting to work was a barrier to employment, and of this group 78% indicated this prevented their working and 21% said it adversely affected their work.

> *"Half of those surveyed reported at least one instance where they had been beaten so badly they were unable to work."*

- In a survey of women on welfare in Wisconsin, a majority of the women surveyed (63%) reported that they had been fired or had to quit a job because their partner threatened them. Half of those surveyed reported at least one instance where they had been beaten so badly they were unable to work. Other kinds of abusive behavior women had experienced included: abuser had disturbed their sleep (63%), abuser had called them at work (53%), and abuser showed up at work (53%). Half of those surveyed reported at least one instance of the abuser promising child care and then refusing. Similarly 33% said their abuser had promised a ride to work and then refused. Most of the women surveyed were employed due to Wisconsin's strict work requirements, but they faced severe work interference.
- In another study of current and former welfare recipients who had experienced domestic violence, 30% had lost a job because of the violence and 58.7% were afraid to go to work or school because of threats.
- Women who sought a protection order because of domestic violence dropped out of an Allegheny County Pennsylvania welfare to work program at six times the rate of women who did not, which is strong evidence that battered women facing a safety crisis in the short term will be unable to comply with welfare reform requirements.

Abusers Often Disrupt Work

Many abusers disrupt survivors' ability to work by actively interfering with her on the job; by making work-related threats; calling her repeatedly at work; stalking her at work as well as in covert ways by deliberately disabling the family car or destroying bus passes.

- Studies indicate that between 35 to 56% of employed battered women were harassed at work—in person—by their abusive partner. Up to 50% of female employees experiencing domestic violence have lost a job, due at least in part to their domestic violence experience.
- Ninety-six percent of battered women reported that they had experienced problems at work due to domestic violence, with over 70% having been harassed at work, 50% having lost at least three days of work a month as a result of the abuse, and 25% having lost at least one job due to the domestic violence.

- In January 1997 about 25% of those seeking services in Ohio domestic violence shelters said their current partner had placed harassing calls to the workplace or job training site; 26% reported that their partner had shown up at their workplace; 40% said their partner had discouraged their attendance at work; and 20% reported other behaviors they believed impacted their chance to get and keep a job.
- Low income women who experienced domestic violence in their adult relationships were more likely to have experienced unemployment and to have had more job turnover than those who had not been subjected to such violence.
- A longitudinal study in Worcester Massachusetts found women who experienced physical abuse during the first 12-months of the study were only one-third as likely to work 30 hours per week for six months or more during the following year as compared to women who had not experienced such aggression.

Battered Women Want to Work

Most battered women work or want to work if they can do so safely and many women use welfare and work as a way to escape an abusive relationship. Although data demonstrates that abusers attempt to interfere with work, domestic violence does not prevent employment for all women who experience it. Indeed service providers noted that many battered women managed to work, and are struggling to overcome work obstacles created by their abusers.

- A study in Washington found that women who had experienced both sexual and physical abuses had held a greater number of jobs than other women, but were employed for *fewer total months*, suggesting they continued to try to work but had trouble keeping jobs.
- Other studies conclude that some battered women try to use work as a way to escape domestic violence.

Federal welfare law requires women to establish paternity and cooperate with child support collection. A distressing invasion of women's privacy, this requirement is particularly threatening to survivors and their children. States are required to have procedures for exempting women with "good cause" such as fear of domestic violence from these requirements, and the Family Violence Option can also be used to waive child support requirements. However, child support enforcement frequently poses increased danger to domestic violence survivors. Court proceedings increase batterers' access to the mother and child and can be used by the abuser as a vehicle for continued harassment. Moreover, child sup-

> *"In another study of current and former welfare recipients who had experienced domestic violence, . . . 58.7% were afraid to go to work or school because of threats."*

port enforcement opens up the issue of visitation and custody, threatening the safety and security of the child. While some survivors may need waivers from the entire process, others may need the state to institute policies and procedures (such as excusing her from court visits, protecting contact information, and ensuring that abusers are not granted unsafe visitation or custody) so that survivors can safely take advantage of pending child support reforms which will aid welfare recipients in achieving economic security.

Most battered women—over 95% in some studies—indicate that they would want to pursue child support *if they can do so safely.*

An Office of Child Support Enforcement study in three states (Colorado, Massachusetts and Minnesota) suggests that abused women want to collect child support, when it is safe for them to do so.

- In Colorado, 40% of the sample disclosed domestic violence and 3% expressed interest in applying for a good cause waiver for child support enforcement.
- In Massachusetts, 36% of the sample disclosed domestic violence and 8% wanted a waiver.
- In Minnesota, 52% disclosed domestic violence and 2% were interested in a good cause waiver.

Battered Women Need Assistance

All evidence clearly points to the need for welfare policies that recognize the special problems and challenges faced by survivors of domestic and sexual violence. Welfare requirements can create dangers for battered women; in particular requirements such as immediate participation in work activities, lifetime assistance limits of five years, and paternity establishment and child support cooperation requirements can present significant roadblocks to accessing benefits and achieving safety. Limitations on access to benefits for immigrant women creates a serious problem for immigrant survivors.

Moreover, due to the violence in their lives, survivors often face multiple barriers to employment, including lingering physical health problems and post-traumatic stress, or substance abuse problems. It has been estimated that between 60–95% of female addicts in treatment have been raped or otherwise sexually or physically abused.

These multiple barriers interact in complex ways, requiring comprehensive holistic services to address all barriers to employment and sufficient time to participate in those services. Programs that are sensitive to the needs of survivors can make a difference.

- *Illinois:* In Chicago, a demonstration project called Options which provided counseling, support groups, legal services and emergency shelter as well as pre-employment training, integrating work and training with traditional domestic violence services, dramatically increased survivors' ability to enter work activities.

• *Minnesota:* Employment increased 64% among welfare recipients after treatment for substance abuse.

The FVO Is Critical

TANF [Temporary Aid to Needy Families] currently contains a provision designed to help domestic violence survivors. The Family Violence Option (FVO), permits states to temporarily waive TANF program requirements for survivors of domestic violence when those requirements "would make it more difficult for individuals receiving assistance . . . to escape domestic violence or unfairly penalize such individuals who are or have been victimized by such violence, or individuals who are at risk of future domestic violence." The FVO was designed to provide states with the ability to craft more flexible responses to meet the individualized needs of battered women on welfare.

Since 1996, a majority of states (38) plus the District of Columbia have adopted the FVO as part of their welfare law. Seven other states have equivalent policies that enable survivors of domestic and sexual violence to obtain waivers from some or all TANF program requirements. Five states to date have not implemented equivalent policies.

The FVO has helped but it needs to be strengthened and improved in the following ways:

1. *Universal Assessment & Services.* Under current law, addressing this issue is optional for states. Given the significant role domestic and sexual violence plays in creating and sustaining women's poverty, all states must be required to certify that they will address domestic and sexual violence in their TANF program. Further, each State plan should describe how trained caseworkers will screen individuals and refer victims to services, waiver program requirements as necessary, and consult with domestic and sexual violence experts to develop and implement policies and programs.

2. *Improved Notice.* Studies show that even local welfare offices of states that have domestic or sexual violence provisions may not fully inform individuals who disclose domestic violence of the protections and services available, or of their rights under TANF. Strengthening notice requirements to applicants and recipients is a crucial enhancement of the current law.

   • *New York:* A study of the New York City welfare agency found it referred less than half of individuals who identified themselves as survivors of violence to special domestic violence caseworkers, as required by state law. Only about one-third of those who were referred to the caseworkers were granted family violence option waivers from any welfare requirement.

   • *Wisconsin:* Approximately 75% of welfare recipients who identified themselves as survivors of violence were not informed about available services, including counseling, housing, or the possibility of using work time to seek help. In addition, while 26.8% reported they were afraid their former partner would harass them if the state attempted to collect child support, only 4.9% were told about the good cause exception to the child support cooperation requirement.

- *California:* Only one in four immigrant women surveyed who identified themselves as survivors of violence had received *any* information from the welfare office about domestic violence waivers for which they were eligible.

3. *Caseworker Training & Coordination with Domestic and Sexual Violence Experts.* Overall, few TANF recipients are disclosing domestic violence to welfare caseworkers. Most states do not track the number of disclosures, but where data exists, the rates are between 5 and 10% of the caseload. This is consistent with research indicating that domestic violence advocates obtain four and five times more disclosures than welfare caseworkers.

> *"Battered women facing a safety crisis in the short term will be unable to comply with welfare reform requirements."*

Issues of trust, expertise and confidentiality work against disclosure to welfare caseworkers. These issues may be mitigated by the use of trained domestic violence advocates, by improved training of caseworkers and by enhanced procedures within welfare offices.

State Office of Child Support Enforcement staff must also be made aware of domestic and sexual violence issues and procedures for FVO waivers should be coordinated with child support exemption procedures. The same concerns about notice and training that have become evident in implementation of the FVO are equally important with respect to child support enforcement. Moreover, paternity establishment and child support enforcement should be made voluntary for all participants, to ensure that no woman is made unsafe by blanket requirements.

All states should be encouraged to build upon and implement the best practices developed in the last five years to address domestic and sexual violence in the TANF program, including enhanced coordination and contracting with experts in the field of domestic and sexual violence.

4. *Pre-Sanction Review:* The foregoing data details the many ways in which domestic violence can interfere with a recipients' compliance with welfare work and program requirements. It is therefore essential that states take steps to avoid unfairly punishing survivors when violence is a contributing factor to the noncompliance. As such, states should put a "pre-sanction review" in place to keep survivors from being sanctioned off welfare, further trapping them in the abuse. . . .

The Secure and Healthy Families Act

The "Secure and Healthy Families Act." (S. 2876), introduced by Senators Patty Murray and Paul Wellstone, is the senate legislation most directly responsive to the needs of survivors of domestic and sexual violence on welfare. [The

Secure and Healthy Families Act was introduced in September 2002 and defeated in February 2003.]

S.2876 extends the FVO to all 50 states, requires caseworker training, and strengthens protections like notice, confidentiality, and pre-sanction review. S. 2876 also authorizes funding for caseworker training and the development and dissemination of best practices for addressing this roadblock to economic security.

While the Senate Finance Mark attempts to strengthen families by investing $1 billion in perilous marriage promotion experiments, S. 2876 focuses on strengthening families primarily through programs designed to enhance income and economic security and escape poverty. Such programs have been tested and proven to enhance family stability and child well-being. This alternative to the Finance Mark will not endanger families. It includes stringent safeguards for domestic and sexual violence, informed participation, and assures non-discrimination based on marital status. The program will be rigorously, independently evaluated to measure effects on family well-being.

Congress Must Do More

With such an overwhelming correlation between violence and poverty, Congress' failure to require states to address domestic and sexual violence in TANF is, to say the least, puzzling. Moreover, given the foregoing statistics, it is incredible that Congress would even consider mandating marriage promotion or providing significant financial incentives . . . for marriage promotion.

Given that so few survivors feel safe addressing the issue with caseworkers, welfare policies that are designed with a blind eye to the realities of domestic violence save the occasional exception for survivors who self-identify, are simply unworkable. Such policies undermine survivors' abilities to escape poverty and abuse. Rather, policies designed for the entire caseload should be created with survivors (the majority) in mind.

At a bare minimum in this year's [2002] TANF reauthorization, Congress should require all states to train caseworkers, screen for domestic and sexual violence, refer individuals to services and modify requirements as appropriate.[1] Congress should invest TANF dollars in caseworker training, study of best practices with respect to addressing domestic violence in TANF, and dissemination of those best practices to all states to help them address this very real barrier to economic security.

---

1. Congress reauthorized TANF in February 2003 without any new provisions addressing domestic and sexual violence. Money for marriage promotion programs was approved.

Patriarchy Encourages Violence Against Women

by Deborah J. Cohan

About the author: *Deborah J. Cohan is a counselor in a battering intervention program and occasional contributor to* Off Our Backs, *a feminist publication.*

The concepts of gender, representation, and social control form a complex nexus of relationships that are ever present in my life. I spend most of my academic life researching the phenomenon of violence against women, specifically battering. And I devote my time as an activist to working to eradicate violence in the lives of women and children. I attempt to do this by being a counselor in a battering intervention program which aims to promote batterers' accountability and women's safety through counseling and education. Though I constantly attempt to merge these two worlds—the academic and activist—I find that I am most often simply struggling to straddle them. My own struggle to narrow the divide between these two spaces could be the topic of another essay. Rather, here I intend to focus my attention on the social construction and social negotiation of space within the context of the battering intervention program.

The fact that the world is not a safe place is not a new idea. Every day we read in newspapers and watch on television about the random, senseless killings that plague our nation, and we also hear about the very patterned and calculated crimes of misogyny, but we hear about these less and they happen more often. I am painfully aware that due to my gender, all of the public and private spaces in which I inhabit make me more vulnerable to all forms of sexual violence. I do not have as much of a feeling of space as I do of what is confining. Most basically, the feeling that due to my gender, I do not have the freedom to choose to occupy any space I want, combined with the feeling that the spaces I can occupy may still render me subordinate or even invisible is terrifying, upsetting, and oppressive.

In her book *The Politics of Reality*, Marilyn Frye deconstructs the meaning of oppression. She explains that its root word is "press," and goes on to say that "something pressed is something caught between or among forces and barriers which are so related to each other that jointly they restrain, restrict, or, prevent the thing's motion or mobility." Furthermore, Frye notes that "the oppressiveness of the situations in which women live our various and different lives is a macroscopic phenomenon." Also, in her book, Frye makes use of the image of a caged-in bird to illustrate that each bar of the cage is confining, but that each bar must be understood in connection to all of the other bars which jointly make the experience an oppressive one for the bird.

Every week I find myself walking into a room without any windows and with only bare white walls and cold, hard, upright chairs. On every chair sits a man. One man shares with me in the process of co-facilitating for the group. All of the other men are there because they have a history of being abusive to their intimate partners. We sit in this room for two hours without a break. First, the men go around in a circle and talk about the past week. They check in by stating their name, the names of their partners, the names of their children, if they have any, and they recall any abusive or controlling behavior that they exerted on their partner during the past week. Each week we call on a few men to do longer check-ins in which they state and explain their most serious and most recent violent episodes. I sit and listen and jot down brief notes to myself on a legal pad. I also ask the men questions which aim to probe more deeply into their behavior and which force them to account for their actions. For instance, if a man states that his partner fell down the stairs, neither I, nor the other group leader, lets him stop

> *"I feel saturated, and enraged by patriarchal norms and ideology which tolerate violence against women."*

there. We are not really interested in what she did, because we do not believe that victims provoke violent behavior or deserve to be beaten, physically or psychologically. Instead, we ask the man what he did, and in a case like I described above, a man typically is encouraged to respond, "Well, I pushed her down the stairs." From the men's accounts of their violent behavior emerges a cold, stark, barren picture of human relations, particularly gender relations. Their accounts are filled with so much contradiction, distortion, rigidity, absolutism, self-centeredness, anger, aggression, fear, jealousy, and misogyny. Sometimes, I feel like a receptacle—a storage bin for their words and stories. Most often, I am filled with rage, fear, and sadness. Above all, I end up feeling empty, and the barren quality of the room itself matches the emptiness and alienation of the accounts of their relationships.

Thus, every week, I find myself deeply entrenched in the oppressive cage that is patriarchy, desperately trying to remove the structural supports which keep it in place. Sometimes I feel as though I am sitting in patriarchy without any way to move. I am never sure if the dizziness and lightheadedness I feel during these two hours is due to not having any windows or fresh air in the room, or if it is because I feel saturated, and enraged by patriarchal norms and ideology which tolerate violence against women. This patriarchal ideology and context of tolerance minimizes or ignores the extent to which some men's violence and acts of intrusion contribute to all women's fear and experience of a lack of safety. Moreover, an integral aspect of this context of tolerance is the way in which male violence is regarded as women's problem.

Violence Against Women Reinforces Gender Hierarchy

Because I contend that battering is not a psychological problem or a relational problem but rather a problem of male dominance, I believe that the men's messages of the gender inequality that they exercise in their own individual relationships reverberates in their more global regard, or disregard for women, more generally. Thus, I, as the only woman in the room, represent to these men the social category that they most vilify and condemn. Before I ever started being a group leader, I observed other groups in session. What always struck me most was the extent to which the men in these groups most often give more credibility and validation to the male leader's words than the female leader's, when they may be saying the very same thing. Moreover, during the time that I observed these other groups, I remember being looked at with an objectifying gaze. I am constantly reminded, both in the battering intervention program and wherever I go and whatever I do, that my body is contested terrain. As a woman, my body is a battleground on which men can strip away my sexuality, my choices, and my freedom. In the battering intervention program, I am constantly reminded of the subordinate position of my gender and am always forced to question the male entitlement that is pervasive and which allows men to make so many woman hating remarks. At first I used to think that the men may have just momentarily forgotten that a woman was sitting in the room and perhaps regarded me as somehow "genderless." Now, after doing this more, I realize that they have not forgotten anything at all; in fact, their words are a reminder to me that I am merely a woman in their eyes. They remind me that violence against women serves to reinforce gender hierarchy and to serve as a mechanism of social control over all women.

Every week, I sit in a room in which my female body is so small, and the male presence is so massive. Sometimes, I hear women who work there remark that they feel lucky that their private, intimate lives are safe and peaceful. When I leave the program at the end of the day, I never feel lucky. What makes me so different from the women in the men's lives?

I walk to my car and finally feel the cold night air on my face, and there is always a voice in my head reminding me that even in that brief walk to my car from the building, I may not be safe. So far, I have always made it to my car, and I have always made it home. I am just always left hoping that one day I will not have to return, that one day, the program will be forced to shut its doors because there are no batterers and no battered women for it to need to exist. Until then, why do I keep going? Because I wouldn't think of doing anything else.

Chapter 3

Are Current Approaches to Reducing Violence Against Women Effective?

Chapter Preface

Once considered a private family matter best left behind closed doors, domestic violence is now recognized as a crime with specific, albeit sometimes controversial, legal and social remedies. Battered women's shelters and programs offer immediate sanctuary and temporary protection for women who leave their abusers. Often, however, just getting away is not enough. Many experts—social scientists and battered women's advocates as well as those in law enforcement—agree that a restraining order (RO) or abuse protection order (APO) is an abused woman's best defense against her abuser. A restraining order is a legal document that limits a man's physical proximity to his alleged victim and also restricts his contact with her by telephone, mail, or e-mail.

Abused women and their advocates insist that ROs offer necessary protection from further abuse by chronically violent men. Experts cite the findings of a six-month American Medical Association analysis of over eighteen thousand male batterers in Massachusetts against whom ROs were issued. The study, they say, revealed just how violent these men are: 74.8 percent of the men had prior criminal records and 48.1 percent had histories of violent crimes.

Provisions in the Violence Against Women Act of 1994 (VAWA) strengthened RO protections by making it a felony for anyone constrained by an RO to travel from one state to another with the intention of harassing or injuring his victim. Further, a man subject to an RO or APO is not allowed to acquire, buy, or own a gun. However, ROs can offer women effective protection only if they are fully enforced. In most states, violation of an RO is a crime punishable by imprisonment or fine or both, but abused women argue that police are often hesitant to arrest RO violators. Further, these women claim that even when violators are arrested, judges are too lenient. Senator Joe Biden (D-DE), the principal author of the VAWA, insists on strict enforcement: "If a stay-away order is issued and there is a violation, what we do is lock the sucker up."

While abused women insist that "stay-away" or restraining orders are crucial to their safety, men's advocacy groups argue that they are issued much too easily. While men's groups such as the Coalition for the Preservation of Fatherhood (CPF) and the Equal Justice Foundation (EJF) acknowledge the horror of battering, they argue that ROs are punitive and discriminatory toward men. Vindictive women can easily obtain ROs even when there has been no abuse, critics argue. Victimized men have little legal recourse because a woman can request an RO against her alleged abuser without a court hearing or even notifying him that the order is in place. Further, a man legally restrained from contact with the woman he allegedly abused is often deprived of his home and contact with his children.

While the intent of an RO is to provide protection for abused women and a cooling off period for both the abused and abuser, it does neither, according to Mark Charalambous of the CPF. "The zealous application of this flawed law is not only failing to protect true victims, but it is directly causing real domestic violence. . . . Far from being a means to effect a 'cooling off' period, as judges and battered women's advocates contend, [restraining orders] arc fire-starters," he argues.

The controversy surrounding the use of restraining orders to protect abused women is part of a larger argument concerning the effectiveness of current legal approaches to abuse. The viewpoints in the following chapter explore other legal and social remedies designed to reduce violence against women.

Mandatory Arrest Laws Reduce Domestic Violence

by Christopher D. Maxwell, Joel H. Garner, and Jeffrey A. Fagan

About the authors: *Christopher D. Maxwell is an assistant professor at Michigan State University. Joel H. Garner is a researcher for the Joint Center for Justice Studies. Jeffrey A. Fagan is the director of the Center for Violence Research and Prevention at Columbia University and a visiting professor at Columbia University Law School.*

After nearly 20 years of research designed to test the effects of arrest on intimate partner violence, questions persist on whether arrest is more effective at reducing subsequent intimate partner violence than such informal, therapeutic methods as on-scene counseling or temporary separation. The most important research efforts addressing this question were six experiments known collectively as the National Institute of Justice's (NIJ's) Spouse Assault Replication Program (SARP). These field experiments, carried out between 1981 and 1991 by six police departments and research teams, were designed to test empirically whether arrests deterred subsequent violence better than less formal alternatives. . . .

The development of a coherent evaluation of the effectiveness of arrest based on the five experiments with published results was complicated by the differences across the experimental sites in case selection, incident eligibility rules, statistical analysis, and outcome measurements. With these differences, prior attempts to synthesize and understand the substantive diversities among and within the experiments proved difficult. Thus, the full potential of SARP to answer questions about the specific deterrent effect of arrest and the safety of victims has not been realized.

Analysis Is Complete

We have previously reviewed and compared the published data from the five replication sites that had reported final results to NIJ by 1993. . . . We pointed out that the comparisons were based on information drawn from different out-come

Christopher D. Maxwell, Joel H. Garner, and Jeffrey A. Fagan, "The Effects of Arrest on Intimate Partner Violence: New Evidence from the Spouse Assault Replication Program," *National Institute of Justice Research Brief*, July 2001.

measures, analytical models, and case selection criteria. Furthermore, we asserted that the inconsistency between sources and measures across sites was not necessarily because of limitations in the experimental designs, but because the SARP design called for multiple data sources and measures that could capture variations in the nature of the deterrent effect. We argued that conclusions about the deterrent effect of arrest therefore should wait until a more careful statistical analysis was completed, one based on data pooled from all five sites and using standardized measures of intervention and outcome. This Research in Brief summarizes the findings of such a statistical analysis.

> *"This research found no association between arresting the offender and an increased risk of subsequent aggression against women."*

We studied the deterrent effect of arrest, using an approach that addressed many problems faced by prior efforts to synthesize the results from SARP. Supported by NIJ and the Centers for Disease Control and Prevention (CDC), the project pooled incidents from the five replication experiments, computed comparable independent and outcome measures from common data intentionally embedded in each experiment, and standardized the experimental designs and statistical models. Using the increased power of the pooled data, this study provides a more consistent, more precise, and less ambiguous estimation of the impact of arrest on intimate partner violence. Key results of this study include the following:

Key Results

• Arresting batterers was consistently related to reduced subsequent aggression against female intimate partners, although not all comparisons met the standard level of statistical significance.

• Regardless of the statistical significance, the overall size of the relationship between arrest and repeat offending (i.e., the deterrent effect of arrest) was modest when compared to the size of the relationship between recidivism and such measures as the batterers' prior criminal record or age.

• The size of the reduction in subsequent intimate partner aggression did not vary significantly across the five sites. In other words, the benefit of arrest was about equal in regards to reducing aggression in all five sites.

• Regardless of the type of intervention, most suspects had no subsequent criminal offense against their original victim within the followup period, and most interviewed victims did not report any subsequent victimization by their batterer.

• This research found no association between arresting the offender and an increased risk of subsequent aggression against women. . . .

The Relationship Between Arrest and Aggression

[We conducted a] statistical analysis of the relationship between arrest and several dimensions of intimate partner aggression. The first analysis (prevalence) uses victim interview data to test for the association between arrest and any subsequent aggression during the period between the experimental incident and the last time the victim was interviewed. This model estimated that if their batterers were arrested, about 25 percent fewer female victims than expected reported one or more incidents of aggression. In other words, when the likelihood of failure (reoffending) is estimated for the typical case, about 36 percent of suspects in the arrest group reoffended, compared with 48 percent of suspects in the nonarrest group. This difference was statistically significant while controlling for differences among sites, the length of time the researchers tracked the victims, and characteristics of the suspect and incident. When examining the rates or frequency of aggression, we again found a statistically significant reduction in subsequent aggression that is related to arrest. On average, female victims whose batterers were arrested reported about 30 percent fewer incidences of subsequent aggression than expected over the followup period. Thus, we found a sizable reduction in subsequent aggression reported by victims whose batterers were assigned to the arrest group. However, because these results are based on a subsample of interviewed victims, rather than on the entire sample of eligible cases, the results from the victim interviews alone should be used with some caution because victims not interviewed may have been involved with suspects who responded differently to their intervention.

Other Factors Related to Aggression

Besides the consistent deterrent relationship between arrest and aggression, other factors were consistently related to aggression, but some factors were not. First, compared with the Omaha victims, a significantly smaller percentage of victims from the other sites (except Milwaukee) reported one or more victimizations by the suspect. On average, victims from these three sites also reported less frequent victimization. These differences in the base rates of aggression across the sites, however, did not translate into significantly different relationships between arrest and aggression in the different sites. In other words, the reduction we find in aggression reported by victims whose batterers were assigned an arrest is of about equal size in each site.

In addition to the comparisons we made across the sites, we looked for differences in aggression reported by the victims across several suspect characteristics. These comparisons

> *"Female victims whose batterers were arrested reported about 30 percent fewer incidences of subsequent aggression than expected over the followup period."*

found that the suspect's age and race were consistently and significantly related to the frequency of subsequent aggression as reported by the victims. These victims reported significantly less aggression when the suspect was older and nonwhite. The suspects' prior arrest records and their marital status with the victim were also consistently related to aggression, but only the prior record was significant in all but one of the analyses. Finally, several other suspect characteristics, such as employment and the use of intoxicants, were inconsistent in the direction of their relationship across the two dimensions of aggression (prevalence and frequency). For example, about 2 percent more victims of employed suspects reported one or more incidents of aggression, though these same victims simultaneously reported about 21 percent fewer incidents of aggression over the followup period.

> *"A consistent deterrent relationship exists between arrest of the suspect and later aggression."*

Official Police Records

We next examined data collected by police departments to measure aggression by the suspect against the victim. The approach to testing whether arrest was related to officially recorded aggression follows the approach to the victim interviews, except we added a statistical analysis that examined the timing of the first new aggressive incident. Overall, the results based on the police data regarding the effectiveness of arrest are consistent in direction with those based on the victim interview data: A consistent deterrent relationship exists between arrest of the suspect and later aggression while controlling for the differences across the sites, the victim interview process, and suspect characteristics. However, the police data show a far smaller reduction in aggression because of the arrest treatment than what was detected using victim interview data, and none of these relationships reached the traditional level of statistical significance. Specifically, in the first analysis (prevalence), we found about 4 percent fewer than the expected percentage of male suspects in the arrest group with one or more incidents of subsequent aggression during the first 6 months of followup. The second analysis, which tested for the relationship between the intervention and the annual rate of aggression, found a reduction of about 8 percent from the expected number of incidents per year for suspects assigned to the arrest group. Finally, the last analysis, which examined the relationship between arrest and the timing of the first new incident, found that the expected risk of a new incident on any given day after arrest or nonarrest is reduced nearly 10 percent among the arrested suspects. Thus, depending on the dimension of the outcome, the average amount of reported aggression by the suspects dropped by between 4 and 10 percent if they were assigned to the arrest group. . . .

Arrest Deters Reoffense

The average survival [nonoffending] rate throughout the followup period varied substantially by site. On the high end was Omaha, where nearly 90 percent of the suspects had not reoffended by the end of their observation period. On the low side was Dade County, where that figure (the cumulative survival rate) was slightly less than 60 percent. These differences between sites, however, did not result in differences in survival rates by intervention group when the five sites were pooled together. . . . Throughout the followup period, which for some suspects lasted nearly 3 years, batterers who were assigned an arrest had a consistently greater rate of survival (nonoffending) than did those assigned an informal intervention.

This consistent, but small, difference in the survival rate by intervention is important because earlier analysis using data from Milwaukee suggested that arrest may have a significant long-term criminogenic effect. . . . During no particular observation period were the suspects assigned to an arrest more likely to batter their intimate partner than those in the control (nonarrest) group. Thus, among this larger sample of male intimate partner abusers, the survival rate for aggression among those assigned an arrest was never less than that of the control group. . . .

Marriage Provided No Protection

Our statistical analysis also showed that the suspects' age, race, employment status, and use of intoxicants at the time of the experimental incident were consistently and significantly related to subsequent aggression against the victim. Contrary to what we found with the victim interviews, white and employed suspects had lower levels of repeat offending according to the police records. Furthermore, suspects who were intoxicated at the time of the experimental incident and those with prior arrests for any crime had, on average, a greater likelihood of aggression recorded by the police. Only the measure of the suspect's marital status with the victim was not consistently or significantly related to aggression. Similar to what we found with the victim interview data, marriage did not appear to provide notable protection against subsequent levels of aggression. Finally, we found that the longer the researchers were able to track the victims for followup interviews, the more initial failures were reported to the police.

> *"Marriage did not appear to provide notable protection against subsequent levels of aggression."*

In addition to our findings about the relationship between arrest and aggression, we observed some patterns in the pooled data. First, we found a general pattern of cessation or termination of aggression that was only moderately related to the suspects' assigned intervention. According to officially recorded data, less than 30 percent of the suspects, arrested or not, aggressed against the same victim during the followup period. Furthermore, only about 40 percent of the interviewed victims reported subsequent victimization of any measured type by the suspects. Other studies that specifically estimated the rate of desistance from intimate violence have also found similar rates over a 1- to 2-year period.

A second pattern concerns the high concentration of repeat aggression among a small number of batterers. During the 6-month followup, the 3,147 interviewed victims reported more than 9,000 incidents of aggression by the suspects since the initial incident. While most victims reported no new incidents of aggression, about 8 percent of them reported a total number of incidents that represented more than 82 percent of the 9,000 incidents. The same 8 percent also accounted for 28 percent of the 1,387 incidents recorded by the police that involved an interviewed victim. . . .

Arrest Deters Aggression

Our multisite pooled analysis of the five replication experiments found good evidence of a consistent and direct, though modest, deterrent effect of arrest on aggression by males against their female intimate partners. The victim interviews indicate that the arrest of the suspect and any subsequent confinement, when compared with the alternative interventions collectively, significantly reduced the expected frequency of subsequent aggression by 30 percent. Similarly, arrest may have reduced by a smaller amount the number of times the police responded to subsequent domestic violence incidents involving the same victim and suspect and may have extended the time between the initial incident and the first subsequent incident. . . .

Arrest Decreases Violence Against Women

The findings of this research have several implications for policy. First, our findings provide systematic evidence supporting the argument that arresting male batterers may, independent of other criminal justice sanctions and individual processes, reduce subsequent intimate partner violence. The size and statistical significance of the effect of arrest varied depending on whether the subsequent aggression was measured by victim interviews or police records; even so, in all measures (prevalence, frequency, rate, and time-to-failure), arrest was associated with fewer incidents of subsequent intimate partner aggression. This finding exists during the first several days after the experimental incident regardless of the period of detention, as well as beyond 1 year. The arrested suspects were detained an average of 9 days, but the reduction in aggression associated with arrest did not vary by the length of the suspects' detention. Thus, our research finds no empirical support for the argument that arrest may eventually increase the risk for violence against women. . . .

While arrest reduced the proportion of suspects who reoffended and the frequency with which they reoffended, arrest did not prevent all batterers from continuing their violence against their intimate partners. In fact, we found a small number of victims who have chronically aggressive intimate partners. Future research needs to build on preliminary efforts to accurately predict high-rate repeat offenders and to find methods of helping their victims before they are victimized further.

Therapy for Abusers Helps Reduce Domestic Violence

by Cindy Baskin, Jean Bernard, Alysa Golden, and Alayne Hamilton, interviewed by the *Education Wife Assault Newsletter*

About the authors: *Cindy Baskin is the coordinator of the Mino-Yaa-Daa therapy program and works within the Aboriginal community in Toronto, Ontario, Canada. Jean Bernard is the executive director of the Changing Ways therapy center in London, England, and is well known in the children's mental health field in Canada. Alysa Golden is a social worker who counsels abusive men. Alayne Hamilton works with abusive men and their abused partners at the Family Violence Project in Victoria, British Columbia, Canada. The* Education Wife Assault Newsletter *is a website publication of Education Wife Assault, a Canadian nonprofit organization that works to decrease the incidence of violence against women.*

Editor's Note: The following viewpoint was originally an interview with Cindy Baskin, Jean Bernard, Alysa Golden, and Alayne Hamilton conducted by the Education Wife Assault Newsletter.

1. What would you define as successful outcomes for a program for men who abuse?

Cindy Baskin: First of all, I think that we are trying to change behaviour. In other words, stopping the physical violence. Then, we are striving to change the values and attitudes that go along with physical violence. My program also considers other things successes. For example, we get a lot of men who are court mandated or pressured to participate. The men who stay in the program after their designated time period are successes. . . .

Jean Bernard: While the focus of the intervention is on men, their behaviours and attitudes, the ultimate reason for the existence of a program like Changing Ways is to have an impact on the safety and quality of life of women, children and men involved. Outcomes must be measured in terms of increased safety for women and children and a reduction of fear and intimidation for the woman whose partner is in the program. There should be a demonstrated increase in men of positive behaviours, pro-social anti-violent attitudes and egalitarian relationships, as well as an increase in their taking responsibility for their behaviour and for their work to change. A relationship may or may not be repaired, but the key factor must be a resulting condition of safety as the only successful outcome.

Alysa Golden: The only outcome that I would define as successful in a men's program is a man being able to

> *"We are striving to change the values and attitudes that go along with physical violence."*

successfully cease all controlling behaviours. Because this outcome is unlikely at the end of a limited group (anywhere from 16–24 weeks) I tend to modify outcome measurement by looking at realistic outcomes. These include: 1) the man being able to reach for an understanding of how his abuse has harmed his partner, 2) the man being able to take responsibility for his abusive and controlling behaviour without minimizing or denying that it happened, 3) the man being able to firmly situate his abusive behaviour within the context of power and control, and not within the context of 'anger'.

Alayne Hamilton: As a member of ACAM, the British Columbia Association of Counselors of Abusive Men, my goals are set out by established Guiding Principles, which are accepted by the provincial government as the standard for programs for abusive men. The primary principle is 'the safety of women and children is paramount'. The treatment goals are to stop violence against women, to reduce the whole array of abusive and controlling behaviours, and to encourage equality in relationships. Successful outcomes, then, include the increase of women's safety, the end of physical violence and the decrease of the whole range of abusive and controlling behaviours.

2. What philosophical frameworks and/or approaches have you found most effective in increasing the success of men's programs?

Baskin: We basically use a combination of a feminist model and a culture based approach. For example, we combine the models based on the cycle of violence and power and control with models based on Aboriginal teachings and culture. We find that the men respond better to the cultural programs and the values of those programs. The programs are more effective when the men are held accountable within our culture and community. We see that it is not enough to try to hold them accountable to the criminal justice system alone, because it does not mean a whole lot to them. Another piece is that we have intentionally chosen an Aboriginal woman to lead this program, making the men accountable to the women in the community. This has a big impact. The principles of culture-based justice to restore balance for all people involved and to the community itself— are a major part of the program. The men become accountable to the victims, their families, and the community. They are responsible for doing something about the harm that they have caused, such as making amends and compensation. In the program, abusive men may be required to make apologies, acknowledge his abusive behaviour, and show what he is doing to change it, to both the victim and the community itself. In terms of making amends and compensation, we hold a lot of ceremonies and healing practices for the women and children which the men are required to prepare. Specifically, the men take care of our sweat lodge, and do the fire keeping for those ceremonies. We believe that when the men are held accountable to the community, then the silence that allows the abuse to continue is broken. Once the silence is broken, it becomes more difficult for men to 'get away with' abusive behaviours.

Bernard: We believe that woman abuse arises out of systemic and systematic abuse of power and control, supported by sexism and male privilege and we have built our program around that paradigm. We focus on keeping men accountable by challenging men's abusive tactics in group therapy, avoiding collusion with them, and constantly returning them to their responsibility for their own behaviours. We take a strong psychoeducational approach and a lesser 'therapeutic' approach.

Men's programs must participate in a coordinated community effort. Any anti-violence program, no matter how strong, sophisticated, or intrinsically effective, will not be effective in a community where anti-violence efforts are not coordinated. A community's coordinated effort must include a judicial response, the consistency of correctional and probation systems, availability of safety mechanisms including shelters and counselling for women, legal assistance for women, and strong public education and advocacy.

> *"Successful outcomes . . .*
> *include the increase of women's*
> *safety, the end of physical*
> *violence and the decrease of the*
> *whole range of abusive and*
> *controlling behaviours."*

Golden: I believe that the most effective philosophical framework and/or approach for increasing the success of men's programs is a feminist philosophy and approach. This framework includes the following elements: 1) vigilant partner contact to make sure that the partner has the counselling and practical supports that she needs. This element sends a message to the man that he needs to work constantly at not being abusive because his partner is no longer isolated and silent. 2) Having at least one woman or man involved in the program who has frontline experience working with women who have experienced abuse. This element ensures that the women's perspective is always front and centre, making it difficult for the man to hide from the impact of his actions. This challenges the man to be accountable for the effects of his actions, which is crucial to stopping his controlling and abusive behaviours. 3) A feminist perspective ensures that the abuse is primarily and consistently dealt with. In non-feminist approaches, the past abuse or other precipitating factors may be the focus, while stopping the abuse is minimized.

Hamilton: It is better to do a men's group program that focuses specifically on a man's abusive behaviour in his relationships with women, rather than doing individual therapy, men's support groups or couple counseling. Although group programs are the accepted approach, we are only beginning to know the success of men's treatment in general, but we do not have enough knowledge to determine which specific programs are most successful. What we do know is that although we need to change men's behaviour, especially physical violence, it is not enough to change behaviour. We need to change the man. Short programs are reasonably successful in changing the physical abuse, but it takes longer to change how a man sees himself and his relationships with women. Getting rid of the array of abusive behaviours involves a long term, concerted effort on the man's part. It is not the program that changes the man; rather it is the man who changes the man. In talking about recovering men, Edward Gondolf describes the process of change in terms of personal growth, in which they accepted responsibility, became empathetic, and redefined their manhood.

3. What steps/measures do you take to increase the safety of women in programs for men who abuse?

Baskin: We are in contact with all of the partners or ex-partners of the men in the program during the man's time in the program. We see how they are doing, how we can help them, and it's a safety check to monitor how honest the men are being in the program. Because it is family and community-based, our program also has programming for children and women. So ideally, the partner of the man would be attending the women's component of the program. Confidentiality is another issue. Confidentiality is limited for men due to partner contact. This is different from a lot of other helping professions, which have a huge emphasis on confidentiality. For example, if we suspect that a man is going to become violent and a woman is at risk, we would contact her.

Bernard: Contact with the men's partners is a crucial element in increasing the safety of women. This strategy brings its own dangers and its implementation is enormously important. Checks on the woman's safety in participating in a partner contact activity and respect for her wishes in this process are essential to the success of this strategy. We ensure that the women are knowledgeable about the program and the material that the men are exposed to. We ensure that they are aware of the uses and potential abuses of program materials and that they have safety plans in place. We refer them to other services in our community. Furthermore, we work with the men to help them develop their plans for keeping their partners and children safe.

> *"When physical abuse decreases, psychological abuse also decreases."*

Golden: It is my belief that the approaches within a feminist framework help increase the safety of the women. The only other element that can significantly increase a woman's safety is if the woman is receiving counselling. Counselling for women whose partners are in a men's program must concentrate not only on practical issues, such as safety plans, and on therapeutic issues such as women finding their voice and reclaiming their power; but counselling for women must

> *"The treatment group showed: more positive behavioural and cognitive skills for coping with anger . . . [and] lower physical and emotional abuse levels."*

deconstruct the hope that women feel when the men are in the program. It is my experience that even though a man is either voluntarily or involuntarily taking part in a program, it is dangerous for women to lose their self-focus by focusing on the hope that the program will help them and their partner. It is a very difficult thing for a man to stop controlling and abusive behaviour to a point where he and his partner will be engaged in an equal and mutually beneficial relationship. If a woman focuses her energy on the hope that the group will cure him, then she is more likely to stay in the relationship even if he is not changing. She may not put as much effort into planning for and keeping herself safe, because 'after all, things aren't as bad now and I need to support him because he is getting help.'

Hamilton: The guiding principles specify some of the issues about women's safety. For example, we must start women's safety programs before beginning men's treatment programs. Then on-going contact is required for assessment purposes and to assure her safety. We can not allow ourselves to hear only the man's story; we have to have the courage and the intelligence to live with the conflict and the ambiguity of knowing the woman's experience. As the woman leader, I talk to the partners of the men in my group, so I know the pain of the woman. We keep contact during the program and have women's programs to help her, focusing on her safety and needs, not on the relationship needs or the man's needs. Although it is true that men are less likely to be violent while in a treatment program, a woman's safety is not assured. We encourage women not to make the Family Violence program their safety plan. We tell her, 'look at his behaviour, not at his attendance in the program because nothing is okay until he is okay'.

4. Do you find that men who abuse increase their emotional/psychologically abusive behaviour as they decrease physically abusive behaviour? How can/does your program address this issue?

Baskin: I would not say that there is an increase in emotionally or psychologically abusive behaviour. However, I would say that these are the forms of abuse that continue after men reduce their physically abusive behaviour. According to Aboriginal culture, abuse happens in different ways: emotional, physical, psychological and spiritual. Physical violence does not exist without these other forms of abuse—it all goes together. Our program works with the men on all of these areas. When we define what violence is, we include all four aspects. We are raising awareness with the men about those issues, getting them to identify their abusive behaviours in all of these forms of abuse, and teaching them how to stop these behaviours while learning new ways that foster equality.

Bernard: It is our basic assumption that this typically happens. Abusive behaviour does not just go away once a man starts our program and stops his physically abusive behaviour. Our program is designed to develop an increased awareness of all of the tactics of abusive power and control. It is designed to help each man discover how he manifests those tactics and how he can develop non-abusive and egalitarian alternatives.

Golden: I have found that it is a lot easier for men to reduce their physically abusive behaviour than to reduce their emotional/psychologically abusive behaviour. Many men have to do a lot of work just to be able to name their behaviour as controlling and abusive and detrimental to their partner if the behaviour is not *physically* abusive. Most men understand that if they hit their partners, it is abuse (even if they feel that it is in self-defense or use other minimizations). He undertakes countless behaviours that are emotionally/psychologically abusive in order to control his partner. If a man feels a need to control his partner, and he is focusing on not being physically abusive, he will often choose a non-physically abusive and controlling behaviour. The programs that I have been involved with address this issue by putting all controlling behaviours in the same abusive pot.

> *"The results are positive, showing that program participants' recidivism rates are half of non-participants."*

Women know that physical abuse and emotional/psychological abuse are equally destructive to them and their children. Many women find that the emotional/psychological abuse is more destructive than the physical because of its constant and sometimes subtle nature. If all of these behaviours are dealt with under the heading 'Power and Control', then they all become equally important to stop. The man needs to become aware of all abusive and controlling behaviours, their impact on his partner, and what he needs to do in order to choose to do something different with his feelings.

Hamilton: This has become an article of faith and yet there is no research to support this statement. In fact, the research shows just the opposite when physical abuse decreases, psychological abuse also decreases, but to a lesser degree. Formal evaluations of BC [British Columbia, Canada] programs show a significant reduction of psychological abuse, although not as large a reduction as physical abuse.

We have to ask ourselves where this belief comes from. Physical violence does not happen in isolation from psychological abuse. Rather, if we eliminate physical abuse, we are left with the enormous psychological abuse that already existed. This abuse is intolerable for the woman, so her experience is absolutely right. However, the emotional/psychological abuse is not born out of the reduction in physical violence because it was there all along. In addition, while a man may change a lot, he still may not be a healthy partner for the woman. If a program does not deal with psychological abuse, we should not expect a significant decrease. In our program, we are very up-front that a decrease in psychological/ emotional abuse is expected and we encourage women to raise their expectations.

5. What experience have you had with evaluating men's programs? What was the methodology? What were the results?

Baskin: We evaluate our men's program once a year. At the beginning and the end of each program cycle, we ask the men to complete a written set of measures about their understanding of violence and their abusive behaviours. Secondly, near the end of the cycle, the men complete a written evaluation form about what they have learned in the program and what changes they have made. Finally, near the end of the cycle, the men are interviewed by an independent researcher. The evaluation also includes information from partners, probation officers, other service providers, and people within the community.

We have just finished our third year and the results indicate that in three years, one man has re-offended.

Bernard: In the early 1990s, we ran a project for 2½ years, to assess our program participants over a period of one year. The research measured a number of behavioural and attitudinal variables in program participants at the time of intake, at the end of the treatment, and approximately one year after the intake. The treatment sample consisted of men who were defined as 'program completers' (men who attended more than 75% of the program) and the control sample were men who had dropped out of the program after three sessions or less. Information was collected from the men themselves, from counsellors and from partners. Data analysis showed significant differences between the treatment and control group in a few areas. The treatment group showed: more positive behavioural and cognitive skills for coping with anger; less maladaptive behaviour and arousal intensity; lower physical and emotional abuse levels; and less traditional views of marriage and family.

We currently have a doctoral candidate conducting research in our program examining characteristics and process of change in program participants. We expect to learn what combinations of characteristics of men and aspects of our program are most likely to lead to positive outcomes.

Golden: I have had no real quantifiable experience in evaluating men's programs. Keeping in contact with the partners of men who abuse and being able to keep in touch with their experience, both in terms of their growth, and his behaviour, seem to me to be a particularly effective way of measuring success.

Hamilton: In the past year, we decided that we will make outcome evaluation an integral part of the program, rather than relying on external evaluations. Our aim is to try to provide indicators of success within the limitations of budget and expertise of a small non-profit agency. What we need to do is admit that we can not prove the success of men's programs, but we can provide strong indicators of success.

We contact the men who complete our program and their partners at 6 month and 18 month intervals after he has completed the first phase. As well as collecting data, this intervention allows supportive contact with the woman and it may increase her safety. It serves as a reminder to the man and may bring him back into treatment if there is a need for it. We are planning to add a three-year follow-up and to compare men who drop out before completing the first phase.

The most interesting indicator is what the woman says; particularly those who have frequent contact with the man. 59% of the couples still live together while 23% live apart but are still in a relationship. It is important to ask the question, 'do you feel safer as a result of his attendance in the program?' In a pilot study of 17 interviews, 100% said they felt safer. This may be either because he has changed or that she ended the relationship. We consider this a success. None of the women interviewed reported physical abuse and 77% reported a decrease in psychological abuse.

The BC Ministry of Attorney General tracks recidivism rates and the results are positive, showing that program participants' recidivism rates are half of non-participants. So these are very positive indicators of success of men's treatment programs, especially when compared to other efforts to change human behaviour.

The Violence Against Women Act Is Necessary to Protect Women

by Judith Resnik

About the author: *Judith Resnik is the Arthur Litman Professor of Law at Yale Law School and coauthor of an amicus brief supporting the constitutionality of the Violence Against Women Act.*

Why, when the issue is violence against women, do some people talk about sex? While some violence directed at women is sexualized, calling it "sex" softens the brutality, implicates the victim as possibly an inciter or a participant, and offers the perpetrator the justification of lust.

Think also about the phrase "domestic violence." True, a good deal of violence against women does occur inside houses, but the coziness assumed to reside within the "domestic" stands in contrast to the cruelty of violence imposed by someone so close.

Linking violence against women to sex and domestic life illustrates more than a problem of rhetoric; it demonstrates the ongoing effects of laws that have treated women unequally. For centuries, state laws wove notions of sex and domesticity into a fabric of toleration of violence against women. And now that federal law is trying to protect women from the residue of that discrimination, objectors are arguing that federal remedies are unconstitutional—because violence against women is about sex and the home, which they say are state, not federal, concerns.

The Sanctity of the Home

Two centuries ago, husbands had the prerogative of beating their wives. One century ago, state courts constructed rules about the sanctity of the home, thereby justifying under a rubric of privacy a reluctance to interfere when men beat or raped their wives. Indeed, up until about 10 years ago, under the United

Judith Resnik, "Citizenship and Violence," *The American Prospect*, vol. 11, March 27–April 10, 2000, pp. 62–64. Copyright © 2000 by *The American Prospect*. Reproduced by permission.

States military code, a man could not be convicted of the rape of his wife because the code defined rape as "the act of sexual intercourse with a female not his wife, by force and without her permission."

In short, the law decided which harms against women were tolerable. And even when those exemptions no longer exist, police, prosecutors, juries, and judges continue to be influenced by the long-standing assumption that women do not have rights of bodily integrity equal to those of men.

But law is not static. Particularly when civil rights are at issue, Congress has often enabled groups that have suffered discrimination under state laws to turn to federal courts for protection.

States' Rights vs. Federal Law

Recall that after the Civil War, some states did not allow African Americans to marry. When Congress considered federal remedies, some opponents responded that marriage was a matter of "domestic relations"—outside the purview of Congress. Congress concluded otherwise; federal civil rights law guaranteed newly freed slaves the right to marry.

In the early part of the twentieth century, labor's opponents argued that employment relations were personal relations, a matter for state, not federal, governance; but Congress began to pass labor laws, including legislation protecting the right of workers to unionize.

These federal laws now seem unremarkable. Yet in a case currently before the U.S. Supreme Court, opponents of the Violence Against Women Act (VAWA), passed by Congress in 1994, are once again raising the familiar themes of personal relations and states' rights.

VAWA Has Federal Provisions

Congress enacted VAWA after four years of hearings and many revisions; it crafted a multifaceted statute that provides substantial funding to state, tribal, and local programs to combat violence against women. VAWA also authorizes federal criminal prosecutions in limited circumstances, for example, if a person crosses state lines to harm an intimate partner already protected by a permanent state court order. And VAWA includes a new civil rights remedy for victims of gender-based violence akin to the remedy already on the books for race discrimination: VAWA lets plaintiffs sue assailants for damages, in either state or federal court, upon proof that a crime of violence was motivated by "animus based on gender."

Now at issue before the Supreme Court is the constitutionality of this one aspect of VAWA, the civil remedy.[1] Thus far, most of the federal judges who have considered it have upheld it. However, one federal appellate court, the Fourth Circuit, thought otherwise, holding that neither the Constitution's Commerce

1. On May 15, 2002, the Supreme Court ruled that the civil remedy of VAWA was not constitutional.

Clause nor the 14th Amendment enabled Congress to create federal court remedies for victims of gender-based violence. . . .

The Majority of States Favor the VAWA

The Fourth Circuit's view that VAWA harms states' rights is not shared by many representatives of state government. When the legislation was pending, the attorneys general of 38 states told Congress that VAWA's civil rights provisions would be a useful supplement to—not a displacement of—state remedies. At the time, few laws in the United States still expressly exculpated men who had attacked their wives. But many prosecutors worried that the residue of both legal and social attitudes about violence against women results in systematically less protection for women victims of violence than for men.

> *"For centuries, state laws wove notions of sex and domesticity into a fabric of toleration of violence against women."*

States did more than worry. In the 1980s and 1990s, the chief justices of more than half the states commissioned task forces to explore the treatment of women in their courts. What they learned was powerful and disheartening. Connecticut's task force concluded, for example, that "women are treated differently from men in the justice system, and because of it, many suffer from unfairness." From states as different as California, Georgia, Maryland, Minnesota, and Kentucky, reports came that women victims of violence faced special hurdles—their claims of injury were often discounted, their testimony often disbelieved.

The record of systemic discrimination was before Congress when it enacted VAWA. And that record explains why, in 1999, the National Association of Attorneys General supported the reauthorization of VAWA and 36 states signed onto a brief filed in the current Supreme Court case, urging that the civil rights remedy be upheld. (Only one state—Alabama—argued for invalidation.)

State and Federal Law Often Overlap

Power is surely at stake here, but not only how to allocate it between state and federal governments. Also at issue is the Supreme Court's ability to override congressional enactments. Will the Court now ignore congressional fact-finding and substitute its own? Will it change its current interpretation of the Commerce Clause and cut back on Congress's power to legislate in this sphere?

To understand why the Court should not, first focus on the Fourth Circuit's argument that violence against women is about sex, crimes, family life, and the home, and that states have exclusive dominion here. That claim is untrue, and as policy it would be unwise.

Federal law oversees state criminal law and family law in a variety of contexts. States cannot, for example, enforce criminal laws discriminatorily, nor can they forbid interracial marriage. Outside the domain of civil rights, many other federal laws define and structure relations that could be termed "domestic"—like welfare law (requiring beneficiaries to work, so that children need to be in child care programs), the Equal Retirement Income Security Act (creating marital property rights in pensions), or tax law (defining economic obligations by reference to marital status).

The point is not that Congress has taken over state law, but rather that state and federal governance—overlapping, often cooperative—is the norm in virtually all fields of human endeavor in the United States, family life and criminal law included.

Violence Restricts Work

Second, focus on Congress's powers over interstate commerce. Since the 1930s, the Constitution has been understood as permitting Congress to regulate not only commercial transactions themselves but activities substantially related to commerce. Since the 1960s, the Constitution has been understood as permitting Congress to remove obstacles to engaging in commerce—especially discriminatory obstacles. Before enacting VAWA, Congress heard testimony from both business executives and individuals detailing not only that violence has an economic effect on the GDP, but that violence against women limits women's full participation as economic actors. Congress learned both that women were beaten to prevent them from going to work and that the threat of violence restricted women's employment options.

At the time, VAWA's opponents predicted its civil rights remedy would open the floodgates to lawsuits having little or nothing to do with commerce. Yet to date, only about 50 decisions have been reported under the civil rights remedy, and of those, more than 40 percent involved allegations of attacks in commercial or educational settings. Indeed, the case before the Supreme Court involves a young woman allegedly raped by two students at her college, one of whom explained publicly that he liked to "get girls drunk and fuck the shit out of them."

Women Are Entitled to Equal Protection

Third, consider Congress's power to enforce the 14th Amendment, forbidding states to deny equal protection of the laws. Opponents of VAWA argue that violence inflicted by individuals is a private act, not state action. But state laws have failed to protect women's physical security equally with men's. State prosecutors have told Congress that inequality continues. Congress can therefore fashion proportionate remedies, as it has done before to protect blacks from racially motivated violence.

VAWA, in other words, is an ordinary exercise of congressional powers, executed in a "federalism-friendly" fashion to provide complementary means of rights enforcement. Its opponents want to identify women with the home, focus on violence in bedrooms, and confine a woman's remedies to whatever is available in the locality in which she finds herself. What they fail to understand is that the federal government has an obligation to secure women's physical safety and to protect women's rights to participate in the national economy free from the threat of targeted violence. VAWA is not about sex, and it is not about a family any of us would want to be in; citizenship in the nation is what is at stake.

Changing Male Attitudes Reduces Sexual Violence

by Andy Peck

About the author: *Andy Peck is the youth coordinator for Men Stopping Violence, an Atlanta, Georgia, social change organization dedicated to ending men's violence against women.*

Editor's Note: This viewpoint was excerpted from the closing keynote address delivered at the Target Violence: A Time to Air It Out conference in Valdosta, Georgia.

I've been asked to talk about sexual violence prevention today. . . .

Maybe it goes without saying that hope is something all of us need in our work—especially work against violence and abuse, work that can be so emotionally and spiritually taxing, which can be so discouraging.

To begin this discussion about hope, I want to share a quote with you, one that has both haunted and inspired me. This is a passage written by Andrea Benton Rushing, taken from an account of her process of healing and recovery after a man raped her while she was living in Georgia. She writes:

> In movie and television versions of rape, the problems are that people think you seduced the man, the police are sexistly hostile, hospital staff are icily callous, but my ordeal wasn't going that way at all. In my apartment, the Georgia police officers who look and sound like rednecks treat me with a courtesy nothing in my childhood summers in segregated . . . Florida, or . . . Alabama, prepared me for. I'm questioned gently. Did I recognize the rapist? A boyfriend? Someone who'd stalked me? Was he a college student my daughter and her friend knew? Did we have oral sex? Anal sex? Did he bite me? They accept my word that I've never seen the man before and don't even ask if I tried to fight him off. At the hospital, the in-take clerk, crisis counselor, lab technician, nurse, doctor, billing clerk are all considerably consoling. At the time I don't notice, but a week later their behavior upsets me. There is, I tell

sympathizers, no plan to end rape. People are just refining their treatment of the inevitable.

I think this is a very challenging and important passage. It offers a perspective I have not often heard but that I suspect is more commonly experienced than it is spoken.

Andrea Benton Rushing describes her experience with people like many of us in this room today—police officers, nurses, hospital staff, crisis counselors. Something about this experience is upsetting to her. I don't think the story here is the failure or futility of those who try to help her, or survivors of rape in general. I think the compassion and care she describes are lifted up. Too often, we know that the experience of

> *"There is . . . no plan to end rape."*

survivors is to be disbelieved, bullied, and harassed in ways that serve as a kind of re-victimization. It has great meaning when we go about our work and our lives in ways that communicate dignity and respect for survivors of sexual violence. It matters.

And maybe the author's mention of race caught your attention? I wondered about leaving it out, or using another passage. I worried about that actually. But, no, here is a woman, a black woman, living in Georgia, who is appreciative (if, yes, surprised) that white police officers could treat her with such courtesy, of a kind she did not experience as a child living in segregation. I thought about finding another passage. Yet, while it is generally uncomfortable to do so, I believe that we need to realize that race and racism shape how people respond to the issue of sexual violence—usually for the worse. This is a time where racism does not stand in the way of compassion and care for someone who needs it.

A Plan to End Rape Is Needed

Yet, despite all that goes well in her account, Andrea Benton Rushing seems to be saying: it is not enough. As a survivor, she wants to know there is "a plan to end rape." Why? What does she mean? . . .

At the rape crisis center [I work at]—at rape crisis centers all over the state and the country—survivors continued to call looking for help and support—in the same numbers, distressingly high numbers. Volunteer crisis counselors continued to make regular trips to the hospital. We continued to hear that the police could be sexist and hostile. We continued to hear that hospital staff could be icy and callous. From that perspective, this whole "plan to end rape" thing just seems pretty pie in the sky. . . .

Maybe the question posed by Andrea Benton Rushing can be approached a little differently. I want to suggest that the question, for me, and maybe for you, is: Are we here today talking about the inevitable? Are we "refining our treatment of the inevitable," as she describes?

Pay attention to how you feel when I say this: rape is inevitable.

This is what Andrea Benton Rushing heard and felt, even as people helped and cared for her. This is what is upsetting. I think it's similar to what we hear when someone tells a joke about rape. I think it's similar to what we hear when people say that rape is human nature, that it's "natural": you know, it's awful but it simply can't be helped. I think it's similar to what we hear when people tell stories about rape that are full of pity: how sad, but what can be done?

What we hear, generally speaking, is that rape is inevitable. And this is oppressive. It is depressing. Even so, many police officers, hospital staff, and crisis counselors, many people nevertheless try to do things to lessen the impact, to minimize the damage. We try to do the right thing, and we do. But maybe something is missing? Something so important? . . .

Rape Is Never Inevitable

You should care about sexual violence prevention because it has something to do with hope. This hope is the hope that rape is not inevitable. Ever. Anywhere.

Now, to me, hope and optimism are not the same. I have hope that we will see a world free of rape. I am not optimistic that this will be soon. There is a lot of sexual violence in this society and few resources devoted to ending it. Yet, to me, there is substantial ground for hope. There have been societies in the past that have been free of rape. There can be again. . . .

> *"In my heart I believe that a world free of rape is possible."*

In my heart I believe that a world free of rape is possible. I have that hope. I believe that human beings are better than that. I believe that we can travel up river, so to speak, to the sources of this trouble and deal with it. And I think that's why I work in prevention. Rape is not inevitable. I absolutely believe this. And I try to put that faith into action. When you get right down to it, that's what "prevention" means to me. . . .

Sexual violence prevention in general, and especially the kind of prevention I want to discuss, is a new and still poorly supported idea. Part of the story here is that to the extent that rape is a matter of public concern today at all, this is a result of the violence against women movement. And how old is this movement? Tracing origins is tricky. But the first rape crisis center was established in [Georgia] in 1974, less than 30 years ago. In DeKalb County, our center is less than 15 years old. The rape crisis center here in Valdosta [Georgia] is about 6 years old. In other parts of the state, for all practical purposes, this movement has not existed.

So, the kind of sexual violence prevention that I want to discuss is new. It is premised on an idea that has been promoted by the violence against women movement and is also new: that rape is not acceptable under ANY circumstances—whether between strangers, acquaintances, on a date, within a marriage, within a family, etc. . . .

Rape Is Never Acceptable

But now, what happens when the idea that rape is unacceptable under ANY circumstances becomes a matter of public concern, of social policy, for all of us? Especially in light of the fact that between 65% and 85% of sexual assaults occur not between strangers but in situations where the perpetrator and victim know one another, this can be a very challenging thing to get people to accept. But this is what activists who helped to found rape crisis centers, raise awareness, and the rest of it have wanted to find out—whether it was possible for a society to say, as a collective, rape is not acceptable under ANY circumstances.

And the idea of prevention has been born. For, if rape is not acceptable, if we are serious about that, then it is to be challenged and eventually stopped. Or, put another way, and even better, it is to be stopped before it starts.

The promotion of this idea has not necessarily worked smoothly. There have been and are significant differences of opinion about what "prevention" means. For example, in 1973—just a year before that first rape crisis center was established at Grady Memorial Hospital—the Governor of Georgia ran a Crime Prevention Month campaign. In that campaign was featured a poster that read, "If you get raped, it might be your fault." This particular campaign, apparently targeted mainly to women, didn't last long, given protests from the Governor's own Commission on the Status of Women and others. In fact, the debate the campaign generated gave momentum to folks working to address rape in a different way. But this message is probably pretty familiar to most of us, even if we didn't catch it back in 1973. We still hear it today. The way of thinking behind that 1973 campaign is still pervasive.

If you get raped, it might be your fault . . . because you wore that dress . . . because you "led him on" . . . because you went out alone with him . . . because you had that drink . . . because you didn't say "no" loudly enough or often enough. The prevention message is, prevention in this case means: don't wear that dress, don't "lead him on," don't go out alone at night, don't drink, say "no" more loudly and more often . . . know your enemy and learn to protect yourself.

I assume that the Governor's office went about this campaign with good intentions—just as I assume that people who promote similar messages today have good intentions. The intention of the message is to protect potential victims, to keep

> *"Rape is not acceptable under ANY circumstances—whether between strangers, acquaintances, on a date, within a marriage, within a family."*

people safe. Yet I think folks protested the Governor's campaign because it stated rather bluntly that at least in a significant number of cases rape is the victim's fault. The message intends to protect potential victims, but in fact mainly what it does is blame them. The person it actually protects is the person who commits a sexual assault, by excusing his sexually aggressive choices.

Primary Prevention

This is not the prevention message I came to sell you on today. The kind of prevention that I want to talk about is sometimes called "primary prevention.". . .

I am asking, to the extent that we suggest that potential victims—primarily women and children—are the first line of prevention . . . to the extent that we suggest that raising their awareness and encouraging their behavior change is the first line of prevention: What's the message in that for men? What are men's roles and responsibilities—as potential perpetrators, or as the fathers, uncles, brothers,

> *"Rape generally happens, primarily because boys and men learn to turn off or disregard this gut feeling, that sick feeling."*

coaches, teachers, and peers of potential perpetrators? What are we as a people doing to prevent sexual aggression in men? What are we as men doing to confront it in ourselves and in other men? . . .

Not long ago, I did some work with young men at a youth detention center. While young men in this setting are often unfairly stigmatized as delinquents and criminals and other things, the young men I worked with in that detention center were not so different from any of the other young men I work with in schools or after-school programs or churches. I think that's important to remember.

In any case, at one point, one of the young men in the group named Robert told a story. I say "young men" though Robert is only 13. He didn't call it this, but the story was in my opinion about a gang rape. According to Robert, who was 11 at the time, a twelve-year-old girl "led" a group of boys and young men into the basement of his home. In this group were 4 or 5 others, including Robert's older cousin and an older brother—the oldest in the group was 16 or 17, Robert said. He said that in the basement this girl began to take off her clothes, and the rest of the group took this as a sign that she wanted to have sex with them. Apparently, all of them did, except Robert.

Why Robert Said No to Rape

Robert said that when the girl began to take her clothes off, he left. I asked him why—especially since older boys, including an older brother and cousin that he was likely to look up to, participated. He said he left because his gut told him it was wrong, because he had a sick feeling about it. Robert didn't call this a rape, but I believe that it was. Not just because she was 12, I don't believe that this girl could have meaningfully consented to what was happening—not in the basement with 4 or 5 older, bigger, stronger boys, not in the presence of other circumstances of force and coercion that Robert either failed to mention or didn't know about. Robert described a gang rape and how he refused to participate in it.

There is more to the story. Robert said something else. He said that if the girl had been 16, he would have stayed and participated in the rape.

Assuming he is telling the truth both about why he left and the conditions under which he would have participated in the assault—but, actually, even if he's not—I think there are at least two very important lessons for us contained in Robert's story.

One is that if rape is to be stopped or prevented, that primarily depends on the choices that men and boys like Robert make. Robert told me that he refused to participate in a gang rape even though in his characterization the girl led the boys into the basement and began to take her own clothes off. He could have attempted, though it would have been wrong, to blame her and hold her responsible for the choices he or other boys were making. He could have said, "If she got raped, it was her fault." But he didn't. The choices those boys made determined whether or not a sexual assault would occur in that basement. Robert proved that by leaving. The other boys proved that by committing the assault. This is the first lesson of Robert's story.

Lack of Empathy Makes Rape OK

The second lesson of the story is that this rape happened, that rape generally happens, primarily because boys and men learn to turn off or disregard this gut feeling, that sick feeling that led Robert out of that basement.

What is this feeling? It may be a sense of right and wrong. I want to think that at a deeper level, it is empathy. It is the ability to see your own humanity in another person's, to try to put yourself in their shoes, to imagine and let yourself feel what they may be feeling or are about to feel. That gut feeling is the biological reminder to treat others with respect, to treat others as you would be treated—and of the principle that human beings are connected, that what we do affects others.

Many people learn to turn off feelings of empathy, or at least disregard them. How? Why? I think there's an important clue in Robert's comment—that if this girl had been 16, he would have stayed. If she had been 16, it would have been OK. . . .

> *"There is so much rape because we teach boys that it is basically OK to rape, to be sexually aggressive."*

I believe Robert's statement reflects the fact that when he draws the line, he is not ultimately using his gut feeling—his empathy, his natural inclination to treat others with dignity and respect. Where he draws the line, in this case, is actually where he turns this feeling off. When Robert draws the line between acceptable sexual behavior and rape, he's not making a distinction between aggressive and consensual sexual behavior. When he draws the line, he is making a distinction between legitimate and illegitimate targets for aggressive sexual behavior—with either denial or lack of concern about the harms that will result. A 12-year-old is not a legitimate target. A 16-year-old is. For this 12-

year-old girl, in this case, that distinction means a lot. For a 16-year-old in her place, it means Robert would probably choose to rape her. . . .

Boys Learn That Rape Is OK

At the risk of over-simplifying a complicated problem, Robert's attitude reflects that there is so much rape because we teach boys that it is basically OK to rape, to be sexually aggressive, especially when this behavior is directed at the so-called "right target." Then, enough of these boys, usually after they've grown into men, find the freedom to act on this belief, at the rate of 100,000s of assaults every year in this country.

Who is the "right target"? In figuring it out, a boy can listen to his gut, which is likely to tell him there is no "right target"—that what he intends to do to another person is the problem and is unacceptable under ANY circumstances. If he learns to listen to his gut, that biological reminder to treat others with dignity and respect, he will not be sexually violent. But he may rape if what his gut tells him is overridden by what he learns from the aggressive mentality and behavior of other men around him. Or if what his gut tells him is overridden because the larger culture and society teaches him that to be a man is to be someone who doesn't take "no" for an answer—a man who takes what he wants, a man who's in charge at all costs, a man who is entitled to sex when and where he wants it. If that is what he learns, then there's a high likelihood that he'll be sexually violent. If he learns that women and girls are sex objects and not partners, there's little chance that empathy will kick in to stop him.

Many boys come to basically accept a sexually aggressive mentality. And they learn how to justify aggressive behavior, like Robert does, as the larger culture does, by blaming the victim—to sort women and girls into "good girls" and "bad girls.". . .

Sexual Violence Prevention Works Through Education

Yet someone who meets all the criteria of a "good girl"—as difficult as this may be, as much effort as this may require—can still be raped. The existence of categories of "good girls" and "bad girls" isn't a truth about women or girls, and certainly not about who is raped. It is evidence of the excuses our culture makes for the persistence of rape.

Without a rapist, there is no rape. So, why would we say: "If you get raped, it might be your fault?" How could this ever be true? It can never be true. We may have the best of intentions, but one of the functions of this statement is always to protect the rapist, to make excuses for him—or, if that is hard to see or accept, the function to protect ourselves from dealing with him, from directly confronting his sexual aggression and sexual aggression generally. . . .

What is primary sexual violence prevention? It is working—through education and other means—to affect the choices of those who commit sexual violence or are likely to do so, bringing about attitude and behavior change that will reduce and eventually end the incidence of rape. This is why it is so important to work with men and boys. Sexual violence prevention is providing boys like Robert with the awareness, guidance and accountability they need to treat all people with dignity and respect—to learn to always listen to that gut feeling rooted in empathy and compassion.

In discussing prevention as I have, I'm suggesting that men's roles and responsibilities are clear and compelling. They are clear and compelling as long as we keep the truth about sexual violence, and our hope that it can end, right here in front of us. Because part of this truth is that men are in the best position to end rape. . . .

> *"Sexual violence prevention is providing boys . . . with the awareness, guidance and accountability they need to treat all people with dignity and respect."*

My co-worker and I were at the detention center for four weeks, four sessions, confronting particular beliefs and behaviors, working toward attitude and behavior change. As a member of the group, we were able to engage Robert pretty directly, face-to-face about beliefs and attitudes that have a high likelihood of leading him to be sexually violent. I think we provided him with the right message and clearly presented the issue of male responsibility.

We were there as older men that he might identify as role models—older men who were telling and showing him something very different from what he saw in that basement. I distinctly remember telling him to pay close attention to that feeling in his gut that led him out of the basement, lifting up his decision and encouraging him to carry it through in all of his relationships and in every situation. He seemed engaged and moved by what we had to say and by the process. He seemed to hear it and take it in. . . .

Sexual Aggression Is Celebrated

Soon enough, Robert will leave the detention center, and return home—rejoining the neighborhoods and schools where most boys and young men live most of the time. He will still be 13, still learning what it means to be a man. Remember that two of the young men in that basement were Robert's older brother and cousin. He may wish for others, we might wish he had others, but they will continue to be potential role-models for him. What will Robert learn from them, or others—again, not in a few hours, but months and years? What will he learn from seeing violence and disrespect toward women—at home or in the neighborhood or on TV? What will he learn from pornography, a $10 billion/year industry that most boys will experience?

We can't be sure what Robert will take as an individual from these kinds of experiences. He always has choices. To some extent, it will always be up to him. But we need to take an honest look at the world most boys are living in. It may require real effort and real courage to look at this honestly. We may resist doing it. But we need to do it. What we find, I think, is that by-and-large boys don't find a lot of reinforcement for what prevention programs might teach about personal responsibility and nonviolence. In fact, they often find the opposite. Sexual aggression in men is regularly condoned and celebrated. Sexual aggression is rooted in traditional norms of masculinity that value dominance and control over others. Sexual aggression is reinforced by pervasive violence and abuse of power of all kinds in this society—in business, in government, in the military. Sexual aggression is itself profitable—through pornography and other industries of explotation. . . .

Rape Behavior Can Be Unlearned

To create education and intervention programs whose goal is behavior and attitude change among boys and young men is the right focus. This is the right thing to do. But, to ask whether these programs alone successfully create attitude and behavior change among their individual participants is the wrong question. It is the wrong question because, in evaluating and understanding the role and effectiveness of these programs, it is important to understand that while they can contribute to the change process for participants they are not solely—or even primarily—responsible for it.

We need to make reinforcement of the prevention message at the heart of these programs part of other institutions that will be in Robert's life. The prevention programs I do with young men and boys seek to engage them in a process of change and growth. For this process to be sustained, these young men and boys and the programs themselves need to be brought into more fundamental social change involving schools, families, neighborhoods, religious institutions, and much more. Until the social and cultural life organized by each of these institutions consistently supports principles of personal responsibility, community, and nonviolence, we have little hope of ending rape.

"Rape is learned behavior and it can be unlearned."

Rape is not inevitable. Rape is not acceptable under ANY circumstances. Rape is a choice. And as we examine the sources that inform this choice, we see that rape is learned behavior and it can be unlearned. Just as our culture and society puts the thought of rape into the heads of boys and men, changes in the culture and society can make rape unthinkable. We need to have that hope.

Mandatory Arrest Laws Do Not Reduce Domestic Violence

by John Klofas

About the author: *John Klofas is a professor of criminal justice and chair of the criminal justice department at the Rochester Institute of Technology in Rochester, New York.*

Domestic violence is a major social problem. Although we fear violence from strangers the most, it's the people we live with that pose the greatest danger—and its women who suffer the most at the hands of their partners.

In about 15% of all murders that are not committed by total strangers, the killer is the spouse, former spouse, boyfriend or girlfriend of the victim. When you look only at murders of women over 18 years old, fully half the victims are killed by their husband, former husband or boyfriend.

Look beyond murder and the statistics are still more alarming. Each year one and half million women and half a million men require medical attention as a result of violence in the home. Pull the curtain back further and the best estimates are that physical assaults occur among as many as two out of three American couples—although most of those assaults are minor—involving slaps or plate throwing—and infrequent over the course of the relationship.

Domestic violence requires condemnation and its victims must know that help is available. For moral and practical reasons, it's good to have this problem out in the open. When a local group of criminal justice officials and women's advocates announced Domestic Violence Prevention Month at a press conference [in 1998] it helped accomplish those goals.

Mandatory Arrest and Prosecution Does Not Work

But there's a mantra for this movement that is troubling—zero tolerance. It calls for defining all domestic assaults as crimes and using the criminal justice system to its maximum—with mandatory arrest and mandatory prosecution.

Supporters of zero tolerance make two claims. They say the criminal justice system ignored domestic violence, and especially its women victims, for too long. And they claim that mandatory arrest and prosecution works. It protects victims and prevents further violence. On the first point the zero tolerance advocates are right. On the second, the best evidence says they are wrong.

Through the 1970s the police response to "family troubles" rarely included arrest. It was official policy that arrest was to be reserved only for the most serious cases of assault.

From the vantage point of 1998, the past pattern of under-enforcement is clear. One 1977 study of police practices across three communities, including Rochester [New York], showed that arrests were made in only 22% of all family assault cases. Other studies showed similar deficiencies.

It was the rising power of the women's movement that led to questions about the policies behind such statistics. They argued that mostly male police officers were discriminating against mostly female victims in favor of mostly male offenders. That conclusion now seems accurate. But we should also recognize that, in that era, there was a whole lot less policing going on. There is also evidence of under-enforcement, by today's standards, in many other areas including drunk driving, drugs, larceny, fighting and other non-stranger assaults.

The Women's Movement Demanded Mandatory Arrests

It was women's advocates who first rejected mediation and called for zero tolerance. And, in 1984 they got a big boost. Researchers in Minneapolis [Minnesota] took a hard look at the effects of mediation versus arrest.

In an unusual social science experiment, responses to domestic violence calls to police were randomly assigned: in some cases the police would make an arrest, in others they counseled the parties, in still others the perpetrator was sent away from the home for a minimum of eight hours. Later, interviews with victims and examination of police records showed that arrest was the most likely intervention to reduce future violence. The study's authors, led by Lawrence Sherman, cautiously endorsed a pro-arrest policy.

These results and recommendations were widely reported even before the research was published. Based on the study and a supportive political climate, police departments adopted mandatory arrest policies in droves. State legislatures passed laws requiring arrest. And the rate of arrest for simple assault soared.

"Mandatory arrest policies don't protect the victims of domestic violence."

But long before New York State joined the herd in 1994, a whole different story had emerged from the research. Good science calls for repeating studies in different settings and under different conditions. When the Minneapolis experiment was repeated in other cities a more complicated picture emerged.

Arrest Deters Only Middle-Class Batterers

There were two important findings. First, arrest reduces domestic violence among employed people but increases it among unemployed people. Class matters. The deterrent power of the police works in the middle classes but backfires among the poor who have less to lose. Second, arrest can reduce violence in the short term but it can increase it in the long run. According to the research, arrest resulted in a doubling of the rate of violence within a year.

Other studies also complicate the picture. It turns out that most serious perpetrators of domestic violence are a lot like other serious criminals. Their violence at home is just part of the violence that they engage in everywhere. They have extensive criminal records and they stand out as different from most other spousal abusers.

> *"The research is clear, mandatory arrest and prosecution does not afford victims of domestic violence universal protection and may increase the danger for some."*

There is also a growing concern among researchers about the harm done by mandatory arrest policies. Murray Straus, perhaps the nation's leading scholar in the area and a past-president of the National Council on Family Relations, has argued against the overuse of criminal penalties. Such penalties can add to the strain on marriages while not protecting victims from serious assault. He and others stress the need to distinguish among cases of domestic violence and to treat different cases differently.

What does that mean for policy? No one is suggesting the return to the days of not-so-benign neglect. And a policy that would treat people differently based on their social class would be offensive. But good policies must address the complexity of a complex world. That's where zero tolerance fails.

Even the researchers who originally recommended mandatory arrest have changed their minds. They support repealing mandatory arrest laws and substituting the discretion of well-trained police officers. In today's climate, they say, we are unlikely to repeat the mistakes of the past.

The research that shows that mandatory arrest policies don't protect the victims of domestic violence is compelling and available to anyone with an interest in the subject. It is, however, largely avoided or ignored by those who push zero tolerance.

Perhaps it is ignored simply because the findings don't square with the experience of zero tolerance supporters. Many of them work in shelters where battered women can find refuge. Such places help the most victimized and most needy; the worst cases of abuse. If this explains the policy blind spot the lesson is simple and already known—extreme cases make for bad laws.

But that doesn't explain the wider acceptance of zero tolerance. Domestic violence policy illustrates how getting tough has become fashionable among a broad coalition of liberal and conservative groups. It illustrates how quick we are today to divide the world into good and evil, even when our own feet are made of clay. Remember that violence occurs in two thirds of all households.

So maybe reducing violence isn't the only or even the most important goal. Maybe our claims of pragmatism serve only to disguise our ideology. We like a world where good and evil are clear, and we will even go so far as to impose that clarity on others' most intimate relationships. Apparently we prefer punishment for the same reason; clarity not utility.

There may be many other ways to explain our acceptance of zero tolerance polices. Legitimate interests may be served by such policies. But the research is clear, mandatory arrest and prosecution does not afford victims of domestic violence universal protection and may increase the danger for some. Those facts should not be ignored, no matter what month it is.

Therapy for Abusers Does Not Help Reduce Domestic Violence

by Martin Dufresne

About the author: *Martin Dufresne is an adjunct professor in the department of criminology at the University of Ottawa in Canada and an internationally known researcher and writer in the area of domestic violence. He is also the secretary of Montreal Men Against Sexism.*

Whether it's called "therapy", "treatment", "counseling", "education", "intervention" or, non-committally, "programs", we are seeing unsupported speculation about "what makes men hit", and the overarching principle of supporting batterers rather than sanction them for their violence is sweeping the industrialized world. This diversion endeavor is achieved via so-called "batterers intervention programs" (BIPs), a low-cost, allegedly "moral" alternative to justice and security for women and to further disruption for the patriarchal system. This despite a dearth of evidence that such programs shield anyone but men from the consequences of wife battering.

Support programs for wife batterers were initiated in the USA in the early eighties as an "alternative" to judicial intervention against this most common form of violence—traditionally tolerated, ignored and often prescribed by a male-supremacist system. Since then, experimental BIPs have sprung up throughout North America, apparently whenever a man or an agency decided to give it a try. Such diversion programs are now being advocated for, referred to and handsomely funded as pilot projects in Europe and Australia. The development of diversion programs seems directly proportional to a) hostility to women's progress in having men held accountable for their "private" violence and, b) conservative administrations' concerns about divorce and the much-alleged demise of the patriarchal Family.

Indeed, the media, the judiciary and the State have endorsed sight unseen any type of BIPs as "the" solution, to the point where no feminist resource for battered women can today avoid being asked the question "But what do you do for the men?" With BIPs being conceptualized as men's right to their share of resources, pressure is being applied and funding is being held back or gutted on the pretext that it would be reverse discrimination not to support the perpetrator as much as his victim, not to direct women's efforts and men's power toward "alternatives" to the very solutions feminists have been advocating for, i.e. extending the reach of justice to men's private crimes against women, and providing entitlement, autonomy and do-or-die resources to the women on the front line of "family violence". . . . At best, BIP providers offer carefully worded optimistic floss ("BIPs can be effective"); at worst they broadcast far and wide grossly inflated claims of success. All of this appears to obfuscate or coddle corporate patrons, lawmakers, judges and the general public whose support for battered women remains hostage to misogynist ideology. In times of budget cutbacks and conservative frenzy over the demise of The Family, siding with batterers instead of sanctioning them, supporting men over women (and children) combines the imperatives of male-supremacist politics and of short-view economic savings.

Indeed these programs and their systematic promotion whenever the issue of male family violence is broached appear to systematically oppose and derail the feminist project of confronting and turning back the tide of male violence against women through substantive accountability for men's violence. Whatever "explanation" they offer for wife battering, BIPs can be seen to simply add allegedly new scientific/humanist sheen to very traditional explanations/attitudes toward male sexist violence. In a world that still resists the notion of men's accountability for assaults against women which they, after all, own in a heterosexist world, BIPs reaffirm and enshrine as "science" the principle that men are entitled to "change" at

> *"Judicial intervention and support for victims were more efficient than [therapy] programs at . . . stopping perpetrators from recidivism against their current victim."*

their own rate, if and how they feel like it, and only inasmuch as their self-interest is re-enshrined and protected as the outer limit of morality in gender relations. We feel that this reversal of feminist advocacy and renewed focus on male self-interest is especially lethal to the victims of intimate violence, implicitly invited to give their batterer yet another chance, to "take him back" for at least the length of the program, over and against their own experience, insights and choices.

This general context of society's acclaim for BIPs may explain why these initiatives' effectiveness in ending sexist violence seems taken for granted ("at least, something is being done"), or sensationalized by the media ("Our guest today is a reformed batterer"). And yet, since BIPs have had to rise to the notion of men's accountability for their actions, set by the feminist movement . . . it makes sense to insist on BIP providers' own accountability. This can be done

by exposing the limits and risks of the experimental "therapies" whose efficiency they misrepresent to woo funding agencies, the judicial system and batterers themselves, by insisting on independent assessment activities. In the
words of R. Karl Hanson and Liz Hart, authors of *The Evaluation of Treatment
Programs for Male Batterers:*

> If important decisions are going to be made based on whether a batterer at-
> tends treatment (e.g., partner stays or leaves, sentenced to jail or probation),
> then it becomes crucial to know the effectiveness of the treatment.

After all, these important decisions can and do cost women their lives. Men
who claim to want to change abusive men should be the first to be or be made
accountable.

In Their Own Words

In the early nineties, Hanson and Hart organized in Ottawa, Canada, a conference bringing together most of the field's North American researchers and prac-
titioners. The following is a point-form presentation of various candid accounts
by conference participants of the limits and risks of their very own programs
for wife batterers, albeit the best in the field by all standards. The supporting
quotes from the conference proceedings appear in our text "Limits and Risks of
Programs for Wife Batterers."

Most of the conference speakers concurred that judicial intervention and support for victims were more efficient than their programs at achieving their stated
aim, stopping perpetrators from recidivism against their current victim. One
only wish that they would be as forthright in their published articles, funding requests and promotion work for BIPs in general or for their specific program.

A realistic psychological exploration of batterer dynamics—men's socially-
sanctioned and lucrative hatred and control of women—remains absent from
these programs, censored from the start as "feminist ideology." This alone is
reason enough to challenge them. For what now presents itself as psychological
theory and practice eludes the actual dynamics of the situation and is much
closer to masculinist politics than to a progressive and indeed realistic analysis
of the dynamics of sexist violence.

Here then is a summary of various points made during conference sessions by the program providers and analysts that convened at the 1990
Ottawa conference assessing the effi-
ciency of "therapies":

> *"Although programs are
> marketed as 'therapy,' research
> has yet to identify any
> pathology in wife battering."*

• Most program providers have neither the time nor the resources to correctly
assess their program's efficiency
  • They feel that a valid assessment would prove ponderous and costly
  • Comparative assessments of programs remain few and far-between

• Experimentation and improvisation remain the rule: an efficient or sufficiently integrated approach to wife-battering has yet to be identified
• Significant questions are being raised concerning the competency and training of most programs' session leaders

Fundamental Problems Exist

• There is no universally acknowledged approach to "treating" batterers or understanding of their process
• Dangerous, victim-blaming theoretical models abound
• A social problem of epidemic proportion is being ignored by BIPs' focus on the individual
• Intrapersonal explanation factors are being grossly over-represented
• Although programs are marketed as "therapy", research has yet to identify any pathology in wife battering
• Attempts to identify a characteristic "batterer profile" on which to base a clinical approach have failed
• Over-represented variables may point to consequences, rather than causes, of battering
• For example, contrary to common media representation, depression has not been shown to be causal factor of battering
• Neither is battering an anger problem, despite the facts that most BIPs build on "anger management" problems. Batterer rarely hit people more powerful than themselves, e.g. bosses or cops
• Stress has not been shown to be the problem either
• Nor is violence visited upon the perpetrator as a child
• Contrary to another common myth, wife batterers suffer no lack of skills
• Recidivism remains impossible to predict in the current psychological paradigm
• Although most programs aim for attitudinal change, providers remain in the dark about how the desired attitude changes might influence recidivism if they were to be attained
• Treatment models still can't integrate the fact that many batterers are now in new relationships and its impact on treatment.
• To sum up, researchers admit being completely in the dark, both theoretically and empirically. But by merely speaking of "therapy" unqualified, all these key issues are obscured at the cost of what would be a scientifically valid protocol. Haphazard intervention creates the risk of iatrogenic impacts. Unable to discern which perpetrators can change, therapists are reduced to trying to weed out those who can't and tend to wash their hands of these, which cuts out of the data and of social intervention a growing number of assaulters. Although programs thus tend to limit themselves to the very best subjects, BIPs legitimize the growing practice of dejudiciarization, extended to all batterers, regardless of treatment availability or prognosis.

Questionable Success Figures

• Why are so much attention and publicity given to programs that reach so very few batterers?

• Subject samples are clearly non-representative of the general batterer population.

• The few follow-up studies done were limited to a restricted and non-representative sample of batterers

• Program effectiveness studies generally rest on biased and unreliable self-assessments by batterers

• Many reasons produce misleading false-positive reports

• Follow-up periods are generally too short to produce evidence of lasting change

• The so-called "honeymoon" period is a big factor in false-positive reports collected after too short a period

• Program effectiveness studies rarely take into account the lack of opportunities to batter (when a partner has left), creating even more false-positive reports

• Some therapists ordain continued contact with the victim as essential to treatment, setting up women for further abuse

• Even non-recidivism cannot be interpreted as caused by "therapy". A number of other likely causes remain unexamined by current studies

• For a number of reasons, most research does not make use of control groups, creating useless data

> *"Recidivism remains impossible to predict in the current psychological paradigm."*

• The influence of judicial intervention on program clients is ignored, despite proof of its efficiency

• Very little importance is given to the social desirability factor in assessing subjects' answers to questionnaires and self-reports about his violence

• In general, self-assessments are poor predictors of real-life behaviors

• Program make-ups are hobbled by middle-upper-class values and unrepresentative of most batterers' attitudes and skills.

• Far from becoming more refined with time, a growing number of programs are sacrificing efficiency considerations in order to maintain attendance and financial input.

• Many program providers seriously question the success possibilities of the stripped-down, shortened programs they find themselves forced to run for lack of sufficient resources.

• Recidivism data generally ignore psychological violence

• The data is sometimes cooked using the lack of violence by victims in order to over-represent program success for "participants"

• Batterers who drop out of programs, whether court-ordered or not, generally suffer no adverse effect whatsoever.

When "Therapy" Becomes Counterproductive

A methodologically valid study of three Maryland programs' outcome (with long-term follow-up and randomly assigned control groups) actually showed slightly *more* recidivism among program participants than in the control groups.

• Analysts acknowledge a general rise of psychological manipulation and violence among program participants

• A reductive notion of conjugal violence can create false-positive results as physical outbursts are replaced by careful and erudite intimidation by someone who managed to beat the system and avoid consequences

• Men can even use program content in order to refine their control strategies, claiming to have become the "experts" on DV and on the victim's alleged power & control strategies

• Men exploit "therapy" to sidestep sanctions that would have a truly dissuasive effect

• Some program providers are openly attacking, along with men's rights activists, support for victims and criminal justice budgets

• The clinical approach serves to obscure the very real benefits of wife abuse for perpetrators

• The multiplication of unverified theoretical "explanations" detracts from acknowledgement of batterers' responsibility

• Structurally, batterers are much more supported than confronted by "therapy" programs

• Program providers show a clear anti-sanctions bias

• Men end up being pitied

• A surprising and dangerous lack of empathy for victims

• Therapies maintain partners in high-risk situations, as compared to safer options

• An idealist "therapeutic" discourse ends up mimicking the batterer's rationale for his violence

• So-called batterer's "profiles" trivialize conjugal violence and ignore the diversity of victims' experience

• "Couple counseling" approaches prove especially risky

In conclusion, we note that, contrary to the notion that perpetrators' hypothetical difficulties are the real reason for the abuse inflicted on their victims and, therefore, sufficient reason to support men, [R.M.] Tolman and [L.W.] Bennett point out empirical evidence establishing that support for battered women is most often the key to substantive change in men's assaultive behavior. This would make the BIPs preferential focus on men actually counterproductive.

The pattern of outcome results does not clearly support psychological intervention as the primary active ingredient in changing men's abusive behavior. The relative success of drop-outs for treatment is problematic for those advocating treatment of men who batter. In all likelihood, positive results purported to be due to a particular intervention are the result of multiple systems of factors.

The Violence Against Women Act Is Unconstitutional

by Anita K. Blair and Charmaine Yoest

About the authors: *Anita K. Blair is deputy assistant secretary of the navy in Manpower and Reserve Affairs. Charmaine Yoest is a Bradley Fellow at the University of Virginia, department of politics, where she conducts in-depth research into social and family policy issues and teaches a course entitled Politics and the Family.*

Remember the Super Bowl Sneak of 1993? Even if you're not a sports fan—stay with us: it wasn't a football play; it was a brilliant public relations campaign. Seven years later, with this year's football festivities just behind us, we would do well to recall how effective a sneaky end-run around the truth can be.

Want to get legislation passed? You need to galvanize public opinion. If you are unconcerned about the truth, a simple way to do that is to *make up* dramatic data. After the truth comes out, people still believe the false factoids.

Case Study: domestic violence. Everyone now knows that the Super Bowl leads to an increase in domestic violence. Why? Because Lenore Walker said so—even though there isn't a shred of evidence to back her up.

It began with a press conference held by a coalition of women's groups just days before Super Bowl Sunday in 1993. The news? After the Redskins won games, there was a 40% increase in police reports of beatings and hospital admissions in Northern Virginia, according to a study done at Old Dominion University.

The Super Bowl Is Blameless

Walker, author of *The Battered Woman*, followed up with an appearance on "Good Morning America" claiming to have compiled a ten-year record showing a sharp increase in violent incidents against women on Super Bowl Sundays.

Then followed nationwide media hysteria, with interviews of domestic violence specialists who surmised, for example, that "provocatively dressed cheer-
leaders at the game may reinforce abusers' perceptions that women are intended
to serve men."

Then again, maybe not. The author of the Old Dominion University study
told *Washington Post* reporter Ken Ringle, "That's not what we found at all."

Lenore Walker referred calls to Denver psychologist Michael Lindsey who admitted to Ringle: "I haven't been any more successful than you in tracking down
any of this," he said. "You think maybe we have one of these myth things here?"

Walker, pressed to detail her findings, said: "We don't use them for public
consumption. We use them to guide us in advocacy projects."

And it worked. The next year, Congress passed the Violence Against Women
Act (VAWA).

VAWA Hurts Women and Families

IWF [the Independent Women's Forum] National Advisory Board member,
Christina Hoff Sommers, devoted two chapters of *Who Stole Feminism?* to an
exposé of this masterful Super Bowl Sneak and the "noble lies" told by gender
feminists to support their claims that the "patriarchy" uses systematic violence
to oppress women as a class.

Sommers concluded: "No study shows that Super Bowl Sunday is in any way
different from other days in the amount of domestic violence." Still today, millions of American women are completely unaware that the story was not true.

Even more troubling, the falsehoods are now enshrined in American law. The
legislative history of the enactment of VAWA is replete with biased statements
and statistics. Senator Joseph Biden chaired four Judiciary Committee hearings,
presenting only witnesses who supported the bill. Those who testified generally
represented the very groups and interests that stood to gain from the $1.6 bil-
lion five-year federal spending authorization under VAWA.

Since its passage in 1994, we have been warning that VAWA is not helpful to
assault victims, and it has produced harmful effects on women and families.

To that end, in December, IWF filed a friend-of-the-court brief in *United
States v. Morrison*, a case currently pending before the Supreme Court. The
case began as *Brzonkala v. Virginia Tech* when Christy Brzonkala sued Virginia
Tech in federal court for civil remedies under the provisions of VAWA over an
alleged forced-sex incident in two male students' dormitory room. After the
Fourth Circuit Court of Appeals decided that the VAWA provisions were uncon-
stitutional, the Clinton Justice Department took Brzonkala's appeal to the
Supreme Court.[1]

In our brief for the court, IWF makes the following arguments:

---

1. On May 15, 2002, the Supreme Court ruled that the civil remedy of VAWA was not constitutional.
Brzonkala lost her appeal.

First, in this legal battle, the Super Bowl Sneak lives on. The deceitful data that appeared in the legislative history of VAWA, now reappear in the legal briefs, as if continued reliance on false statistics and nonexistent studies somehow gives VAWA constitutional credibility. Besides advocacy research, the plaintiff and the groups supporting her, like the groups that originally supported VAWA before Congress, have omitted some key facts.

> *"VAWA is not helpful to assault victims, and it has produced harmful effects on women and families."*

Second, most violent crime is committed by men, against men. For every violent crime except rape, male victimization rates are higher than female rates. The one violent crime that disproportionately victimizes women, rape and sexual assault, has declined steadily since 1980. This is true even after "rape" was recently redefined to include attempts, verbal threats, and "psychological coercion" in the National Crime Victimization Survey.

Professor Richard Gelles, Ph.D., one of the nation's foremost experts on domestic violence, states that reported rates of domestic (or intimate) violence against women declined between 1976 and 1986, when he and his colleagues conducted the First and Second National Family Violence Surveys, and have continued to decline since. He recently wrote that female-to-male violence showed no decline and was actually higher and about as severe as male-to-female violence.

Gelles emphasizes that women, usually smaller and weaker than men, are more likely to be injured as a result of partner violence, but rates of assault are about equal for men and women.

Statistics from the Department of Justice Office of Juvenile Justice and Delinquency Prevention show that between 1981 and 1997, "violent crime by girls increased 107%, compared to a 27% increase for boys." Even Bonnie J. Campbell, director of the Department of Justice Violence Against Women Office, admits, "We are seeing numbers that suggest that young women are getting more aggressive." These facts belie the underlying premise of VAWA, that women as a group are subject to oppression by men as a group. The truth is far more complex.

VAWA Hurts Victims

Third, VAWA is not only unconstitutional, but often harmful to the victims it purports to help. IWF's science fellow, psychiatrist Sally L. Satel, M.D., reviewed numerous VAWA programs and concluded in an article for the Summer 1997 *Women's Quarterly:* "A single complaint touches off an irreversible cascade of useless and often destructive legal and therapeutic events. This could well have a chilling effect upon victims of real violence, who may be reluctant to file police reports or to seek help if it subjects them to further battery from the authorities."

Additionally, VAWA provides grant incentives for states to adopt mandatory arrest policies, which require police to make an arrest of the partner they judge to be at fault (or both partners) when called to a domestic assault scene. These policies have produced an unexpected result: There have been substantial increases in arrests of women.

Lastly, why is Christy Brzonkala suing in federal court? VAWA's civil remedy provisions, which put "gender violence" under federal purview, are unconstitutional and counterproductive. The personal safety of women, and men, will be best secured by holding state and local authorities responsible for effective enforcement and prosecution against violent crimes, no matter what the "gender" of the victims.

We could scrap VAWA and start over, and nothing would be lost. Only this time we would observe the Constitution, examine all the facts—not the false factoids—and do what's best for all crime victims, not just "gender" victims. As Professor Sommers notes, "Battered women don't need untruths to make their case before a fair-minded public that hates and despises bullies; there is enough tragic truth to go around."

Chapter 4

What Is the Extent of Violence Against Women Worldwide?

Worldwide Violence Against Women: An Overview

by Charlotte Watts and Cathy Zimmerman

About the authors: *Charlotte Watts and Cathy Zimmerman are researchers with the Health Policy Unit, Department of Public Health and Policy, at the London School of Tropical Medicine in London, England.*

In the past few years, WHO [World Health Organization], the American Medical Association, International Federation of Obstetricians and Gynaecologists, Royal College of Nursing, and other professional medical organisations have made statements about the public-health importance of violence against women. Several organisations have developed guidelines on how health workers can better identify, support, and refer victims of violence. These actions result from a growing recognition that violence represents a serious violation of women's human rights, is an important cause of injury, and is a risk factor for many physical and psychological health problems. Understanding gender-based violence and the appropriate case management of women with a current or previous history of violence are now recognised as core competencies for health workers. . . .

Violence Against Women Is Rooted in Sex Inequality

The UN Declaration on the Elimination of Violence Against Women defines violence against women as . . . "any act of gender-based violence that results in, or is likely to result in, physical, sexual or psychological harm or suffering to women."

Although broad in its scope, this statement defines violence as acts that cause or have the potential to cause harm, and emphasises that these acts are rooted in sex inequality. This focus on women does not deny the fact that men experience violence. Indeed, war, ethnic cleansing, and gang and street violence are significant causes of male morbidity and mortality. However, as violence against men often differs in its aetiology and response strategies, it warrants separate consideration.

In practice, the term violence against women encompasses an array of abuses targeted at women and girls, ranging from sex-selective abortion to the abuse of elder women. The term includes geographically or culturally specific forms of abuse such as female genital mutilation, dowry deaths, acid throwing, and honour killings (the murder of women who have allegedly brought shame to their family), as well as forms of violence that are prevalent worldwide such as domestic violence and rape. There are many potential perpetrators, including spouses and partners, parents, other family members, neighbours, teachers, employers, policemen, soldiers, and other state employees.

> *"Violence against women is not only a manifestation of sex inequality, but also serves to maintain this unequal balance of power."*

Violence against women is not only a manifestation of sex inequality, but also serves to maintain this unequal balance of power. In some cases, perpetrators consciously use violence as a mechanism for subordination. For example, violence by intimate partners is often used to demonstrate and enforce a man's position as head of the household or relationship. For other forms of violence, the subordination of women might not be the explicit motivation of the perpetrator, but is nevertheless a consequence of his actions. For example, a man who rapes a woman whom he judges to be sexually provocative might justify his act as being an appropriate punishment for her transgression of socially determined rules of female behaviour. Women themselves frequently do not challenge accepted norms of female behaviour because of the fear of being attacked or raped. Thus, women's unequal status helps to create their vulnerability to violence, which in turn fuels the violence perpetrated against them.

Global Research on Violence Against Women

Over the past 20 years, the evidence of the extent of violence perpetrated against women has increased and is beginning to offer a global overview of the magnitude of this abuse. We will now discuss the magnitude of some of the most common and most severe forms of violence against women. When reviewing the findings it is important to note that because of the sensitivity of the subject, violence against women is almost universally under-reported. Thus, these findings might be more accurately thought of as representing the minimum levels of violence that occur.

Although there are many different forms of violence against women, they nonetheless often share certain characteristics. For example, most forms of violence, including intimate partner violence, child sexual abuse, and much non-partner sexual abuse do not occur as unique incidents, but are ongoing over time, even over decades. Often, the woman not only knows the perpetrator before the first incident, but might live with or interact regularly with him. Also particular to most forms of violence against women is the way in which society attributes blame to female victims. Women experiencing intimate partner violence, for example, are frequently accused of having provoked the violence by their disobedience, failure as a wife, or infidelity. Girls or women who have been sexually assaulted or raped are frequently said to have "asked for it" by the way they were dressed or behaved—even when the victim is a child.

Intimate Partner Violence

One of the most common forms of violence against women is that perpetrated by a husband or other intimate male partner. Intimate partner violence—often termed domestic violence—takes various forms, including physical violence ranging from slaps, punches, and kicks to assaults with a weapon and homicide, and sexual violence takes forms such as forced sex, or forced participation in degrading sexual acts. These are frequently accompanied by emotionally abusive behaviours such as prohibiting a woman from seeing her family and friends, ongoing belittlement or humiliation, or intimidation; economic restrictions such as preventing a woman from working, or confiscating her earnings; and other controlling behaviours.

> *"Violence against women is not only a manifestation of sex inequality, but also serves to maintain this unequal balance of power."*

The most accurate data on the prevalence of intimate partner violence comes from cross-sectional population surveys. Over the past 16 years, more than 50 population-based surveys on violence by intimate partners have been done in various parts of the world. In these studies, women are asked directly about their experiences of specific acts of violence—e.g., "has a current or former partner ever hit you with his fist or with something else that could hurt you?"

The findings of these surveys indicate that between 10% and 50% of women who have ever had partners have been hit or otherwise physically assaulted by an intimate male partner at some point in their lives. In a review of surveys, between 3% and 52% of women reported physical violence in the previous year.

Women Report Sexual Assault by Their Partners

Research also suggests that many women are sexually assaulted by their partners. For example, in a cross-sectional household survey in one province in Zimbabwe, 26% of women who had ever been married reported being forced to have sex when they did not want to, with 20% reporting that this occurred in the year before the survey. When asked about the type of force used, 23% reported physical force, 20% reported that their partner shouted, 12% reported being forced while they were asleep, and 6% reported the use of threats.

Findings on the prevalence of physical and sexual violence by intimate partners varies greatly between studies. This variation can be attributed not only to the differences in the levels of violence between settings, but also to differences in research methods, definitions of violence, sampling techniques, interviewer training and skills, and cultural differences that affect respondents' willingness to reveal intimate experiences. For these reasons, it is not possible to make direct comparisons between cultures or countries, or to make judgments about in which society intimate partner violence is worst. However, the extent that prevalence varies between local communities can be explored within the same study. For example, a survey of married men in four districts of Uttah Pradesh noted that the extent to which men reported ever forcing their wife to have sex varied substantially between neighbouring districts (14–36%), as did the extent to which they reported having hit their wives in the past year (10–33%). In-depth research is needed to identify context-specific factors affecting such variation.

Rape and Sexual Coercion

Representative studies of violent and coerced sex by non-intimate partners are few. Most available data come from police and justice records, rape crisis centres, and retrospective studies of child sexual abuse. From the population studies that have been done, it is clear that although the common image of rape is a violent attack by a stranger, in reality, most forced sex is perpetrated by individuals known to the victim, such as intimate partners, male family members, acquaintances, and individuals in positions of authority. Sexual violence by men who are not intimate partners may involve physical force or, more usually, non-physical coercion to compel girls and women to have sex against their will. Non-physical pressure often includes blackmail, trickery, and threats. Rape can occur while women are asleep, under the influence of alcohol, recreational drugs, or other drugs such as the date-rape drugs rohypnol and

> *"The extent of violence perpetrated against women has increased and is beginning to offer a global overview of the magnitude of this abuse."*

gamma hydroxybutyrate. Although sexual assaults by strangers are widely acknowledged as crimes, by contrast, rape in marriage, sexual coercion in schools, sex in return for a job, and forced marriage are tolerated or socially condoned in many countries. Rape of women by gangs of men are common in South Africa, Papua New Guinea, and some parts of the USA. These attacks have been associated with gang initiation, rites of passage, ethnic hatred, and racism, as well as with punishment.

Data on forced sexual initiation come from reproductive health studies exploring the context of sexual initiation both within and outside marriage. Well designed cross-sectional studies of forced first sex have been implemented in many countries, including Tanzania, South Africa, and New Zealand. In these studies, 28%, 40%, and 7% of women, respectively, reported that their first sexual intercourse was forced. Research also suggests that the younger a woman is at first intercourse, the more likely it is that force was used. In the New Zealand study, for example, 25% of girls reporting first sex before age 14 years stated that it had been forced.

Sexual Abuse of Girls

Child sexual abuse includes rape, sexual touching of a child, forcing a child to touch another individual sexually, exposure to or participation in pornography, and forcing a child to have sex with another person. Frequently, these sexual violations occur between an adult and a child (defined as statutory rape), or involve non-consensual sexual contact between a child and a peer. Abuse often persists over time, and perpetrators frequently use threats and other manipulative tactics to keep children from disclosing abuse to others. The most common perpetrator of child sexual abuse is a father or another male family member. Abuse by teachers, child-care workers, family friends, religious leaders, and neighbours has also been reported in many countries.

Current statistics of child sexual abuse come mainly from retrospective population-based studies. However, even in retrospective studies there are substantial barriers to disclosure that make the collection of representative data on the extent of childhood sexual abuse extremely difficult. For example, in three countries in an ongoing WHO multicountry study on women's health and domestic violence, the percentage of women who reported sexual abuse before age 15 years during face-to-face interviews almost doubled when researchers used an anonymous method of disclosure compared with direct questioning. Despite the potential for under-reporting, findings suggest that child sexual abuse is not uncommon for girls, and to a lesser degree boys, and that, regardless of the sex of the victim, most perpetrators are male, and known to the victim. A review by Finkelhor of studies from 20 countries, including ten national representative surveys, showed rates of childhood sexual abuse of 7–36% for girls, and 3–29% for boys, with most studies reporting 1.5 to 3 times more sexual violence against girls than boys. Again, the variation in prevalence may be attributed partly to methodological and context-specific factors.

Trafficking, Forced Prostitution, Exploitation of Labour, and Debt Bondage

During the past decade, a rapidly growing worldwide industry has developed in trafficking women and girls for forced labour and sexual exploitation. War, displacement, and economic and social inequities between and within countries, and the demand for low-wage labour and sex work drive this illicit trade in women. Often controlled by mafia, gangs, or highranking police and military figures, trafficking in women and girls is a highly profitable business. Most definitions of trafficking, including that in the United Nations Palermo Convention, highlight the use of violence, coercion, deception, or debt-bondage; the exploitative relationship between trafficking agents and victims; and the misuse of power and control over women for profit.

There are no reliable statistics on the number of women and children who are trafficked. Rough estimates suggest that 700 000 to 2 million women and girls are trafficked across international borders every year. Importantly, this figure does not include the substantial number of women and girls who are bought and sold within their own countries, for which there are scant data. Reports of trafficking in women come from nearly every world region. The greatest number of victims are thought to come from Asia (about 250 000 per year), the former Soviet Union (about 100 000), and from central and eastern Europe (about 175 000). An estimated 100 000 trafficked women have come from Latin America and the Caribbean and more than 50 000 from Africa. The former Soviet Union and central and eastern Europe may currently be the largest source countries for women trafficked into prostitution.

> *"Most forms of violence . . . do not occur as unique incidents, but are ongoing over time, even over decades."*

Women are often deceived into believing they have secured jobs as nannies, waitresses, or dancers, only to discover that they have been trafficked into bonded or forced prostitution and other forms of slavery-like situations, such as domestic servitude, sweatshop labour, and begging. Many women are confined, beaten, and raped, and most have vital documents, such as their passports and visas, confiscated. Data from the International Organization for Migration office in Kosovo show that, of the 130 women who were assisted during the first 4 months of 2001 (most of whom were Moldovan), 72% were promised false opportunities abroad, 11% were kidnapped, and 91% received no payment for their services. 60% had no access to medical services despite the high-risk nature of their work.

Physical and sexual violence towards prostitutes has seldom been the focus of public or academic interest. However, research is beginning to show that prostitutes often face physical and sexual violence from clients and other individuals such as pimps, club owners, and law enforcement workers. For example, in a UK survey of 240 prostitutes in Leeds, Glasgow, and Edinburgh 50% of prostitutes working outdoors and 26% of those working indoors reported some form of violence by clients in the past 6 months. Among prostitutes working outdoors, 81% had experienced violence by clients. Of these women, 33% had been beaten, 30% threatened with a weapon, 25% choked, 27% raped vaginally, and 9% slashed or stabbed. In a survey of 540 female prostitutes in Bangladesh, 49% had been raped and 59% beaten by police in the past year. These figures show the extent to which women in sex work are vulnerable to violence as a result of the conditions of their work and their marginalised status.

Rape in War

The wars in the former Yugoslavia and Rwanda focused international attention on the use of rape as a deliberate strategy to undermine community bonds, weaken resistance to aggression, and, in the former Yugoslavia, to perpetrate ethnic cleansing through impregnation. But, the rape of women in war is not a new phenomenon. Japanese troops raped civilian women systematically in Korea, China, and the Philippines during World War II. Rape has also been documented in the war of independence in Bangladesh; in civil wars such as those in Liberia, Uganda, and Rwanda; and during social and political uprisings such as the recent anti-Chinese riots in Indonesia. There are no accurate data on rape during war. For example, estimates of the number of Muslim women raped by Serb soldiers during the 1992–95 conflict in Bosnia-Herzegovina vary from 20 000 to 50 000—ie, by as much as 1.2% of the total prewar female population.

Until very recently, violence against women was thought an insignificant form of collateral damage. It was only [in 2002] that the International Criminal Tribunal in The Hague defined sexual offences as a crime against humanity and convicted three Bosnian Serb soldiers of raping and torturing Muslim women and girls who they enslaved, abused, and rented and sold to other soldiers. Similarly, it is only relatively recently that sexual violence in refugee camps has been identified by relief agencies as an issue that needs formal attention and response.

Sex-Selective Abortion, Female Infanticide, and Deliberate Neglect of Girls

In countries such as China, Taiwan, South Korea, India, Pakistan, and some sub-Saharan African countries the ratio of men to women is higher than would be expected from the typical sex ratio at birth and the typical differential mortality. High female mortality rates resulting from sex-selective abortion, female infanticide (the deliberate killing of female infants soon after birth), and systematic and often fatal neglect of the health and nutritional needs of girls cause this demographic inequality. It is estimated that worldwide between 60 and 100 million women and girls are "missing". For example, in the latest Indian census in 1991, only 929 girls and women were counted for every 1000 boys and men. After adjustment for expected differences in fertility and life-expectancy, these census figures suggest that between 22 and 37 million Indian girls and women are "missing", with the greatest excess mortality in girls younger than 4 years.

"Most forced sex is perpetrated by individuals known to the victim, such as intimate partners, male family members, acquaintances, and individuals in positions of authority."

The increasing availability of ultrasonograph examination has facilitated early termination of female fetuses. South Korea has the highest sex ratio at birth, at 117.2 boys for every 100 girls in 1990. Sex ratios increase with parity, and for third children, 185 boys are born for every 100 girls. Despite the magnitude of this social and ethical problem, female infanticide has received little international attention from policymakers, public-health professionals, and the medical profession.

Millions of Women Experience Violence

We have reviewed some of the most prevalent and severe forms of violence that are widely perpetrated against women. Our list is not exhaustive. We have not, for example, included several important forms of violence against women, including elder female abuse, dowry deaths, acid throwing, and female genital mutilation.

Research into violence against women is increasing, but there are no widely agreed definitions of the different forms of such violence that could be used to standardise research findings. Furthermore, context-specific variations in the willingness of respondents to disclose experiences of violence and differences in the populations in which the studies are done make cross-country and cross-study comparison difficult. The figures presented here are minimum estimates, and still they suggest that globally, millions of women are experiencing violence or living with its consequences. . . . Ultimately, the sheer scale of violence against women forces the question of what it will take to translate increasing recognition of the global prevalence of this abuse into meaningful, sustained, and widespread action.

The United Nations Has Helped Reduce Worldwide Violence Against Women

by Mary Robinson

About the author: *Mary Robinson was United Nations high commissioner for human rights from 1997 to 2002.*

Women's rights are human rights. This affirmation seems self-evident, yet women waited until 1995 to see it stated unequivocally in an international document. That year, the overwhelming majority of the world's nations adopted the Beijing Declaration and Platform of Action at the end of the Fourth World Conference on Women in China. The inclusion of these documents in the final act of that historic gathering is not to be underestimated. The recognition of women's rights as human rights, one of the goals of the international women's movement, came about only after decades of struggle. More importantly, it visibly illustrates evidence of women's transformation of the human-rights discourse, pointing toward the recognition of the human rights of all people.

The 1948 Universal Declaration of Human Rights and the international covenants that followed it proclaim equality between men and women and proscribe discrimination, but the traditional human-rights framework has not fully incorporated the rights of women. The concept of equality means much more than treating all persons in the same way, for equal treatment of persons in unequal situations will perpetuate rather than eradicate injustice. Feminists and others quickly realized that a critical rethinking of what human rights meant to women was required. As Rebecca J. Cook has observed, "International human rights and the legal instruments that protect them were developed primarily by men in a male-oriented world. They have not been interpreted in a gender-sensitive way that is responsive to women's experiences of injustice."

To transform international human rights in order to take the concerns of women into account is to tackle notions that have held firm sway for decades,

Mary Robinson, "A Selective Declaration: Women's Human Rights into the New Millennium," *Harvard International Review*, vol. 21, Fall 1999, pp. 60–63. Copyright © 1999 by *Harvard International Review*. Reproduced by permission.

some even before the birth of the human rights movement. Among these notions is the primacy accorded to civil and political rights over economic, social, and cultural rights—an imbalance which in itself belies the supposed "gender neutrality" of rights.

Gender and Human Rights

The Universal Declaration of Human Rights enshrines the inherent dignity and equal and inalienable rights of all members of the human family. The Vienna Declaration and Program of Action of 1993 forcefully reiterates that all human rights—civil, cultural, economic, political, and social—are interdependent. With the benefit of 50 years of experience, it has become clear that all human rights must be respected with the same degree of affirmation and conviction. Freedom of speech and belief are as important as freedom from fear and want; the right to fair trial and the right of participatory and representative government should be considered side by side with the rights to work, health care, and education.

This vision continues to be challenged, however. Some still hold that economic, social and cultural rights are not right at all but goals, albeit laudable ones, that governments should strive to achieve. For many in this camp, only civil and political rights are universal. This attitude may help explain why fundamental rights to decent living conditions, food, basic health care, and education, all laid down in the International Covenant on Economic, Social, and Cultural Rights, are widely denied. The *1999 State of World's Children* report of the United Nations Children's Fund (UNICEF) warns that nearly a billion people, one-sixth of humanity, are functionally illiterate. Two-thirds of them are women. Meanwhile, the latest World Bank report indicates that the recent financial and economic crisis has driven many into poverty, measured by the World Bank as income of less than US$1 per day.

The victims of poverty are in fact denied almost all rights—not only to adequate food, health care, and housing, but also to participation in political processes, access to information and education, fair legal treatment, and the benefits of citizenship. These conditions are exacerbated for the most vulnerable, in particular women and children, who in some parts of the world are being increasingly exploited through drug trafficking, forced labor, and prostitution. Thus, the separation of economic, social, and cultural rights from civil and political rights does not reflect the reality of women's positions in society, in which the violation of these rights is not so neatly separated.

> *"In fighting violence against women from a human rights perspective, women have challenged doctrines of privacy and the concept of the sanctity of the family."*

As gender inequality creates conditions of exploitation or subordination in the economic sphere for women, the lack of attention to these rights is of particular concern. At the same time, women are increasingly demanding progress in areas of health care, food, shelter, and employment. The lesser status given to these rights complicates this articulation. As Charlotte Bunch writes, "Women's rights advocates need to show how socioeconomic rights are central to the achievement of women's rights . . . Women fighting for recognition of their human rights advocate a holistic understanding of human rights as indivisible and interconnected. Socioeconomic and political-civil rights should not be seen as competitive but as equally important needs that must be sought together, not one before the other."

The holistic approach to human rights has, at least officially, gained much new ground in the last decade. The Vienna Declaration and Program of Action recognize in Chapter 1, Paragraph 18: "The human rights of women and the girl child are an inalienable, integral, and indivisible part of universal human rights." In the same section, the Program of Action established that "the full and equal participation of women in political, civil, economic, social, and cultural life, at the national, regional, and international levels, and the eradication of all forms of discrimination on the grounds of sex are priority objectives of the international community." At the Third International Conference on Population and Development, held in Cairo in 1994, the world's governments validated sexual and reproductive rights for the first time, recognizing the right of women to make their own decisions on issues of sexuality and reproduction, as well as the right to information about and access to contraceptive services.

Reproductive Rights Are Important

The exercise of sexual and reproductive rights is clearly described in the Cairo Programme of Action as "the basic right of all couples and individuals to decide freely and responsibly the number, spacing, and timing of their children and to have the information and means to do so, and the right to attain the highest standard of sexual and reproductive health." It also includes a couple's right to make decisions concerning reproduction "free of discrimination, coercion, and violence." The Beijing Platform for Action, for its part, stresses that "all human rights—civil, cultural, economic, political, and social, including the right to development—are universal, indivisible, interdependent, and interrelated."

These commitments on paper have been translated into governmental "plans of action" to implement the goals fixed in Vienna, Cairo, and Beijing. The United Nations is carrying out a program of "mainstreaming the gender perspective" in all its activities, ensuring that women benefit equally from development and other programs.

Certainly, these formal commitments have yet to be realized. However, the history of the international women's movement over the last 30 years demonstrates how women can bring issues to the world agenda and obtain concrete commitments from governments and institutions that can then be translated into effective change at the grassroots-level. The special session of the UN General Assembly to be held [in 2000] to assess the progress made since the Fourth World Conference in Beijing in 1995 will provide another opportunity for women to make their voices heard as they have done so effectively in the cycle of such gatherings that began in Nairobi in 1985.

Gender-Based Violence

One example of the potential of the international women's movement is the growing global recognition of violence against women as a human rights issue. Putting the issue on the human rights agenda has also meant successfully challenging other firmly entrenched notions of a traditional human rights framework like the public-private distinction in enforcing human rights and the principle of state responsibility.

The issue of violence against women has only recently found its place on the international human rights agenda. In the 1970s women's issues were generally related to problems of political and economic discrimination and to equitable participation in the development process by women of the Third World. The major international legal instrument concerned with women's rights *per se*, the 1979 Convention on the Elimination of All Forms of Discrimination Against Women, concentrated on the vague concept of "discrimination." The issue of gender-based violence is not specifically addressed in the Convention, although it is clearly fundamental to its provisions.

Similarly, at the World Conference to Review and Appraise the Achievements of the United Nations Decade for Women: Equality, Development and Peace, held at Nairobi in July 1985, the issue of violence against women arose only as an afterthought to the issues of discrimination, health, and economics. Still, it was acknowledged that violence against women—in the family, in the community and by states—has inhibited women from enjoying the full benefits of human rights. Women have since focused the issue on the agenda around the world, conducting successful grassroots campaigns that made international forums take notice.

Gender-Based Violence Is Included

In 1992, the UN Committee on the Elimination of Discrimination Against Women (CEDAW) formally included gender-based violence under gender-based discrimination (formally known as CEDAW General Recommendation 19, entitled "Violence against women," 1992). The process of anchoring the issue of violence against women firmly on the international agenda culminated in the adoption, without a vote, of resolution 48/104 by the General Assembly on December 20, 1993, entitled the "Declaration on the Elimination of Violence Against Women." The following year, the UN Commission on Human Rights appointed the first Special Rapporteur on the issue, Sri Lankan human rights expert Radhika Coomaraswamy.

In fighting violence against women from a human rights perspective, women have challenged doctrines of privacy and the concept of the sanctity of the family. In the past, the state and the law intervened with regard to domestic violence only when violence became a public nuisance. Otherwise, the doctrine of privacy allowed for violence against women to continue unabated. Indeed, much of the blame for violence against women can be placed on government inaction. There appears to be a permissive attitude, a tolerance of perpetrators of violence against women, especially when this violence occurs in the home. Governments rarely acknowledge the gravity of the crime. A failure to recognize crimes such as domestic violence, marital rape, sexual harassment, and violence associated with traditional practices persists in many countries. Even where crimes of violence against women are recognized in the law, they are rarely prosecuted with vigor. But according to norms recently established by the international community, a state that fails to prosecute crimes of violence against women is as guilty as an individual perpetrator. States have a positive duty to prevent, investigate, and punish crimes associated with violence against women.

State Responsibility

The public-private distinction, which has been at the root of most legal systems, including human rights law, has created major problems for the enforcement and recognition of women's rights. It is a positive development that states are reaching into the privacy of the home, and are now increasingly being held responsible for human rights offences committed within the home.

The problem of violence against women brings into sharp focus an issue that has been troubling the international community: state responsibility for the actions of private citizens. In the past, a strict judicial interpretation held the state responsible only for those actions which it or its agents were directly accountable. In this case the interpretation would encompass issues such as women in custody and in detention, and perhaps the issue of women involved in armed conflict. The questions of domestic violence, rape, and sexual harassment were seen as the actions of individuals, and thus beyond the responsibility of the state.

However, it is now a recognized part of general international human rights law that states are responsible for the protection of the rights of individuals to exercise their human rights, the investigation of alleged violations of human rights, the punishment of the violators of human rights, and the provision of effective remedies for the victims human rights violations.

States Do Not Consider Women's Rights as Human Rights

Yet states are rarely held responsible for ignoring their obligations with regard to women's rights. The reason for this is twofold. First, states do not consider women's rights as human rights, especially those rights that are exercised in the home or the community, and they do not see such violations as an "internationally recognized justiciable wrong." Second, states do not consider themselves responsible for violations of women's rights by private actors.

Except for categories such as "pirates" and "international war criminals," private individuals and agencies are not generally bound by international human rights law. But states may be responsible for their failure to meet international obligations even when violations originate in the conduct of private individuals. State responsibility for the violation of women's human rights by private actors is anticipated by customary international law.

> *"States are rarely held responsible for ignoring their obligations with regard to women's rights."*

Using the existing human rights and international legal framework and transforming it simultaneously, state responsibility for the violation of women's human rights by private actors is anticipated by customary international law. States are held legally responsible for acts or omissions of private persons when, among other instances, the states fail to exercise due diligence in the control of private actors. . . .

State Action Against Violence Is Necessary

Discrimination under the Convention is not restricted to actions by or on behalf of the state; this is expressly acknowledged, in regard to violence, in General Recommendation 19. Article 2(e) of the Convention specifies that states' parties are required "to take all appropriate measures to eliminate discrimination against women by any person, organization or enterprise." This provision covers state responsibility for violations by private actors. Article 16 explicitly refers to discrimination in the family and Recommendation 19 clearly includes family violence within its purview.

The Declaration sums up the current standards in operation as they relate to the question of violence against women. Article 4(c) of the Declaration proclaims that states should "exercise due diligence to prevent, investigate and, in accordance with national legislation, punish acts of violence against women, whether those acts are perpetrated by the State or by private persons." All states are not only responsible for their own conduct or the conduct of their agents, but are now also responsible for their failure to take the necessary steps to prosecute private citizens for their behavior, in compliance with international standards. This emergence of state responsibility for violence in society plays an absolutely crucial role in efforts to eradicate gender-based violence and is perhaps one of the most important contributions of the women's movement to the promotion and protection of human rights.

Women's Rights Movement Is Critical

The experience of the international women's rights movement and it's successes in specific areas are instructive for other human rights defenders around the world. The analyses women have applied and their redefinition of human rights to make them truly universal can find a parallel in other "readings" of the human-rights discourse.

Rights are not gender-neutral, for the instruments that contain them are the product of particular circumstances, places, and authors. Similarly they are not "culture neutral." The founding human rights document of our era, the Universal Declaration, is an informative example.

The basis in personal dignity that it and other UN human rights instruments indicate has a Western philosophical, even religious tone. But the developing phase in the history of human rights over the last 50 years of interpretation and implementation of the Declaration has opened it up to new perspectives and challenges in cultural conditions much more diverse than its Western roots had offered.

The Declaration's capacity to be translated into very different languages and cultures is undeniable, even if much of the work of translation has yet to be carried out. This work is essential if the Declaration is to be relevant to people around the world. Women are taking up the challenge and showing the way.

The United Nations Has Not Helped Reduce Worldwide Violence Against Women

by the Independent Women's Forum

About the author: *The Independent Women's Forum is a conservative non-profit organization offering an alternative to the feminist viewpoint.*

CEDAW [Convention on the Elimination of All Forms of Discrimination Against Women] is a U.N. convention that was signed in 1980 by President Jimmy Carter but never ratified by the U.S. Senate—for good reasons. Now Senators Joseph Biden and Barbara Boxer are leading a fight to ratify CEDAW, and it looks like the vote will be close.[1]

Ten Reasons Why This Misnamed Treaty Should Be Rejected

1. CEDAW Assails Our Federal System and National Sovereignty at a Time We Can Least Afford It: Those who support CEDAW say that it won't affect our states' laws or national sovereignty—that it is merely an international treaty with no binding force. They are wrong. Remember that our Constitution says that "all treaties made . . . under the authority of the United States, shall be the supreme law of the land, and the judges of every state shall be bound thereby, anything in the Constitution or laws of any State to the contrary notwithstanding." So any issue covered by CEDAW—which includes almost all domestic policy—shall be transferred from state to federal power without so much as a national debate. CEDAW's dictates shall become "the supreme law of the land." The ratification of CEDAW turns American policy making over to unelected foreign bureaucrats. No U.S. senator was elected to do that!

2. CEDAW Trivializes the Meaning of Human Rights: CEDAW has been ratified and accepted by states with abominable human rights records such as

---

1. As of March 2003, the Senate had not ratified CEDAW.

China, Iraq, The Congo, Cuba, Libya, and Saudi Arabia. Conversely, America is the world's strongest defender of human rights and needs neither to verify nor improve its position through CEDAW. We have been partner since 1948 to the Universal Declaration of Human Rights and later to the International Covenant on Civil and Political Rights, which establishes the international principle of equality for women. When the Senate rejected CEDAW in 1994, four senators, including Nancy Kassebaum (R.,Kan.), warned of the risk of "cheapening the coin" of human rights.

Socialism and Big Sister

3. CEDAW Is Socialism by Another Name: Article 11 calls for governments to set wages so that jobs of "equal value" (e.g. firemen and kindergarten teachers) are granted "equal remuneration." This is "comparable worth," a system of government wage setting that Americans have rightly rejected as inefficient and antithetical to free market principles. Article 11 also demands that governments guarantee "maternity leave with pay" and provide . . . a "network of childcare facilities." Moreover, CEDAW wants government-set quotas for political candidates, office holders, government officials—everything from politicians to polevaulters.

4. CEDAW Is Not Taken Seriously by the Worst Offenders: In Saudi Arabia 15 schoolgirls were forbidden to leave their burning school and perished; in Nigeria a woman is to be stoned to death for adultery; and in other signatory countries practices

> *"In other signatory countries practices such as genital mutilation, honor killings, and socially sanctioned rape and domestic violence go on."*

such as genital mutilation, honor killings, and socially sanctioned rape and domestic violence go on. To women in such countries, quotas and wage setting are both preposterous and useless.

5. Big Sister Will Be Watching: If signed by the United States, the treaty would be a powerful weapon in the hands of hard-line feminist groups like the National Organization for Women [NOW] who would use it to continue their assault on American institutions. Expect rancorous lawsuits targeting our armed forces for not allowing women in combat, Cub Scouts for not including girls, and Little League teams for male overrepresentation. Why? Because Article 1 of the Treaty outlaws "any distinction . . . on the basis of sex" in "any . . . field." Working with them will be Non Governmental Organizations—unaccountable global interest groups which issue "Shadow Reports" attacking democratic governments.

No More Mother's Day

6. CEDAW Hates Your Mother: Last year the U.N. Commission responsible for enforcing the treaty censured Belarus for celebrating Mother's Day. Why? Because Article 5 of the treaty calls for governments to "modify the social and

cultural patterns of conduct of men and women with a view to achieving the elimination of . . . all . . . practices which are based on . . . stereotyped roles for men and women." Significantly, the only stereotype cited by the CEDAW enforcers is motherhood!

7. Here Come the Gender Police: Article 10 of the treaty calls for the "elimination of any stereotyped concepts of the roles of men and women . . . in particular, by the revision of textbooks and school programs." Do we—our state educators—want UN gender monitors revising our textbooks and school programs?

8. Australia Tried It and Balked: Australia was one of the first countries to ratify CEDAW and to implement its own sexual discrimination laws. By 2000, intrusion of U.N. monitoring committees and their non-governmental allies into the Aussies' domestic laws and policy prompted a pullback. The country restricted U.N. inspectors' visits, called for an overhaul of U.N. committees, and refused to ratify the ever more intrusive CEDAW Optional Protocol. The Australians officially complained of the U.N.'s criticism of democratic countries— and its willful blindness to the egregious violations perpetrated by signatory nations such as Iraq.

9. If You Liked the Old Soviet Constitution, You Will Love CEDAW: Like the old Soviet Constitution that claimed to "break the fetters of oppression," CEDAW lays claim to lofty human rights principles that only democracies take seriously. Just like the Soviets, CEDAW puts power in the hands of a few unelected and unaccountable "experts." The "experts" then define their feminist wish list as "human rights" to be imposed upon nations and individuals, while—sad to say—not succeeding in "breaking the fetters" of the worst economic and social oppression among its signatories.

CEDAW Will Harm America and Not Help Any Women

10. It Doesn't Work: It is sad to see Third World delegates place their hope in a mechanism that has not—will not—rescue women from true abuse and oppression, but will spend more time concentrating on minor issues in democratic countries. Remember, it was America—not CEDAW—that liberated the women and girls of Afghanistan from the Taliban.

Unless there is a strong effort to stop it, political pressure from N.O.W. and other activist groups will make ratification likely. Signing on to CEDAW would do serious harm to the United States while doing nothing for women around the world, who need the protection of stable societies, not the bitter gender politics of this misguided treaty.

Rape Is Often Used as a Weapon of War

by Joanne Barkan

About the author: *Joanne Barkan is a New York–based writer.*

A glass wall covered by blinds separated the courtroom participants from the spectators in the public gallery, but a hush enveloped both sides when the witness known as FWS-50 began to speak. Although a voice modulator screened her identity from the public, other microphones in the room occasionally picked up the undisguised sounds of her anguish. Indicating one of the defendants, she said,

> I only know that he was very forceful, that he wanted to hurt me as much as possible. But he could never hurt me as much as my soul always hurt me.

When the prosecutor asked why she had decided to testify after remaining silent for almost eight years, she said,

> [to] let it be known that it really happened. It's not easier for me to speak about it today, but nevertheless, I wanted everyone to hear about it.

The Sexual Enslavement of Muslim Women

She wanted everyone to hear about this: in the summer of 1992, at age sixteen, she was taken prisoner by soldiers near her village in Bosnia, held for two months, and raped so often that she lost count of how many times and how many men; she was raped vaginally, anally, and orally; she was gang raped by ten men at a time; she was raped by soldiers and paramilitary thugs; she was threatened with guns and knives while being raped; she was trapped in an apartment where she had to clean for the soldiers who raped her all night.

FWS-50 was one of thousands—some say twenty thousand—Muslim women sexually enslaved and tortured by Bosnian Serbs, Serbs, and Montenegrins during the Bosnian War of 1992–1995. She was one of sixteen women from the town of Foca (pronounced Fo'-cha) and its surrounding villages in southeastern Bosnia who agreed to testify in 2000 before the International Criminal Tribunal

Joanne Barkan, "As Old as War Itself: Rape in Foca," *Dissent*, Winter 2002, pp. 60–66. Copyright © 2002 by the Foundation for the Study of Independent Social Ideas. Reproduced by permission.

for the former Yugoslavia, located in The Hague. FWS-50 faced the men she was accusing—all three Bosnian Serbs, all three soldiers in the war, all three, like herself, born in Foca. . . .

Serbs Begin Ethnic Cleansing

On April 8, 1992, Serb forces supported by artillery and heavy weapons attacked Foca. By April 17, they had taken the town, although fighting in the surrounding villages continued into the summer. The occupying forces included army units, paramilitaries, and military police; the men were Bosnian Serbs, Serbs, and a smaller number of Montenegrins. Their mission was to rid the Foca district of its Muslim citizens so the territory could be annexed, along with other parts of Bosnia, to create a Greater Serbia. The Serb forces began the job immediately. As soon as they took over a village or a neighborhood in town, they rounded up any Muslims who had not already fled and separated them into two groups: men and older boys in one group: women, children, and the very elderly in a second group. The Serbs slaughtered some men on the spot and transferred the rest to prisons and camps where starvation, filthy conditions, and torture killed many more.

Everyone in the second group went to the rape camps. The Serbs had a fairly regular procedure. They usually transported a new batch of these prisoners to a temporary detention center where some of the women—most often the younger ones—were raped for the first time, frequently by

> *"The camps had a specific function: . . . Serb forces could find their designated target— Muslim women—and carry out a campaign of systematic mass rape."*

more than one soldier. After a day or two, the prisoners were trucked to one of the main rape camps. These included Foca High School and Partizan Sports Hall ("Partizan" for short), which was a gymnasium near the central police station. Those who went first to the high school stayed anywhere from several days to several weeks. From there, most were transferred to Partizan, where roughly seventy-five people (two-thirds of them women and teenage girls) were trapped at any one time. Escape from either camp was nearly impossible; resistance to rape utterly impossible. Armed guards never hesitated to beat their prisoners into submission; they beat two to death.

Terrorize, Humiliate, and Stigmatize

The label "rape camp" describes the high school and Partizan quite well. Like prison camp inmates, the detainees had little to eat, they slept on the floor, they had no hygienic facilities or medicine, and they had only the clothes on their backs. The elderly and the small children suffered some beatings, but otherwise the Serb soldiers left them alone; they were irrelevant. The camps had a specific function: they served as convenient collection sites where Serb forces could find their designated target—Muslim women—and carry out a campaign of systematic mass rape. The strategy was to terrorize, humiliate, and stigmatize the women so completely—and through them, the men and children—that all Muslims would leave the territory and never return.

The Serbs also aimed to impregnate as many women as possible, certainly for the added trauma this would produce, but also to expend the procreative capacity of Muslim women on Serb-sired babies. The Serbs regularly taunted their victims while they were being raped: "Now you'll have Serb babies." Forty of the women and

> *"The reports depicted a systematic policy, rape as a primary tactic in a war strategy."*

teenagers in Partizan became pregnant. Nearly every unmarried woman taken to the camps was a virgin, so the sexual torture had an added dimension of shock and pain for them. But all the women who survived the ordeal knew they might be ostracized by their families and their Muslim community. . . .

Rape Was the Original Collateral Damage

Wartime rape is as old as war itself. It has always served at least two purposes: to intimidate the enemy and to reward the troops as booty. But military commanders rarely drew attention to its usefulness. Instead, the ubiquity of wartime rape allowed them to portray it as inevitable; it was simply one of the ghastly things that happened during war because war was ghastly. Conventional wisdom classified wartime rape as an unfortunate byproduct of war, not as an instrument of war. It was the original collateral damage.

But no one could plausibly dismiss the Bosnian war rapes as collateral damage. The international media began reporting on the rape camps almost immediately, and the reports depicted a systematic policy, rape as a primary tactic in a war strategy. Roy Gutman, *Newsday*'s Europe correspondent, was interviewing refugees and filing stories by summer 1992. He wrote a grisly piece on Foca in April 1993. The images from Bosnia broadcast on television, with their unnerving resemblance to Nazi concentration camps, shocked Americans. But despite public outcry in the United States and abroad, the European governments and two U.S. presidents (George Bush I, then Bill Clinton) refused to intervene to stop the atrocities. Human rights groups and organizations devoted specifically to human rights for women kept up the pressure. But instead of intervention, Clinton consented, reluctantly, to an international tribunal under the auspices of the United Nations to prosecute crimes already committed.

ICTY Set New Precedents

From the start, most observers considered the International Criminal Tribunal for Yugoslavia (ICTY) a sop to human rights and feminist activists who wanted intervention. The tribunal also served to soothe public opinion. But it had little funding, no means to arrest suspects, and no credibility. Almost no one expected it to succeed. And yet to some extent, at least for women, it did.

When the United Nations voted the ICTY into existence on May 25, 1993, the only precedents for the new court were the international war crimes tribunals at Nuremberg and in the Far East after the Second World War. As for prosecuting mass rape, there was precious little to build on. The body of international law of war, which sovereign states had been assembling since the 1860s, largely neglected rape. The record for enforcing whatever law did exist and prosecuting sexual assaults was "a wholesale failure" in the words of Diane Orentlicher of the War Crimes Research Office at American University's law school. Clearly, international law needed amending if it was going to include women in its system of justice. The ICTY would have to set new precedents; it would have to pry open key judicial categories—genocide, crimes against humanity, war crimes, violations of the laws or customs of war, grave breaches of the Geneva Conventions—and insert the words "rape, sexual assault, and sexual enslavement."

Opportunity Was Lost at Nuremberg

There had been an opportunity to expand justice for women in 1945–1946 when the Allies prosecuted high-ranking Nazi officials in Nuremberg. The opportunity was lost. The Allies drafted a statute that laid out the rules for trial procedure and defined the crimes to be tried. The statute they wrote—called the London Charter of the International Military Tribunal—did not contain the word rape although rape was rampant during the war in Europe. Rape and sexual crimes could have been prosecuted as "ill treatment" under war crimes and as "inhumane acts" under crimes against humanity, but they weren't. In one of the subsequent trials held in Nuremberg, the United States (as one of the occupying powers) prosecuted lower-ranking Nazis under the Allied Control Council Law No. 10, which did include rape in its definition of crimes against humanity. Yet the tribunal did not prosecute anyone for rape.

The record improved slightly under the Tokyo tribunal (1946–1948), where the Allies prosecuted high-ranking Japanese officials for crimes committed in the Far East. The indictment listed rape as a crime. The prosecutors used the mass rape atrocities in Nanking in 1937, along with other crimes, to convict the Japanese leaders. But the indictment never mentioned the sexual enslavement of some two hundred thousand women—the "comfort women"—in the countries occupied and colonized

> *"The body of international law of war, which sovereign states had been assembling since the 1860s, largely neglected rape."*

by the Japanese Imperial Army. This was a glaring omission given that a Dutch military court in Batavia (Indonesia) in 1948 prosecuted and convicted twelve Japanese army officers of sexually enslaving thirty-five Dutch women.

Chapter 4

Wartime Rape Changed After World War II

After the Batavia trial, no court prosecuted rape as a war crime or crime against humanity under international law for almost fifty years. During that time, wartime rape changed along with war. Ethnic conflicts, which were increasingly in the news, targeted civilian populations; this kind of war lent itself to sexual violence. Mass rape carried out methodically and publicly could terrorize an entire community. Military forces in Rwanda, Sierra Leone, the Democratic Republic of the Congo, Cambodia, and East Timor, as well as the Balkans used it as an instrument of terror for ethnic cleansing and genocide. In an interview, Kelly Askin of American University's War Crimes Research Office contrasted this use of rape with aspects of rape during the Second World War.

> Because Nazi law forbade sex with a Jew, more attempts were made to cover up the crime or at least not draw attention to it. Thus the pervasiveness was not as well recognized. . . . In Asia, the situation of the former "comfort women". . . was part of the war machine in that the soldiers did not have to go out looking for sex. . . . But the sexual slavery was not used to terrorize the enemy, but for protecting the soldiers from venereal diseases, etc.

Against this background, the new International Criminal Tribunal for Yugoslavia looked like an exceptional chance in 1993 for advocates of human rights for women to make some progress. But every step forward, as it turned out, required a lobbying campaign. Nongovernmental organizations and university-based institutes wrote briefs and letters, requested meetings, did press work, and held seminars and conferences. They wanted the following: rape and sexual slavery specified as crimes in the ICTY statute, more women as judges and prosecutors, a senior official in the prosecutor's office experienced in prosecuting sexual offenses, nondiscriminatory wording in ICTY documents, women on evidence-gathering teams in the field, funding for a victims unit to protect women and all traumatized witnesses during trials, and, of course, aggressive prosecution of sexual offenses.

Rape as a Crime Against Humanity

The advocates' work had to be thorough, and there was a lot of it. Take, for example, the wording of the first document prepared by the office of chief prosecutor Richard Goldstone. This was a motion in a case involving several camps where mass rapes of women had taken place. According to Felice Gaer, director of the American Jewish Committee's Blaustein Institute for Human Rights, the motion made cursory reference to the rapes, and "then the phrase 'what was worse' was used to describe a single atrocity—one man being forced to bite off the testicles of another. The rapes were mentioned in passing, like road accidents." The Blaustein Institute, the Women's International Human Rights Clinic, and the Harvard University Human Rights Program made their critique in an *amicus* memorandum, and the prosecutor's office reworded the motion.

Overall, many prosecutors and judges were responsive, some even courageous. The human rights advocates got some, but definitely not all, of what they wanted. The ICTY statute, for example, lists rape under crimes against humanity but not under other headings; sexual slavery appears nowhere in the statute.

History—in so far as it will deal with human rights for women—will likely judge one strategic decision made by the ICTY as invaluable: the decision to put together "the rape case." Even in the early stages of the tribunal's work, the lobbying to get prosecutors to pay attention to sexual offenses paid off.

> *"No court prosecuted rape as a war crime or crime against humanity under international law for almost fifty years."*

Before long, more than 20 percent of the charges filed at the ICTY involved allegations of sexual assault— an extraordinarily high percentage in light of the past record. But in any individual case, the rape of women was only one crime among many being prosecuted. If rape were overshadowed in most trials by other crimes, the possibility of breaking new legal ground for women's rights decreased. But, hypothetically, a case devoted to just one type of crime, just one category of victim, and just one place might have significant impact on the law and on public opinion. In late 1994, the ICTY office of the prosecutor, supported by women's rights advocates, began the investigation for a rape case. The prosecutors would investigate only sexual crimes and only those committed against women. The place they chose to investigate was Foca.

Eight Men Were Indicted

On June 26, 1996, the ICTY indicted eight men from Foca on sixty-two counts of crimes against humanity, grave breaches of the Geneva Conventions of 1949, and violations of the laws or customs of war. All eight were born in the municipality. When they joined in the ethnic cleansing of the district in 1992, their ages ranged from twenty-three to thirty-seven. Before the war, they did various jobs—café owner, car mechanic, waiter, electrician. Some had wives and children. When the fighting began, five of them became paramilitary leaders in Foca as well as sub-commanders in the Bosnian Serb military police, two joined a special reconnaissance unit of the Bosnian Serb army, and one was appointed chief of police in Foca. The charges against them included rape, torture, outrages upon personal dignity, persecution on political, racial and/or religious grounds, willfully causing great suffering, enslavement, and inhuman treatment—all directed against the Muslim women of their hometown.

After indicting the men, the ICTY had to apprehend them. This was a stumbling block in almost every case because the tribunal had no police force of its own. If the accused did not turn themselves in, the ICTY had to rely on Bosnian Serb authorities or NATO peace-keeping troops. The leaders of the new Republika Srpska (the country created by Bosnian Serbs from the territory they took over and "ethnically cleansed") stonewalled or, in a ploy that amounted to the same thing, they claimed that local authorities had jurisdiction. This was senseless: local authorities would not arrest the accused because often they were the accused. . . .

Three Men Were Arrested and Tried

Between the original indictment and the start of the trial (almost four years), NATO troops arrested two of the eight accused. A third turned himself in because he expected, incorrectly, that the charges would be dropped. A fourth, Foca's police chief, was killed when NATO troops tried to arrest him. (He was charged with overseeing the rape camps and raping a young prisoner the day after she asked him to help stop the atrocities.) The fifth—recognizable by the tattoo on his forehead that read, "I was dead even before I was born"—blew himself up with a hand grenade during his arrest. The other three accused men remained at large.

The prosecutors prepared for the trial with only three defendants in custody (the ICTY does not try anyone in absentia). Like every other ICTY case, the Foca case depended almost entirely on witness testimony. Unlike the prosecutors in Nuremberg who made use of the voluminous records kept by the Nazis, the ICTY prosecutors had almost no documentation.

Rape charges are especially difficult to prosecute because few survivors agree to testify. From the beginning of the Foca investigation, the prosecutor's office had to find the right balance between encouraging women to testify and not pressuring anyone to do so. The trial would be an ordeal: it would go on for months, the witnesses had to face the accused during their testimony, some of the women had never before spoken about what happened in Foca. The tribunal could screen their identities from the public, their names would never appear in court documents, but they still risked being re-traumatized. Those women whose families had survived the war knew they could be ostracized for speaking about rape in public. Many rape survivors had lost their families and all property; they were destitute, homeless, and too frightened to testify. In other ICTY cases, women who planned to testify occasionally withdrew at the last moment because anxiety overwhelmed them. Foca was no different. Of the scores of women and girls brutalized there, sixteen were able to testify.

> *"Chief defense counsel . . . asserted that the prosecution 'did not prove that the alleged victims of rape were exposed to any severe physical or psychological suffering.'"*

Sixteen Survivors Testified

The rape trial—the first of its kind in history—began on March 20, 2000. The accused were Dragoljub Kunarac, commander of a special reconnaissance unit of the Bosnian Serb army: Radomir Kovac, a sub-commander of the military police and paramilitary leader; and Zoran Vukovic, also a sub-commander of the military police and paramilitary leader. The prosecution called thirty-three witnesses during the trial. The six-teen survivors described the assaults they had suffered, when and where these took place, who else was present, and the crimes they saw carried out against other women and girls. Because the soldiers, including the

> *"For the first time in history, an international war crimes trial focused exclusively on crimes of sexual assault."*

accused, usually took more than one prisoner at a time for raping, the survivors were often able to corroborate each other's testimony. Other witnesses provided background or expert testimony; some were relatives of the survivors or Foca residents who managed to flee the region.

The defense lawyers called twenty-nine witnesses and used various arguments to refute the charges. Sometimes they relied on witnesses to establish alibis for the whereabouts of the accused. One witness, a physician, testified that an accident in the summer of 1992 had left Zoran Vukovic impotent for three weeks and incapable of rape during that period. The defense rejected the charge of enslavement because the accused had not been in permanent possession of the women. Regarding dozens of other rapes, the defense did not deny that rape had taken place but argued that the prosecution had not proved rape because some of the women, according to the defense, liked the soldiers. Chief defense counsel Slavisa Prodanovic also asserted that the prosecution "did not prove that the alleged victims of rape were exposed to any severe physical or psychological suffering." He added, "The rape in itself is not an act that inflicts severe bodily pain."

All Were Found Guilty

The lawyers took eight months to present their cases. Closing arguments ended on November 22, 2000. The court reconvened on February 22, 2001 to hear presiding Judge Florence Mumba of Zambia read out the verdicts and sentences.

Dragoljub Kunarac (who, among other offenses, offered to let a soldier rape FWS-186 in the presence of FWS-191 for 100 Deutsche marks) was found guilty of rape, torture, and enslavement as crimes against humanity and rape and torture as violations of the laws or customs of war. The tribunal sentenced him to twenty-eight years in prison.

Radomir Kovac (who, among other offenses, raped FWS-75 and FWS-87 as he played a recording of *Swan Lake*) was found guilty of rape and enslavement as crimes against humanity and rape and outrages upon personal dignity as violations of the laws or customs of war. The tribunal sentenced him to twenty years in prison.

Zoran Vukovic (who, among other offenses, raped sixteen-year-old FWS-50 and then told her that he could do much more but he had a daughter the same age) was found guilty of rape and torture as crimes against humanity and rape and torture as violations of the laws or customs of war. The tribunal sentenced him to twelve years in prison.

The Foca Trial Was Historic

The Foca trial will surely have an impact on international human rights law. For the first time in history, an international war crimes trial focused exclusively on crimes of sexual assault. For the first time in history, an international court found that crimes of sexual assault, under certain conditions, amount to enslavement as a crime against humanity. For the first time in an ICTY trial, rape was successfully prosecuted as a crime against humanity (the International Criminal Tribunal for Rwanda made this breakthrough for the first time in history in 1998). In addition, the document read by Judge Mumba (which was a summary of the three-hundred-page judgment) established, on the basis of the evidence, that rape was used as an instrument of terror to drive Muslims out of the Foca district.

Appreciative Critics

Even critics of the ICTY and resolute skeptics of all international tribunals appreciate what the Foca trial accomplished. Human rights activists celebrated the progress, but they had hoped for one additional precedent. The ICTY statute lists both rape and enslavement as crimes against humanity, but neither word fully captures what happened to the women and girls in Foca. According to Kelly Askin, the judgment could have and should have used the term sexual slavery. "The judgment," she maintained, "treated the rapes as merely one of a number of things that indicated that enslavement occurred, instead of clarifying that the sole reason for the enslavement was to effectuate continuous rape. All the other acts—the selling, the physical mistreatment, the manual labor—were not the reason behind the enslavement."

The other disappointment—a bitter one for the survivors—was the sentencing. Jurists consider the ICTY's sentencing practices lenient in general, but the Foca sentences seemed excessively so. "They reflect an appropriate sentence for a single act of rape as a war crime," Askin said. "But these [men] were serial rapists, people who raped untold numbers of victims over and

> *"The sole reason for the enslavement was to effectuate continuous rape."*

over again and were also responsible for countless others raping the detainees."

After the war ended, after the women and girls who survived Foca left the refugee camps, many made their way to Sarajevo, now the capital of what is left of Bosnia-Herzegovina. That is where they heard the news about the verdict and sentencing. Nezira Zolota, spokesperson for a Sarajevo-based association of female camp survivors, talked to some of the Foca women when the report came in. The leniency of the sentences left them "seriously shaken," she said. The "minimum punishment . . . actually minimized the suffering of the victims."

Everyone who followed the trial agrees that much harsher sentences would have been appropriate and perhaps given the rape camp survivors a small measure of relief. But the women and girls of Foca and the human rights advocates knew from the start that the rape trial, the ICTY, and all international war crimes tribunals represent a failure more than anything else, a human failure to intervene and stop whatever produces crimes against humanity.

Worldwide Sex Trafficking Promotes Violence Against Women

by Janice Shaw Crouse

About the author: *Janice Shaw Crouse is a member of the Coalition Against Sexual Trafficking of Women and Children based in Washington, D.C.*

In colonial times, slave traders abducted men, women and children from Africa and brought them to the new world—often in ball and chain—for a life of slavery on plantations. Centuries later, that dark practice still spawns painful emotions.

In today's post-modern age of technological progress and moral decay, the tentacles of sexual slavery have spread around the globe. The U.S. estimate of 1 million victims worldwide is considered low. They consist of children and young, naive women who have been lured, coerced, kidnapped or trapped into 21st century slavery: the evil that is sexual trafficking.

Tragic Statistics

Dr. Laura Lederer has been studying the issue of sexual trafficking for 20 years. She serves as the director of Harvard University's Protection Project, an effort by the John F. Kennedy School of Government to address issues of violence against women and children. Dr. Lederer reports, "Over the last 10 years, the numbers of women and children [who] have been trafficked have multiplied so that they are now on par with estimates of the numbers of Africans who were enslaved in the 16th and 17th centuries."

An international conference on sexual trafficking was held in Manila, Philippines, in March 2000 and attended by representatives of 20 Pacific Rim countries and the United States. Organizers said sexual trafficking is organized crime's third largest source of money, surpassed only by drugs and guns.

They reported that 250,000 people are bought and sold every year in Asia alone.

Women Are Drugged and Beaten

Two women told their tragic stories [in fall 2000] at a conference on sexual trafficking held in Washington, D.C. "Anita," a young mother in rural Nepal, became destitute after her husband left. To survive, she began selling vegetables. One day, on her way to market, a kindly couple offered her a banana. When she became sick and dizzy, they helped her off the bus and gave her a drink of "tea." When Anita woke up, days later, her kind helpers were her captors, and she was a sexual slave.

Half a world away, "Jane's" story is heartrendingly similar. A young woman befriended this poor Mexican teenager and offered her a job as a waitress in the United States. The woman convinced Jane's mother that she would have a better life in America and smuggled her into a remote area of Texas. Her captors forcibly detained Jane in a trailer. Never leaving her alone, they monitored her phone calls and beat her until she agreed to "work off her debt" through prostitution.

> *"In today's post-modern age of technological progress and moral decay, the tentacles of sexual slavery have spread around the globe."*

The testimony of these courageous women helped expose prostitution's underbelly, and the bodyguards standing behind Anita and Jane gave mute testimony to the truth: They continue to face danger from the prostitution mafia.

The Associated Press lists eight top countries where traffickers take women and children: Germany, Greece, Italy, Kosovo, Netherlands, Spain, Turkey and the United States. But they end up in many more. The victims are taken to cities or remote areas where their captors control them through threats, abuse and terror. Battered into submission, these children and women service the basest sexual appetites of a succession of men.

Children Exploited

"Sex tourism" is another dimension of sex trafficking. Every year, the National Center for Missing and Exploited Children reports, thousands of Americans travel abroad to engage in sex with children or to make pornographic pictures of them. Costa Rica holds the dubious distinction as the "Mecca" of child prostitution, *The Miami Herald* reported. Experts say those who participate in sex tourism are often supposedly respectable men—doctors, lawyers, teachers and military personnel. Some think that having sex with a child carries less risk of HIV infection. Others say the kids need the money anyway.

If the children don't die of disease or brutality, they are left emotionally destroyed. In developing countries, brothels employ boys and girls as young as age 10. In some countries, for extra money, pimps will find children as young as 6 years old.

In [an] interview, . . . Senator Sam Brownback (R-Kansas) said, "Just look at an American child between the ages of nine and 13. Imagine her being tricked away from her family, promised a year's wages (to a family that doesn't have anything), taken to Bombay, locked in a seedy room, not fed for three days, beaten until she agrees to submit herself to the sex trade. That's this horrifying, inhumane thing that's taking place."

Organized Crime Is Involved

Concerned Women for America [CWA] is part of a coalition of conservative and religious leaders fighting against sexual trafficking. "The sexual exploitation of children and young women is an atrocity. Adults are meant to protect children and young women, not exploit them," says Mrs. Beverly LaHaye, CWA's founder and chairman. "It has become an international crisis made even more corrupt with the involvement of organized crime."

CWA's legislative department is building support for legislation introduced by Representative Christopher H. Smith (R-New Jersey), who has called sexual trafficking "commercial rape." Sen. Brownback introduced a companion bill in the Senate in April [2000]. [The Victims of Trafficking and Violence Prevention Act of 2000 became law on October 28, 2000.]

Sex Is Big Business

Sex trafficking has been around for years, but it was largely hidden in the sleazy clubs and brothels of major cities. Now, this increasingly big business has exploded onto Main Street and cannot be ignored. According to the U.S. State Department, more than 50,000 foreign women and children are brought into the United States every year. Torn from their families and cultures, these victims have lost everything. Most of us cannot fathom the problem; it seems too cruel and inhumane to be real.

In Thailand, according to Dr. Lederer, the overall estimated national annual income from prostitution is between $22 and $27 billion. In Indonesia, estimates are "only" $1.2 to $3.3 billion. So while the victims are poor and vulnerable, the traffickers get rich and powerful. Unless they are caught and punished, the "business" will continue to expand. Already, the market is pushing for younger children, according to the National Center for Missing and Exploited Children.

"We must view sexual trafficking as evidence of violence against women."

Human Price Tags

A young Asian girl sells for about $16,000. "Unlike other products, a girl can be sold over and over again." Dr. Lederer says. Women from Eastern Europe are considered exotic and, because of poor economic conditions, they readily believe ads offering them jobs as "models" and "dancers."

The United States has documented Russian and Latvian nationals who were forced to dance nude in Chicago. According to charges filed, traffickers met the women at the airport, seized their documents and return tickets, locked them up and beat them into submission. They were told if they refused to comply, the Russian mafia would kill their families.

War and international conflicts often lead to children and women forced into sexual bondage. In Sierra Leone, more than 5,000 children have been forced to spy, kill and sexually service rebel forces, and 4,000 more are missing. "If you were not made a wife of a commando, then you had to prepare yourself for sex with countless numbers of men," reported Musa, one of the captured girls.

These stories also occur in the United States. [In 1999], an illegal alien from Mexico, Rogerio Cadena, was convicted of heading a sex-slave ring in Florida. Cadena used a massive ring of family and friends to smuggle girls as young as 14 into the United States. They paid Cadena $3,000 to get jobs as nannies, waitresses and housekeepers. Once here, the girls were kept in camps where their captors forced them to service men every 15 minutes for 12 hours a day. They were allowed to keep $3 per customer, but had to pay their "fee" and "expenses" from that income. The women were terrorized with threats to their families.

Sexual Trafficking Is Not Opposed by All

It seems obvious that sexual trafficking is a tragedy anyone would oppose. But some leftists fear that a crackdown on sexual trafficking will inhibit access to prostitution as a "career option" for women. Some feminists who oppose sexual trafficking as an abuse of women have reservations. [Renowned feminist] Gloria Steinem fears efforts to eradicate sexual trafficking will be contaminated by a "cult of virginity."

In a United Nations report released in August 1999, author Lin Lim writes, "All child prostitution is intolerable, but adults choose it for a variety of reasons. Many choose it as the most viable, lucrative alternative." Lim continued, "The revenues generated by [the sex trade] are crucial to the livelihoods and earnings potential of millions of workers beyond the prostitutes themselves."

No One Consents to Exploitation

But truth is coming out. William Bennett of Empower America and Charles Colson of Prison Fellowship wrote in *The Wall Street Journal*, "There can be no meaningful 'consent' to one's own sexual exploitation—particularly when one lives in poverty and desperate circumstances." We must view sexual trafficking as evidence of violence against women, otherwise law enforcement agents would be required to interview international thugs to determine if the women they pimp "consented" to their degradation.

Requiring victims to prove they were forced into prostitution cuts the heart out of legislation to prevent sexual trafficking. Victims would have to prove they helped in the investigation and prosecution of their captors and that they would suffer hardship if they were returned home. Only children 16 and under would be protected from deportation and the almost certain revenge of traffickers. Condemning only "forced" prostitution would protect the perpetrators and punish the victims.

Female Genital Mutilation Is a Serious Problem

by Khadi Diallo

About the author: *Khadi Diallo is an activist and volunteer for the French section (GAMS) of the Inter-African Committee on Traditional Practices Affecting the Health of Women and Children.*

[Unesco Courier:] A Malian woman who underwent excision [female genital mutilation] at the age of 12 recalls the experience which led her to combat this ritual practice.

[Khadi Diallo:] That day will remain etched in my memory forever. At the time, in 1966, I was 12, my sister 10. Like every summer, we were visiting our paternal grandparents in our village 15 kilometres from Bamako in Mali. Early one morning, we went to see my aunt, my father's sister, whom we were always happy to visit because she spoiled us.

I didn't suspect a thing. My aunt called me into the bathroom. Several women jumped on me and held me down. They spread my legs open. I was screaming. I couldn't see the knife but felt them cutting me. I was crying as the blood flowed everywhere. They said, "Don't cry, it's shameful! You're a woman, what we're doing to you is nothing." They started clapping. They dressed me in a white skirt. No bandages, just something they had prepared with shea oil and leaves. I left. It was my little sister's turn. I heard her crying and begging me for help, and that hurt even more.

The excision was a plot. We were betrayed. We were living in Senegal, where my father was a civil servant. My parents were educated people, they were against excision. But at that time, it was a widespread practice in the country-side and city. Most little girls were excised much younger than us, and the occasion was followed by a party. We stayed with our aunt for almost three weeks. A woman she knew helped us because we couldn't stand up by ourselves. It hurt so much we avoided going to the bathroom. Our mother cried and kissed us the first time she came to see us, but she couldn't do anything. In

Africa, the father's family decides whether children live or die.

Meanwhile, we were given our female education. We were told that a woman must be strong, tough, secretive and not too talkative. Sex was a taboo topic.

The Mutilation Never Heals

I was filled with hatred and rage. I had not been brought up with that mentality. But I was resigned, despite the pain. I got married at 22. I never talked about the feeling of being incomplete, of missing a part of my body. Women were not allowed to express desire or pleasure. I could only talk to close friends about the fact that excision is not a wound but a mutilation. A wound heals, but a mutilation means disfigurement. It means removing a part that never grows back. When I had daughters of my own, I told my husband that I did not want them to be excised. He agreed. I protected them by not sending them to visit Africa when they were little.

It was not a sacred or religious rite, but a ritual passage. There is an expression in Bambara that says "taking the dress," which means becoming

> *"Men invented excision to control women's sexuality."*

a real woman. Before excision, a girl is innocent, she can walk around bare-chested or even naked. After excision, she must keep her body covered. The person who has his or her child excised does so because that's the way things have been for generations. They are afraid that evil will befall the child if they don't. They have always heard, "when you have a daughter, you must have her excised so that she can become a perfect woman." But Islam never said "excise your daughters," even though many people think the Koran orders them to do so. Men invented excision to control women's sexuality. To be a real woman, her clitoris, which is considered to represent a man's sex, is removed. Excised mummies dating back prior to the appearance of Islam have been found.

African women have been denouncing excision since 1924, but at that time they were considered crazy. More recently, we have been lucky enough to have support from European women and the media to make ourselves heard. When I came to France, I started campaigning with several organizations, including GAMS [the French section of the Inter-African Committee on Traditional Practices Affecting the Health of Women and Children]. Today, we are invited to clinics and maternity wards to tell mothers that excision is against the law. We campaign for prevention in schools and with social workers. We also see families individually. Psychologically, it's more difficult for girls born in France to undergo excision. Those who are 18 or 20 today will have or have had problems during their first sexual experience. The men of my generation learned to accept the unacceptable. But today's boys will not want girls who are undergoing excision now and will be old enough to marry around 2020. I know a girl who had to leave her neighbourhood because people made fun of her.

We are against excision in all its forms, even if it takes place under anesthesia in the hospital. Our campaign isn't just against the pain at the time of excision, but against the mutilation of our bodies.

When Tradition Becomes Abuse

[Unesco Courier:] More than 130 million girls and women have undergone genital mutilation, according to the World Health Organization (WHO), which estimates that another two million are at risk every year. The mutilation (known as FGM) can take many forms but about 80 percent of cases involve the removal of the clitoris and often the small lip-like structure surrounding the vulva. The most extreme form is infibulation: the external genitalia are partially or entirely removed and the vaginal opening is stitched closed. FGM is concentrated in 28 African countries, although a growing number of cases are being reported among immigrant groups in Europe, Australia, Canada and the U.S. Cases have also been reported in the Middle East and Southeast Asia.

FGM is considered a human rights abuse by a growing international movement of NGOs [nongovernmental organizations] and UN agencies. These activists seek to eliminate the practice, not legitimate it on the grounds of cultural or religious tradition. They also reject its medicalization in which health professionals reduce the risk of infection. . . .

Public awareness campaigns target communities, families and health authorities, while efforts are underway to develop laws to ban and sanction the practice. Some groups are also pushing for provisions to offer asylum to those at risk of mutilation in their countries of origin.

Honor Killings in the Middle East Are a Serious Problem

by Hillary Mayell

About the author: *Hillary Mayell is a writer for* National Geographic.

Hundreds, if not thousands, of women are murdered by their families each year in the name of family "honor." It's difficult to get precise numbers on the phenomenon of honor killing; the murders frequently go unreported, the perpetrators unpunished, and the concept of family honor justifies the act in the eyes of some societies.

Most honor killings occur in countries where the concept of women as a vessel of the family reputation predominates, said Marsha Freemen, director of International Women's Rights Action Watch at the Hubert Humphrey Institute of Public Affairs at the University of Minnesota.

Reports submitted to the United Nations Commission on Human Rights show that honor killings have occurred in Bangladesh, Great Britain, Brazil, Ecuador, Egypt, India, Israel, Italy, Jordan, Pakistan, Morocco, Sweden, Turkey, and Uganda. In countries not submitting reports to the UN, the practice was condoned under the rule of the fundamentalist Taliban government in Afghanistan, and has been reported in Iraq and Iran.

Honor Killings Are Only Part of the Problem

But while honor killings have elicited considerable attention and outrage, human rights activists argue that they should be regarded as part of a much larger problem of violence against women.

In India, for example, more than 5,000 brides die annually because their dowries are considered insufficient, according to the United Nations Children's Fund (UNICEF). Crimes of passion, which are treated extremely leniently in Latin America, are the same thing with a different name, some rights advocates say.

"In countries where Islam is practiced, they're called honor killings, but dowry deaths and so-called crimes of passion have a similar dynamic in that the women are killed by male family members and the crimes are perceived as excusable or understandable," said Widney Brown, advocacy director for Human Rights Watch.

The practice, she said, "goes across cultures and across religions."

Complicity by other women in the family and the community strengthens the concept of women as property and the perception that violence against family members is a family and not a judicial issue.

"Females in the family—mothers, mothers-in-law, sisters, and cousins—frequently support the attacks. It's a community mentality," said Zaynab Nawaz, a program assistant for women's human rights at Amnesty International.

Women as Property

There is nothing in the Koran, the book of basic Islamic teachings, that permits or sanctions honor killings. However, the view of women as property with no rights of their own is deeply rooted in Islamic culture, Tahira Shahid Khan, a professor specializing in women's issues at the Aga Khan University in Pakistan, wrote in *Chained to Custom*, a review of honor killings published in 1999.

"Women are considered the property of the males in their family irrespective of their class, ethnic, or religious group. The owner of the property has the right to decide its fate. The concept of ownership has turned women into a commodity which can be exchanged, bought and sold."

Honor killings are perpetrated for a wide range of offenses. Marital infidelity, pre-marital sex, flirting, or even failing to serve a meal on time can all be perceived as impugning the family honor.

Amnesty International has reported on one case in which a husband murdered his wife based on a dream that she had betrayed him. In Turkey, a young woman's throat was slit in the town square because a love ballad had been dedicated to her over the radio.

Even Victims of Rape May Be Killed

In a society where most marriages are arranged by fathers and money is often exchanged, a woman's desire to choose her own husband—or to seek a divorce—can be viewed as a major act of defiance that damages the honor of the man who negotiated the deal.

Even victims of rape are vulnerable. In a widely reported case in March of 1999, a 16-year-old mentally retarded girl who was raped in the Northwest Frontier province of Pakistan was turned over to her tribe's judicial council. Even though the crime was reported to the police and the perpetrator was arrested, the Pathan tribesmen decided that she had brought shame to her tribe and she was killed in front of a tribal gathering.

The teenage brothers of victims are frequently directed to commit the murder because, as minors, they would be subject to considerably lighter sentencing if there is legal action. Typically, they would serve only three months to a year.

In the Name of Family Honor

Officials often claim that nothing can be done to halt the practice because the concept of women's rights is not culturally relevant to deeply patriarchal societies.

"Politicians frequently argue that these things are occurring among uneducated, illiterate people whose attitudes can't be changed," said Brown. "We see it more as a matter of political will."

The story of Samia Imran is one of the most widely cited cases used to illustrate the vulnerability of women in a culture that turns a blind eye to such practices. The case's high profile no doubt arises from the fact that the murder took place in broad daylight, was abetted by the victim's mother, who was a doctor, and occurred in the office of Asma Jahangir, a prominent Pakistani lawyer and the UN reporter on extrajudicial, summary, or arbitrary executions.

> *"Officials often claim . . . nothing can be done to halt [honor killings] because the concept of women's rights is not culturally relevant to deeply patriarchal societies."*

In April 1999 Imran, a 28-year-old married woman seeking a divorce from her violent husband after 10 years of marriage, reluctantly agreed to meet her mother in a lawyers' office in Lahore, Pakistan. Imran's family opposed the divorce and considered her seeking a divorce to be shaming to the family's honor. Her mother arrived at the lawyer's office with a male companion, who immediately shot and killed Imran.

Imran's father, who was president of the Chamber of Commerce in Peshawar, filed a complaint with the police accusing the lawyers of the abduction and murder of Imran. The local clergy issued *fatwas* (religious rulings) against both women and money was promised to anyone who killed them.

The Peshawar High Court eventually threw out the father's suit. No one was ever arrested for Imran's death.

Most Honor Killings Are Ignored

Imran's case received a great deal of publicity, but frequently honor killings are virtually ignored by community members. "In many cases, the women are buried in unmarked graves and all records of their existence are wiped out," said Brown.

Women accused by family members of bringing dishonor to their families are rarely given the opportunity to prove their innocence. In many countries where the practice is condoned or at least ignored, there are few shelters and very little legal protection.

"In Jordan, if a woman is afraid that her family wants to kill her, she can check herself into the local prison, but she can't check herself out, and the only person who can get her out is a male relative, who is frequently the person who poses the threat," said Brown.

"That this is their idea of how to protect women," Brown said, "is mind boggling."

Ending Violence Against Women

Violence against women is being tackled at the international level as a human rights issue. In 1994 the UN's Commission on Human Rights appointed a special rapporteur on violence against women, and both UNICEF and the UN Development Fund for Women have programs in place to address the issue.

But the politics of women's rights can be complex. [In 2001] the special rapporteur on extrajudicial, summary or arbitrary executions was criticized by a coalition of member countries for including honor killings in her report, and a resolution condemning honor killings failed to pass.

Amnesty International is preparing to launch a worldwide campaign to halt violence against women in 2003. . . .

Local Cooperation Is Key

"Police officers and prosecutors need to be convinced to treat these crimes seriously, and countries need to review their criminal codes for discrimination against women—where murder of a wife is treated more leniently than murder of a husband, for instance," said Brown.

Countries that don't recognize domestic violence as a crime at all need to bring their penal codes up to international standards, she said, adding that increased public awareness and greater education about human rights would also help.

Some progress has been made.

In a *National Geographic* documentary, Michael Davie investigated honor killings in Pakistan, where it is estimated that every day at least three women—including victims of rape—are victims of the practice.

The case of one of the victims Davie examined is heartbreaking but also hopeful. Zahida Perveen, a 29-year-old mother of three, was brutally disfigured and underwent extensive facial reconstruction in the United States. She is one of the only survivors in Pakistan to successfully prosecute the attacker—her husband.

"The reason honor killings have emerged as a human rights issue is that it's the only way ultimately that it can be addressed," said Freeman. "Naming the problem and bringing international attention to it highlights the refusal of some of these governments to shine any kind of light on their failure to protect their own citizens.

"Change can't happen if it's just people working inside the system; they're overwhelmed. International campaigns and media attention give them some ballast and the ability to say 'Look, the world is watching what is going on here,' and provides support for making change in their own countries."

Ritualized Slavery in Ghanaian Shrines Is a Serious Problem

by Brian Edwards

About the author: *Brian Edwards is a London-based television producer/ director.*

About an hour east of Ghana's capital, Accra, lies the Volta delta, a fertile plain criss-crossed by a few metalled roads, and speckled with Ewe villages that have changed little for centuries.

Among the Ewe nothing happens without cause. They are fervent believers in Einstein's maxim that 'God does not play dice'. If someone dies, it is for a reason. There is the superficial cause—malaria, drowning, etc. And there is the profound cause—the displeasure or vengeance of the gods. A family who has experienced notable misfortune—deaths, illness or just a failing crop—may well seek out a soothsayer, a man or woman who can make contact with the spirit world, in order to divine *why* the family has so displeased the gods.

Once the cause of the offence has been divined, the soothsayer will communicate what offering the gods will accept as compensation. According to the elders, for hundreds of years these offerings have comprised cattle, perhaps some rolls of calico and a few crates of the local moonshine, *apeteshe*. Then, around a hundred years ago, an unfortunate change occurred. A family unable to buy the prescribed cattle offered the shrine priest one of their virgin daughters instead. This offer was accepted, and a new tradition was born.

Visiting Ghana for a Channel 4/Home Box Office project, *Innocents Lost*, on the exploitation of children around the world, we filmed several thousand of these women and girls serving at shrines throughout the delta. Called *trokosi* in the Ewe language, they are, in theory, wives and servants to the gods. In practice, their role ranges from the purely ceremonial, to working as the priests' cooks, farmhands, cleaners and mistresses.

Girls Serve for Life

In one shrine we were able to speak to some *trokosi* in private while they were working the fields owned by the shrine. Christy was typical. A slight, pretty 12-year-old, her parents had brought her to the shrine two years before. All she knew about her captivity was that her older sister had been a *trokosi* before her, but the *fetish* or god had killed her, so Christy had been sent to replace her. As far as she was aware, she was serving a life sentence for a crime someone else had committed. 'It's for ever,' she told us. 'Even when I die my family will have to bring somebody else and, when she dies, they will bring another person.'

We asked another girl, Atuishe, if she was happy in the shrine. 'Happy? Oh no, I am a *trokosi*, not a normal person. Others live free, but I am suffering in bondage here. If I could have got some poison I would have taken it long ago.'

Many Are Abused

No one is quite sure now many *trokosi* are enslaved in Ghana, partly because the conditions in which they live vary so much. In some shrines, the priests regard the girls as sexual property and, although they are only supposed to have sex with them 'after their third menstruation', we met several girls who had children by the priests when they were as young as 12.

One girl told us how the priest had come to her in the night when she was just 10. She knew what he wanted but kept refusing to comply. Several nights later he raped her. Afterwards, as she lay on the ground crying, the other girls begged her to be quiet. They warned that if the priest was disturbed he would come back and not only beat her, but beat them as well.

Conversely, in another shrine, the priest, Obosumfor, was appalled when we told him how other priests treated their *trokosi*. He believed that the offer of service made by a family was to the gods, not to him. If a family offered their daughter, he ordered a feast and told them to return in a week's time to celebrate. Obosumfor, his family, the girl and her family would eat and drink late into the night, singing and drumming to attract the gods' attention. As dawn broke he would perform a ritual in which the girl became a *trokosi*. Then, everyone, including the girl, would simply go home. As far as Obosumfor was concerned, the girl would serve the gods in the spirit world (their domain), but would continue a normal life in the material world.

Only a *Trokosi* Will Appease the Gods

As film-makers we were there primarily as observers. Our plan was not to get involved. Then we met Juliet, a frightened 14-year-old. Her mother had whisked her away from her village to the capital to prevent her in-laws sending the girl to a shrine as a *trokosi*. Ten years earlier, Juliet's father, Joshua, had stolen a tape recorder from his friend, Willie. Willie went to the priest and the priest told Joshua he must return the tape recorder, pay Willie compensation and pay a fine to the shrine. Joshua ignored this ruling and, in so doing, went against the will of gods.

Eight years later Joshua's father and mother died. Two deaths in swift succession sent the family elders scurrying to the soothsayer. He confirmed their worst fears: the gods were angry with the family for ignoring the earlier judgment. Unless the family paid not only the original fine, but also compensation to the shrine in the form of a *trokosi*, the deaths would continue.

Negotiating Their Daughter's Release

We joined Joshua and his family on the way to the shrine to try to negotiate a reduction in the fine, and in particular to try to secure Juliet's freedom. The shrine was a mud hut with a corrugated iron roof in the centre of a village of 20 or so buildings about two hours from the nearest metalled road. The outside was painted with caricatures of the reigning priest's most recent ancestors. The bottles of vodka we had brought as an offering smoothed permission for us to enter the shrine and to film. After a couple of hours of formalities, negotiations began in earnest.

'Negotiation' is an entirely inaccurate description. First Joshua, then each of the relatives who had accompanied him, threw themselves on the earth floor in front of the priest in turn and begged for mercy. Faces pressed into the hard-packed clay, they reached out and touched his feet and asked for the 15 head of cattle to be reduced to five, the five crates of *apeteshe* to be reduced to one, the three rolls of calico to be forgotten.

> *"I am a trokosi, not a normal person. Others live free, but I am suffering in bondage here."*

We had arrived mid-morning. Six hours later the small patch of sunlight that filtered into the shrine through the one opening near the roof was beginning to move up the opposite wall. Negotiations were drawing to a close, yet Juliet's name had not been mentioned.

Finally we asked our interpreter.

'Why haven't they mentioned Juliet?'

'I don't know.'

'Can you ask them why Juliet's freedom has not been discussed.'

The girl, we were told, was not up for negotiation; she had to come to the shrine; it was what the gods wanted.

The Filmmakers' Presence Inflates the Price

When we asked if the gods would accept money or cattle in her place, the priest and his acolytes retired for a private conference. When they returned the priest threw his cowrie shells on the floor and considered the pattern before announcing that the gods had decreed that Juliet's freedom could be bought for 5 million Cedis (US$2,415). This was Joshua's entire earnings for about 10 years.

Without doubt our presence had massively inflated the price.

We knew the danger of getting involved because we had heard tales of German and US charity workers arriving at shrines laden with donations from church collections to 'free sex slaves in Africa'. Word of these charities spread fast and the number of *trokosi* at any one shrine became increasingly exaggerated. Girls from other villages would be drafted in and several thousand dollars would be handed over, the girls would be 'freed' but the real *trokosi* remained enslaved.

New Law Makes *Trokosi* Illegal

Many priests are vehemently opposed to these liberations. One, Gidisu, threatened to put a curse on any 'liberator' setting foot on his island. He told us all his *trokosi* were very happy, and none of them wanted to leave, but he wouldn't let us speak to them. When we raised the question of cattle in exchange for girls, he was very clear: a girl had a lot more uses than a cow.

After our film and another exposé by ABC's *60 Minutes* were broadcast, the Ghanaian government passed a law in late 1998 making it illegal to send a child away from home for a religious ritual. However, the real challenge is to implement this. In the Volta delta few policemen will act against the priests. Instead elders and chiefs have been recruited to try to persuade priests to give up their girls for cattle.

It was this approach we adopted to try to secure Juliet's freedom. With the help of the local charity, International Needs, Juliet's freedom was secured in exchange for just three cows.

Despite their successes International Needs estimates that there are still up to 3,000 girls living in bondage in the region. Liberations continue but the emphasis now is on getting the priests who have already liberated their *trokosi* to persuade those still holding girls that the game is up.

Organizations to Contact

The editors have compiled the following list of organizations concerned with the issues debated in this book. The descriptions are derived from materials provided by the organizations. All have publications or information available for interested readers. The list was compiled on the date of publication of the present volume; the information provided here may change. Be aware that many organizations take several weeks or longer to respond to inquiries, so allow as much time as possible.

Advocates for Abused and Battered Lesbians (AABL)
PO Box 85596, Seattle, WA 98105-9998
(206) 547-8191
e-mail: aabl@isomedia.com • website: www.aabl.org

AABL provides services for lesbians and their children who are or have been victims of domestic violence. Through community education and outreach, its members encourage communities to recognize and eliminate lesbian battering, homophobia, and misogyny. AABL provides information on intimate abuse, and its website includes stories from survivors of domestic violence.

American Bar Association Commission on Domestic Violence
740 Fifteenth St. NW, Washington, DC 20005-1022
(202) 662-1737 • fax: (202) 662-1594
e-mail: abacdv@abanet.org • website: www.abanet.org/domviol/home.html

The commission researches model domestic violence programs in an effort to develop a blueprint for a national multidisciplinary domestic violence program. The commission provides information on domestic violence law and publishes several books, including *Stopping Violence Against Women: Using New Federal Laws* and *The Impact of Domestic Violence on Your Legal Practice: A Lawyer's Handbook*.

Battered Women's Support Services (BWSS)
PO Box 1098, Postal Station A, Vancouver, BC, Canada V6C 2T1
(604) 687-1868 • fax: (604) 687-1864
e-mail: infobwss@telus.net • website: www.bwss.org

Battered Women's Support Services provides education, advocacy, and support services to assist all battered women in Vancouver. BWSS works from a feminist perspective and seeks the elimination of all woman abuse. The organization publishes a quarterly newsletter, *The Wave*, and several educational pamphlets and fliers.

Center for the Prevention of Sexual and Domestic Violence
936 N. 34th St., Suite 200, Seattle, WA 98013
(206) 634-1903 • fax: (206) 634-0115
e-mail: cpsdv@cpsdv.org • website: www.cpsdv.org

The center is an interreligious ministry addressing issues of sexual and domestic violence. Its goal is to engage religious leaders in the task of ending abuse through institutional and social change. The center publishes educational videos, the quarterly newsletter *Working Together*, and many books, including *Violence Against Women and Children: A Christian Theological Sourcebook* and *Sexual Violence: The Unmentionable Sin—an Ethical and Pastoral Perspective*.

Concerned Women for America (CWA)
1015 Fifteenth St. NW, Suite 1100, Washington, DC 20024
(202) 488-7000 • fax: (202) 488-0806
website: www.cwfa.org

CWA seeks to protect the interests of American families, promote biblical values, and provide a voice for women throughout the United States who believe in Judeo-Christian values. CWA believes pornography contributes to abusive behavior in men. The organization publishes the monthly magazine *Family Voice*.

Family Research Laboratory (FRL)
University of New Hampshire
126 Horton Social Science Center, Durham, NH 03824-3586
fax: (603) 862-1122
website: www.unh.edu/frl

FRL is an independent research unit devoted to the study of the causes and consequences of family violence, and it also works to dispel myths about family violence through public education. It publishes numerous books and articles on violence between men and women, marital rape, and verbal aggression. FRL's website offers a complete listing of available materials, such as the article "Stress and Rape in the Context of American Society," and the book *Understanding Partner Violence: Prevalence, Causes, Consequences, and Solutions*. However, many of the publications are intended for research scholars rather than the general public.

The Fatherhood Coalition (CPF)
PO Box 700, Milford, MA 01757
(617) 723-DADS
website: www.fatherhoodcoalition.org

The Fatherhood Coalition is an organization of men and women advocating the institution of fatherhood. They work to promote shared parenting and to end the discrimination and persecution faced by divorced and unwed fathers, in society at large and specifically in Massachusetts. CPF is active in the fight against the abuse of restraining orders, especially in divorce cases. The organization's website offers articles and links to other pro-fatherhood and male advocacy groups.

Feminist Majority Foundation
National Center for Women and Policing
8105 W. Third St., Suite 1, Los Angeles, CA 90048
(213) 651-2532 • fax: (213) 653-2689
e-mail: womencops@aol.com • website: www.feminist.org/police/ncwp.html

The center is a division of the Feminist Majority Foundation, an activist organization that works to eliminate sex discrimination and social and economic injustice. The center's members believe that female police officers respond more effectively to incidents of violence against women than do their male counterparts. It acts as a nationwide resource for law enforcement agencies and community leaders seeking to increase the number of female police officers in their communities and to improve police response to family violence. Its publications include *Equality Denied: The Status of Women in Policing, 1997* and *Police Family Violence Fact Sheet*. The Feminist Majority Foundation also publishes the quarterly *Feminist Majority Report*.

Independent Women's Forum
PO Box 3058, Arlington, VA 22203-0058
(800) 224-6000
e-mail: info@iwf.org • website: www.iwf.org

The forum is a conservative women's advocacy group that believes in individual freedom and personal responsibility and promotes common sense over feminist ideology. The forum believes that the incidence of domestic violence is exaggerated and that the Violence Against Women Act is ineffective and unjust. It publishes the *Women's Quarterly.*

National Clearinghouse on Marital and Date Rape
2325 Oak St., Berkeley, CA 94708
website: www.members.aol.com/ncmdr/index.html

The clearinghouse operates as a consulting firm on issues of marital, cohabitant, and date rape. It attempts to educate the public and to establish social and political equality in intimate relationships. Its publications include *Marital Rape Victims Fight Back, Prosecution Statistics on Marital Rape*, and the pamphlet *State Law Chart on Marital Rape.*

National Coalition Against Domestic Violence (NCADV)
PO Box 18749, Denver, CO 80218-0749
(303) 839-1852
website: www.ncadv.org

NCADV is dedicated to the empowerment of battered women and is committed to the elimination of personal and societal violence in the lives of battered women and their children. The organization's work includes coalition building at the local, state, regional and national levels; support for the provision of community-based, nonviolent alternatives—such as safe home and shelter programs—for battered women and their children; public education and technical assistance; policy development and innovative legislation; focus on the leadership of NCADV's caucuses and task forces developed to represent the concerns of organizationally underrepresented groups; and efforts to eradicate social conditions that contribute to violence against women and children. Publications include *General Information Packet: Every Home a Safe Home* and the *National Directory of Domestic Violence Programs: A Guide to Community Shelter, Safe Homes, and Service Programs.*

National Coalition of Anti-Violence Programs
The New York City Gay and Lesbian Anti-Violence Project
240 W. 35th St., Suite 200, New York, NY 10001
(212) 714-1184
website: www.avp.org

The project serves lesbian, gay, transgender, bisexual, and HIV-positive victims of violence, and others affected by violence, by providing free and confidential services enabling them to regain their sense of control, identify and evaluate their options, and assert their rights. By educating law enforcement and social service agency personnel and calling attention to inadequate official and professional responses, the project works to hold law enforcement and social service agencies accountable to their obligation for impartial service. The project also tracks and publishes statistical reports of hate crimes and domestic violence. All reports and media releases are available on its website.

National Criminal Justice Reference Service (NCJRS)
PO Box 6000, Rockville, MD 20850
(800) 851-3420
e-mail: askncjrs@ncjrs.org • website: www.ojp.usdoj.gov/nij

A component of the Office of Justice Programs of the U.S. Department of Justice, NCJRS supports and conducts research on crime, criminal behavior, and crime prevention. It also acts as a clearinghouse for criminal justice information. Many reports are available from the clearinghouse, including *Domestic Violence, Stalking, and Antistalking* and *Civil Protection Orders: Victims' Views on Effectiveness.*

The National Organization for Men Against Sexism (NOMAS)
PO Box 455, Louisville, CO 80027-0455
(303) 666-7043
e-mail: info@nomas.org • website: www.nomas.org

The National Organization for Men Against Sexism is an activist organization of men and women supporting positive changes for men. NOMAS advocates a perspective for enhancing men's lives that is pro-feminist, gay-affirmative, antiracist, and committed to justice on a broad range of social issues, including class, age, religion, and physical abilities. The organization publishes a quarterly journal called *Brother*, as well as occasional position papers and briefs. All publications are available on its website.

NOW Legal Defense and Education Fund (NOW LDEF)
99 Hudson St., New York, NY 10013-2871
(212) 925-6635 • fax: (212) 226-1066
website: www.nowldef.org

NOW LDEF is a branch of the National Organization for Women (NOW). It is dedicated to the eradication of sex discrimination through litigation and public education. The organization's publications include several legal resource kits on rape, stalking, and domestic violence, as well as information on the Violence Against Women Act.

U.S. Department of Justice Violence Against Women Office
Tenth St. & Constitution Ave. NW, Room 5302, Washington, DC 20530
National Domestic Violence Hotline: (800) 799-SAFE • fax: (202) 307-3911
website: www.ojp.usdoj.gov/vawo

The office is responsible for the overall coordination and focus of Department of Justice efforts to combat violence against women. It maintains the National Domestic Violence Hotline and publishes a monthly newsletter. An on-line domestic violence awareness manual is available at the office's website along with press releases, speeches, and the full text of and news about the Violence Against Women Act.

Women's Freedom Network (WFN)
4410 Massachusetts Ave. NW, Suite 179, Washington, DC 20016
(202) 885-6245
e-mail: wfn@american.edu • website: www.womensfreedom.org

The network was founded in 1993 by a group of women who were seeking alternatives to both extremist ideological feminism and antifeminist traditionalism. It opposes gender bias in the sentencing of spouse abusers and believes acts of violence against women should be considered individually rather than stereotyped as gender-based hate crimes. WFN publishes a newsletter and the book *Neither Victim nor Enemy: Women's Freedom Network Looks at Gender in America.*

Bibliography

Books

Robert M. Baird and Stuart E. Rosenbaum, eds.	*Pornography.* Amherst, NY: Prometheus Books, 1998.
Elisabeth L. Beattie and Mary Angela Shaughnessy	*Sisters in Pain.* Lexington: University Press of Kentucky, 2000.
Robinette Bell	*Violence Against Women in the United States.* Collindale, PA: DIANE, 1999.
Maria Bevacqua	*Rape on the Public Agenda.* Boston: Northeastern University Press, 2000.
Drucilla Cornell, ed.	*Feminism and Pornography.* New York: Oxford University Press, 2000.
Clare Dalton and Elizabeth M. Schneider	*Battered Women and the Law.* New York: Foundation Press, 2000.
Rebecca Emerson Dobash et al.	*Changing Violent Men.* Thousand Oaks, CA: Sage, 1999.
Andrea Dworkin and John Stoltenberg	*Just Sex.* Lanham, MD: Rowman & Littlefield, 2000.
Zvi Eisikovitz and Eli Buchbinder	*Locked in a Violent Embrace.* Thousand Oaks, CA: Sage, 2000.
James E. Elias	*Porn 101.* Amherst, NY: Prometheus Books, 1999.
Lynette Feder, ed.	*Women and Domestic Violence.* Binghamton, NY: Haworth Press, 2000.
Luke Ford	*The History of X.* Amherst, NY: Prometheus Books, 1999.
Robert Geffner and Alan Rosenbaum	*Domestic Violence Offenders.* Binghamton, NY: Haworth Maltreatment and Trauma Press, 2002.
Nicholas A. Groth	*Men Who Rape.* Cambridge, MA: Perseus, 2001.
Rhonda Hammer	*Antifeminism and Family Terrorism.* Lanham, MD: Rowman & Littlefield, 2002.

Kerry Healey et al.	*Batterer Intervention.* Collingdale, PA: DIANE, 1999.
Neil S. Jacobson and John Grottman	*When Men Batter Women.* New York: Simon and Schuster, 1998.
Adam Jukes	*Men Who Batter Women.* New York: Routledge Taylor and Francis, 1999.
Ellyn Kaschak, ed.	*Intimate Betrayal.* Binghamton, NY: Haworth Press, 2001.
Fauziya Kassindja	*Do They Hear You When You Cry?* New York: Doubleday, 1998.
Kathryn Kolbert and Zak Mettger, eds.	*Justice Talking.* New York: New Press, 2001.
Anne Llewellyn Barstow	*War's Dirty Secret.* Cleveland, OH: Pilgrim Press, 2000.
David J. Loftus	*Watching Sex.* New York: Avalon, 2002.
Thomas C. Mackey	*Pornography on Trial.* Santa Barbara, CA: ABC-CLIO, 2002.
Katherine S. Newell et al.	*Discrimination Against the Girl Child.* Washington, DC: Youth Advocate Program International, 2000.
Robbin S. Ogle and Susan Jacobs	*Self-Defense and Battered Women Who Kill: A New Framework.* Westport, CT: Praeger, 2002.
James M. O'Neil and Joseph R. Biden	*What Causes Men's Violence Against Women.* Thousand Oaks, CA: Sage, 1999.
Susan M. Okin et al.	*Is Multiculturalism Bad for Women.* Princeton, NJ: Princeton University Press, 1999.
Dolly M. Palmer	*Means of Escape.* Catskill, NY: Press-Tige, 2001.
Francine Pickup	*Women and Violence.* Oxford, UK: Oxfam, 2000.
Jody Raphael	*Saving Bernice.* Boston: Northeastern University Press, 2000.
Ann Russo	*Taking Back Our Lives.* New York: Routledge Taylor and Francis, 2001.
Elizabeth M. Schneider	*Battered Women and Feminist Lawmaking and the Struggle for Equality.* New Haven, CT: Yale University Press, 2000.
Sabine Sielke	*Reading Rape.* Princeton, NJ: Princeton University Press, 2002.
Joseph W. Slade	*Pornography in America.* Santa Barbara, CA: ABC-CLIO, 2002.
Randy Thornhill and Craig T. Palmer	*A Natural History of Rape: Biological Bases of Sexual Coercion.* Cambridge, MA: MIT Press, 2000.
Cheryl Brown Travis, ed.	*Evolution, Gender, and Rape.* Cambridge, MA: MIT Press, 2003.
Lenore E. Walker	*The Battered Woman Syndrome.* New York: Springer, 1999.
Susan Weitzman	*Not to People Like Us.* New York: Basic Books, 2000.

Bibliography

Kathleen Winkler	*Date Rape*. Berkeley Heights, NJ. Enslow, 1999.
Yoshimi Yoshiaki	*Comfort Women*. New York: Columbia University Press, 2001.

Periodicals

Ileana Arias et al.	"Violence Against Women: The State of Batterer Prevention Programs," *Journal of Law, Medicine and Ethics*, Fall 2002.
Louise Bill	"The Victimization and Revictimization of Female Offenders," *Corrections Today*, December 1998.
Mark Blackburn	"Know Thyself," *Ms.*, October/November 2001.
Diane Boudreau	"A Matter of Rape," *ASU Research Magazine*, Fall 2000.
Lucy M. Candib	"Primary Violence Prevention: Taking a Deeper Look," *Journal of Family Practice*, October 2000.
Lynne Cohen	"Bad News on Porn: A Major Study Concludes That Even the 'Mild' Stuff May Do More Harm than Previously Assumed," *Report Newsmagazine*, April 1, 2002.
Ann Coulter	"Annie's Got Her Gun," *George*, August 1999.
Cara Feinberg	"Hitting Home: Domestic Violence Is the Issue That Embarrasses Traditionalists," *American Prospect*, April 8, 2002.
Maggie Gallagher	"Violence Is Gender Neutral," *Conservative Chronicle*, December 8, 1999. Available from PO Box 29, Hampton, IA 50441.
Jan Goodwin	"The Ultimate Growth Industry: Trafficking in Women and Girls," *On the Issues*, Fall 1998.
August Gribbin	"Congress Targets Traffic of Sex Slaves into U.S.," *Insight*, August 2, 1999. Available from 3600 New York Ave. NE, Washington, DC 20002.
Jacky Hardy	"Everything Old Is New Again: The Use of Gender-Based Terrorism Against Women," *Minerva: Quarterly Report on Women and the Military*, Summer 2001.
Andy Klein	"Andy Klein's Letter," *National Bulletin on Domestic Violence Prevention*, June 1999.
G. Krantz	"Violence Against Women: A Global Public Health Issue," *Journal of Epidemiology and Community Health*, April 2002. Available from BMJ Publishing Group, BMA House, Tavistock Square, London WC 1H 9JR UK.
Richard D. Krugman and Felicia Cohn	"Time to End Health Professional Neglect of Cycle of Violence," *Lancet*, August 11, 2001.
Hillary Larkin and Nancy O'Malley	"In Favor of Mandatory Reporting," *Western Journal of Medicine*, August 1999. Available from 111 Franklin St., 11th Floor, Oakland, CA 94607.

Sharmila Lawrence	"Domestic Violence and Welfare Policy: Research Findings That Can Inform Policies on Marriage and Child Well-Being," Research Forum on Children, Families, and the New Federalism, December 2002. Available from 154 Haven Ave., New York, NY 10032.
John Leo	"Pervasive Male-Bashing Isn't Good for Society," *Conservative Chronicle*, May 13, 1998. Available from PO Box 29, Hampton, IA 50441
Paul Mandelbaum	"Dowry Deaths in India: Let Only Your Corpse Come Out of That House," *Commonweal*, October 8, 1999.
Kate Millet	"What Is to Be Done," *Chicago-Kent Law Review Symposium of Unfinished Feminist Business*, 2000. Available from 565 West Adams St., Chicago, IL 60661-3691.
Kelly Patricia O'Meara	"Dyncorp Disgrace," *Insight*, February 4, 2002. Available from 3600 New York Ave. NE, Washington, DC 20002.
Joy D. Osofsky	"The Impact of Violence on Children," *Future of Children: Domestic Violence and Children*, Winter 1999. Available from The David and Lucile Packard Foundation, 300 Second St., Suite 200, Los Altos, CA 94022.
Daphne Patai	"Do They Have to Be Wrong?" *Gender Issues*, Fall 2000.
Jennifer L. Pozner	"Not All Domestic Violence Studies Are Created Equal," *Extra*, November/December 1999. Available from 130 West 25th St., New York, NY 10001.
Scott Raab	"Men Explode," *Esquire*, September 2000.
Simon Robinson	"The Last Rites," *Time International*, December 3, 2001.
Jennie Ruby	"It's Time to Stop Tolerating Rape," *Off Our Backs*, September/October 2002. Available from State Historical Society of Wisconsin, attn. James Buckett, 816 State St., Madison, WI 53706.
Suzanne Ruggi	"Honor Killings in Palestine," *Middle East Research and Information Report*, Spring 1998. Available from 1500 Mass. Ave. NW, Suite 119, Washington, DC 20005.
Dean Schillinger and Ariella Hyman	"In Opposition to Mandatory Reporting," *Western Journal of Medicine*, August 1999. Available from 111 Franklin St., 11th Floor, Oakland, CA 94607.
Adriene Sere	"Men and the History of Rape," *Said It*, March 2000. Available from PO Box 75035, Seattle, WA 98125.
Silja J.A. Talvi	"The Suffering Within: The Plight of Battered Women Who Kill in Self-Defense," *Z Magazine*, October 2002.
Gale Goldberg Wood and Susan E. Roche	"Situations and Representations: Feminist Practice with Survivors of Male Violence," *Families in Society: The Journal of Contemporary Human Services*, November/December 2001. Available from 11700 W. Lake Park Dr., Milwaukee, WI 53224.

Index

Index